Model Rebels

The publisher gratefully acknowledges the
generous contribution toward the publication of this book provided by the
Wang Family Foundation.

Model Rebels

The Rise and Fall of China's Richest Village

Bruce Gilley

UNIVERSITY OF CALIFORNIA PRESS

Berkeley   Los Angeles   London

CONTENTS

ILLUSTRATIONS

TABLES

Prologue

In the late summer of 1993, a fuzzy-headed Chinese peasant with bushy eyebrows and big ears was sentenced to twenty years in prison. The charges against him were both plentiful and serious: stealing state secrets, harboring criminals, obstructing justice, and much else. But what made the trial a national, even an international, sensation was the identity of the accused: Yu Zuomin, the celebrated Communist Party secretary of China's richest village, Daqiu.[1]

When the verdict had been read aloud to the packed courtroom in the northern China port city of Tianjin, a deflated Yu Zuomin (pronounced "yoo zoe-meen") leaned forward in the wooden-railed dock and donned his gold-rimmed glasses to read aloud a prepared "statement of regret." It would be his last words before disappearing from the world, perhaps for good. "There are ideological as well as historical reasons for my crimes," he said in a ponderous voice barely familiar to the hand-picked audience. "As the village grew, my head swelled and I forgot about the law and about spiritual things. I was muddle-headed and unaware of the serious crimes I had committed."[2]

Along with Yu, another twenty-five officials, workers, and party cadres from Daqiu (pronounced "da-chew") Village—a hamlet of just four thousand people in the nearby countryside—were sent to jail on that day. Several of them have since served their terms. Others will languish in prison for life. None of them will ever regain their positions, or their fame.

The mass trial of Daqiu marked the end of a unique, yet portentous, tale of power and protest in rural China. The trial centered on the beating to death of a factory worker in the village in late 1992, which precipitated an armed standoff between the village and the national paramilitary police. But the charges, the testimony, and the official statements heard during the one-month trial left little doubt that much more was at stake. During a fifteen-year ride to fame, Yu Zuomin had led his village in a constant struggle of political and ideological resistance against the Communist state in China. At first, this struggle was aimed at narrow objectives, mainly having to do with the village's economic policies. But by the early 1990s it widened to include political goals: an end to discrimination against the new rural rich; the formulation of an unabashedly materialistic new ideology; and, most explosively, the effective abolition of Communist Party rule in the Chinese countryside. Yu Zuomin sat in court that day accused of waging a war of liberation for all of China's eight hundred million peasants.[3]

The fall of Daqiu was the most sensational purge in rural China since Dazhai, the model village of the 1960s and 1970s, was revealed to be a fraud and its charismatic leader, Chen Yonggui, stripped of his national vice premiership in 1980. But the story of Daqiu could not have been more different. For not only was its economic miracle for real, but its political fame came from grassroots power, not high-level patronage.

Still, many observers initially dismissed the Daqiu incident as a freak. Protest in the Chinese countryside is traditionally associated not with wealth and fame but with poverty and oppression. But Daqiu was different: a village that rebelled *because* it was wealthy, not in spite of it. And one where growing autonomy, not growing oppression, spurred resistance. The changing goals of that resistance were also a seeming anomaly: an initial focus on more typical economic goals soon widened into a less common struggle for political and ideological goals. In short, Daqiu was seen as a rich and cocky aberration.[4]

Recent research on peasant politics in China is fundamentally recasting this view, bringing the story of Daqiu back to center stage. For a start, rather than concentrating on grievances alone, which are seen as more of a constant, scholars are shifting their attention to the ability of peasants to mount resistance. What leads to resistance is the *ability* of the peasants to mobilize and organize, not just their *desire* to do so. In addition, the new study of peasant politics significantly broadens the definition of resistance. No longer is it confined to the stereotyped massings of peasants armed with picks and shovels. Instead, it includes a broad array of actions, everything from flaunting state policies to using senior allies in the party and media to manipulate policies. Looked at in these terms, the rise and fall of Daqiu is an important example of a new form of political struggle in rural China, and possibly in China as a whole. The Chinese countryside is now bristling with similarly wealthy villages that, having flourished under the state and enjoyed its praise, now often turn the tables and become a challenge to its rule. These are the "model rebels" of which Daqiu was the prime example. As one Chinese official wrote, "The fall of Yu Zuomin is a rarity among outstanding peasant entrepreneurs; but the 'Yu Zuomin phenomenon' is not at all unusual."[5]

This book is an attempt to describe the events and forces that shaped the extraordinary story of Daqiu. In particular, it will trace the rise of the village's protest, which eventually led to its downfall. A second aim is to reevaluate Yu Zuomin by telling the story from the perspective of the village itself. The official verdict held that Yu was a criminal and a tyrant, a conclusion taken up with alacrity by a foreign press eager to discredit what was seen as the latest in a string of bogus "model villages" in China. Certainly, Yu was a flawed leader. Yet the contention here will be that he was jailed mainly because he was a political rebel, not because of the crimes perpetrated in his village.

I visited Daqiu once, in the summer of 1992, just months before its slide into oblivion. Reporting on the village since then has been a particular source of fascination to me. Media reports on the village in the mainland China and overseas Chinese press are plentiful. So too is the extensive section on the village in the annals of Tianjin's Jinghai county, published in 1995, even if Yu Zuomin has been entirely airbrushed from the narrative. That information has been supplemented by interviews with Daqiu and Tianjin officials at various times, as well as the sage advice of several scholars outside China. Key village statistics are summarized in tables in the appendix.

Many scholars and journalists both inside and outside China have helped me with this project. I owe a special debt of gratitude to Kevin O'Brien of Ohio State University, who encouraged me at an early stage and helped to identify the importance of the Daqiu story, and to Lin Nan of Duke University for his keen insights and profound knowledge of the village. Li Lianjiang of Hong Kong Baptist University, Richard Baum of the University of California at Los Angeles, and Thomas Gold of the University of California at Berkeley were also generous with their time and wisdom. I would also like to thank Professor Fu in China, who shared so much at great personal risk to help me understand the story of Daqiu.

Most of this manuscript was completed during a salubrious 1998–99 academic year as a visiting scholar at the Graduate School of Journalism at the University of California at Berkeley. I am grateful to the dean of the school, Orville Schell, for affording me this opportunity.

ONE

Yanzhao Elegy

We peasants have paid a stiff price for leftism. We still have nightmares about a return to the leftist persecutions and the poverty of the
past. I have been poor and so has this village. We must never go back
to that period!

Yu Zuomin, 1979

Once you pass the pear orchards and vegetable fields of suburban Tianjin on your way south toward the village of Daqiu, the landscape
changes suddenly. The tree-lined roads and lotus ponds of the former
colonial port city and its environs disappear. So too do the brick houses
and well-paved roads that mark the current-day prosperity of Tianjin.
By the time you reach Jinghai, the capital of the county by the same
name, the countryside is dry and bleak. Corn fields and dust bowls en-
velop the scene. Adobe and mud huts, known collectively by the Chinese peasants as "dirt houses" (*tufang*), dot the bleak terrain.

The village of Daqiu can be reached along a winding dirt and asphalt
road about fifteen kilometers southeast from Jinghai, forty-five kilometers from Tianjin. Hedged in today by the Tuanpowa reservoir to the
northeast and the Dagang oil field to the southeast, it is one of literally

thousands of villages here. Most of them, including Daqiu, date from a period of large-scale migration from nearby Shandong province following the establishment of China's last native dynasty, the Ming, in the late fourteenth century. Among the migrants of that era was a family surnamed Qiu (pronounced "chew"). They named their settlement Qiu Family Village, or Qiu-jia-zhuang. When another family named Qiu began farming on a nearby hillock, the name was changed to today's Big Qiu Village (Da-Qiu-zhuang), or Daqiu for short.[1]

The low-lying plains that surround Daqiu were previously under the sea and as a result the soil is heavily alkaline. The winters are harsh and the spring rains are unpredictable. Nothing ever came easily to the Qiu family and others who settled here over time. Neither cooking oil nor tea leaves. Not clothing or education, grain or water.

While other parts of northern China were touched by the sprouts of industrialization and westernization that attended China's growing contacts with the West from the mid–nineteenth century onward, the changes completely bypassed Daqiu and its environs. People from surrounding regions sang many a disparaging ditty about the area, which became known as the "old eastern townships" of the new province of Hopeh (now spelled Hebei) after the fall of the last dynasty, the Qing, in 1911. One of them went:

> Old eastern townships,
> Watching the dusk,
> Drinking bitter water,
> And eating vegetable husk.
> If you've a son,
> Don't find a bride there.
> If you've a daughter,
> You too should beware.

Within the eastern townships, Daqiu was the poorest of the poor. Male suitors from the village had little luck finding spouses from other villages. Overtures from its men were spurned with scornful rhymes such as:

Better to eat husks for a year or two,
Than to be in your Daqiu,
Married to you.

Even for those who could find a bride, weddings were often impossible because of the costs. Chinese tradition dictated an elaborate wedding banquet, and that meant proper marriages were rare. In Daqiu, the problem was so acute that a whole songbook of rhymes evolved around the plight of bachelors:

Bachelorhood is best!
Bachelorhood is best!
Lying on the wall,
Taking a long rest!

and, more poignantly:

A man reaches forty,
Living in a house of dreams.
Clutching the pillow
And counting the beams.

In 1929, the Year of the Dog in the Chinese calendar, Yu Zuomin was born in this village to a typical family of poor peasants. He was the third of four boys. Just fifteen landlords held a quarter of the village's arable land at this time, the rest being shared by more than 250 households like Yu's. With his trademark big ears and easy smile, Yu was a pleasant if unremarkable boy. Like most children in the village, he began working the fields at a tender age and did not learn to read or write. His parents collected enough surplus grain to put him through just one semester of private tuition, offered during the winter months by itinerant scholars in long gowns who had failed to enter the civil service.

Most of Yu Zuomin's childhood memories would have been of social unrest. The lengthy inter-regnum between the fall of the Qing dynasty in 1911 and the rise to power of the Chinese Communist Party

(CCP) in 1949 visited untold miseries on rural China: warlords, corrupt and incompetent rule by the republican Nationalist Party, Japanese invaders, and finally a bloody civil war exacted a heavy toll. Yu's father was swept away by floods while working the fields in 1938 because nearby dikes had not been repaired. Then, during the three-year civil war that began in 1946, Jinghai county was thrust into the center of battle as village-based Communist armies attacked Nationalist garrisons in Tianjin and Jinghai town. By the time the CCP seized power across the land in 1949, China's peasantry was poor and depleted.

Yu Zuomin's generation had high expectations of the Communists. The new party promised land reform, education, health services, and, most important of all, "liberation" from the iniquitous economic system of the past. In Jinghai county alone, 30,000 people who were deemed remnants of the old order (10 percent of the population) were investigated, and 5,600 of them sent to labor camps. But for others in the county, the early years of Communist rule brought many welcome changes, including running water and basic health services. If nothing else, the assertion of political stability was a welcome change for the region's beleaguered peasants. Daqiu and the twenty-three other villages that made up the "old eastern townships" of Hebei were put under a new township called Caigong, which belonged to the new county of Jinghai. To spur its development, Jinghai county was put under the direct administration of the affluent port city of Tianjin.

Yu Zuomin, aged thirty-five, joined the party in 1954 and learned to be an accountant in the village's agricultural cooperative. He was a popular figure in Daqiu even then, marrying a girl from the village's powerful Li family. He was not a born leader because there were no born leaders in these parts; but the spirit of the times encouraged the likes of Yu—uneducated and unused to rallying others—to step forward. Like many others joining at this time, he was drawn to the party in the midst of the period of its greatest revolutionary élan. Everyone felt they were part of a great enterprise. In the words of the new state's founder, Mao Zedong, China had "stood up."

Mao Zedong was the son of a peasant from Hunan province who believed that he alone could fathom the hearts and minds of China's then five hundred million peasants. By the mid-1950s, however, sixty-three years old and already suffering from the early stages of Parkinson's disease, Mao was beginning to lose touch with the realities of the country over which he ruled. In the following two decades, the miseries he laid on the doorstep of rural China were unprecedented.

In late 1955, after touring southern China, Mao convinced himself that China needed an "upsurge" in collective farming in order to leapfrog past the Soviet Union to become the communist world's new economic superpower. Eager to discredit cautious rivals within the party, he ordered China's peasants to be forcibly organized into twenty-six thousand huge collective organizations called communes (*gongshe*). The communes, which replaced entire townships (*xiang*), sat atop a three-tiered structure. Below them were production brigades (*shengchan dadui*) based on villages (*cun*), each of which contained several production teams (*shengchan dui*). Daqiu became a production brigade under the new Caigong commune in 1958. Yu Zuomin, who already headed a twenty-person farming group which became a production team, was made a deputy party secretary of the brigade.

Collective farming, with its emphasis on top-down direction and low incentives, was a disaster for rural China—all the more so because the rural sector was simultaneously drained of capital in order to finance a crash industrialization program in the cities. The combined result of this so-called Great Leap Forward was a famine of epic proportions. Somewhere between 10 million and 40 million people died of starvation and its effects in China in the three years between 1959 and 1961, humanity's worst-ever famine. No records exist of the number of "unnatural deaths" in Daqiu during these years, but they must have been substantial. In Jinghai county as a whole, according to official figures, 11,800 people died in the two worst years, 1960 and 1961, about 5,600 more deaths than would be expected based on the previous decade's annual death rates. Births also fell to roughly a third of their historical rate.[2]

The party's unflinching attitude during the Great Leap Famine was to encourage peasants to "recall the sufferings of the past and rejoice in newfound happiness" (*yi ku si tian*). As grain harvests fell, peasants were told to do more with less, or to "launch a sputnik," a reference to the Soviet Union's startling launch of the first satellite to orbit the earth in 1957. Certainly, no one in Daqiu dared to compare the woeful situation directly to the depredations of the past. But they did find some solace, and wry humor, in a village song of old that made reference to the bloated condition of edema that accompanies starvation:

> Daqiu Village, the poorest to be found,
> Alkaline soil and mud huts abound.
> Swollen tummies, bitter water slaked,
> Half the year eating husks and straw baked.

As morale, even the will to live, was sapped from the villagers, leaders became scarce. Most production team leaders in Daqiu simply stayed home, hoping to survive. But Yu Zuomin, angered by the miserable state of affairs, allowed his team's members to grow private crops. He almost lost his job for the outrage. Nonetheless, his team survived without a single death from starvation.

The Great Leap Famine, as it is now called, is arguably the seminal event in Communist China's history. A party that had come to power on the backs of the peasantry unleashed a mad campaign in which the peasants suffered most. To be sure, most of the peasants believed that the famine was caused by insubordination in the ranks of the radiant Mao and by unusually bad weather. But in later years, as the truth emerged, the poverty and death caused by Mao would remain indelibly marked on the rural imagination. As Yu Zuomin later recalled:

> It was considered glorious to be poor and useful to carry out leftist policies. It was considered a good thing to tell lies, put up fake sput-niks, dress in shabby clothes as if it were handsome, and keep say-

ing, "The situation is not just pretty good, it's really good," even when the peasants could only eat chaff and no one could get married. . . . Everyone cared about the upper levels and about documents. Nobody cared about the truth. Doing things together was considered an honor. Everything had to be done across the board and by everybody all at once. The feeling was that peasants did not know how to grow crops and should submit to the blind leadership of others. Everything also had to be on a "great" scale, like a Great Leap Forward, even if the only result was "great" harm for the common people. And public things were used to oppose private things, so everything had to be both "great" and "public." Everything also had to be equal and egalitarian. Everyone had to eat from the same rice bowl. And all this was passed off as true communism. As a result, people were afraid of taking risks or making breakthroughs or tackling sensitive issues. To sum it all up, poverty begot leftism, which in turn begot more poverty. The result was that the country's economy was brought to the verge of collapse.[3]

What makes the memory of the Great Leap Famine all the more bitter to this day is that the party has never admitted it caused the famine or tried to make a full accounting of the number who died. The peasants remember, though. And that memory undermines any faith in the perspicuity of those who issue orders from Beijing. "In his later years, Mao Zedong said so many erroneous things and made so many mistakes, bringing great misfortunes on the common people," Yu later said, scowling at a room full of visiting cadres from Beijing. "But I never saw one of you dare to criticize him."[4]

The Great Leap Famine finally ended in the early 1960s, when the most outlandish industrialization goals were shelved and peasants were allowed to regain some measure of control over agriculture. But

life remained a struggle for peasants living with a predatory state officially committed to draining rural wealth to build urban prosperity.

In 1963, torrential flooding across the Tianjin plains forced the evac-
uation of Daqiu as the central government, ordering Tianjin spared,
sacrificed the surrounding villages to the raging waters. Yu Zuomin,
who had emerged from the famine as Daqiu's de facto leader, led a
haggard trek of the by-then 1,900 villagers to safety in the eastern sub-
urbs of Tianjin. Like a small-scale reenactment of the Long March that
had both consolidated and irrevocably changed the Chinese Communist Party itself, the 45-kilometer trudge created and fortified the
village's identity, and Yu's leadership. Gaunt and trailed constantly by a
shaggy dog, Yu became the person on whose shoulders the fate of
Daqiu rested. His sense of responsibility now went beyond his wife,
three sons, and two daughters. He was the village leader, and the village was a team. When they returned to their sodden homes the following year, the villagers endorsed Yu as their party secretary, a consensus formally approved by the county.[5] He was the village's tenth
party secretary since 1949, the others having all died of starvation or
disease or been sacked for political reasons. By that standard, he would
last only a few years.

While waiting out the floods Yu had organized the villagers to col-
lect discarded rice straw to sell to the Tianjin Paper Mill for use in
making pulp. That successful foray inspired him when they returned
home. After an abortive attempt to build a small-scale flour mill, he invested Rmb 400 of brigade money to buy a crusher to make pulp for
sale to the same Tianjin Paper Mill. The idea worked brilliantly at
first. The small factory earned Rmb 10,000 in 1967, and the proceeds
were reinvested in seven more machines that brought in Rmb 70,000
the following year. But the risks of depending on the erratic state sector
soon ruined the enterprise. When the Tianjin Paper Mill was ordered
to make its own pulp rather than rely on outside suppliers, Daqiu's flir-
tation with industry came to a rusty end.

Other winds were also blowing at this time that further constrained Daqiu's entrepreneurial urge. In 1966, Mao launched the Great Proletarian Cultural Revolution, an ideological purity campaign through which the increasingly sick and paranoid leader sought to rout his perceived enemies within the party. The movement's worst excesses took place in the cities, but some aspects spilled into the countryside as well. Peasants were held up as role models during the Cultural Revolution, and millions of party officials and youths were rusticated in order to learn from their idealized country cousins. One of the youths sent to Daqiu was a strong-minded woman from Tianjin named Shi Jiaming. Yu Zuomin protected her, along with several university teachers and scientists sent to the village, from anything worse than hard labor. All of them would return the favor in later years.

Yu himself, along with thirteen thousand cadres in Jinghai, was briefly dismissed from his post as village party chief at the outset of the Cultural Revolution. With nothing objectionable in his family or class background, he was accused by youthful Red Guards from the city merely of being a "dog's head chief of staff" (*goutou junshi*), a term of abuse roughly meaning a good-for-nothing. Buckets of human excrement were poured over his head as punishment. Fortunately for the village, the guards soon left and Yu was restored to his post.

Were it only a question of billeting rusticated guests and an occasional brush with pubescent Red Guards, the Cultural Revolution might have been forgotten in the Chinese countryside. But the peasants too were expected to display their revolutionary brio. Besides daubing slogans on their mud walls and sitting under trees to study the works of Mao, this meant mimicking the achievements of "model villages." China's most famous model village of this period gained its fame as a result of the same 1963 floods that had brought Yu Zuomin to power in Daqiu. In August of that year, the party's mouthpiece, the *People's Daily,* praised the party secretary of a remote hamlet in the northwestern province of Shanxi for bringing his village through the torrential rains without any loss of life or aid from the state. When reporters dispatched to Dazhai village found that its irrigation systems and field terracing had been rebuilt through round-the-clock work, a model was born. The propaganda system was soon hard at work promoting Dazhai as a paragon for native self-sufficiency. A year later, Mao appealed to the nation's peasants to "learn from Dazhai." Rural cadres were encouraged to become "Dazhai cadres" and meetings were called to encourage "Dazhai-style production." The local newspaper in the area, the *Xiyang Daily,* was renamed *The Dazhai Raging Flame.*

The party secretary of this seventy-eight-household hamlet was Chen Yonggui, a simple but charismatic peasant instantly recognizable by the garb he adopted, which was unique to the northwest peasants: a plain buttoned tunic called a *duijin,* a grass belt, and, most distinguishing, a white towel wrapped around his head to ward off the sun, known colloquially as a lamb's tummy (*yang duzi*). Chen, then forty-eight, was fond of drawing attention to his peasant roots: "I've never been to school, never studied a day in my life. I have no culture, and my understanding of communist theory is really awful," he would say.[6] He was a perfect embodiment of the anti-intellectual, rural-based spirit of the party. Known affectionately as "Uncle Chen," he was made a party politburo member in 1973 and a state vice premier in 1975.

Dazhai was a heartening story at a time when rural China was still recovering from the Great Leap Famine. Unfortunately, what began as a flicker of hope soon turned into a sham. Caught up in the media attention lavished on him, Chen began to lie and distort the truth. The miracle harvests and effortless mechanization he announced to reporters turned out to be mostly lies. Yu Zuomin, who made four pilgrimages to Dazhai during the Cultural Revolution, knew it from the start. "They were a big hoax off stage," he would recall. "The peasants of the village were poor, and so were the leaders."[7]

It took several years before those cold truths were admitted in full. The first suggestion that Dazhai had falsified grain production figures surfaced in the *People's Daily* in 1980. After that, the true story emerged slowly, like a mournful lament. In a revealing book published in 1994, two Beijing academics showed that the village's grain yields had been grossly inflated by shrinking the reported amount of land under cultivation by nearly 40 percent, to 53 hectares, and by borrowing grain from elsewhere.[8] Dazhai had also been showered with free equipment and materials from around the nation, they wrote, totaling about Rmb 850,000—an overwhelming amount in those days. What's more, Dazhai's revolutionary zeal had harmed the very people it was supposed to represent. Red Guards killed 141 people in and around Dazhai during the Cultural Revolution, 124 of them simple farmers. Chen Yonggui was dismissed from his posts in 1980 and held under house arrest at a state-run orchard in suburban Beijing. There he died of lung cancer in 1986.

More than anything, Dazhai gave model villages a bad name in China. The party refrained from using the term "model village" any longer. But even those villages it praised were deemed a hoax by a skeptical public. For a long time, it would be hard to convince anyone in China that a wealthy village—especially one noticed by the national press—was for real. That was the true legacy of Dazhai.

Closer to home, the Cultural Revolution also produced the riotous model village of Xiaojin (pronounced "shee-ow-gin"), north of Tianjin.[9] Unlike Dazhai, Xiaojin's repute was built solely on its political correctness. Rather than spending their days in backbreaking field work, Xiaojin villagers stomped away the hours in revolutionary song and dance troupes. In the late 1960s, Mao's actress-wife, Jiang Qing, visited the village and praised its fervor. Her Gang of Four clique, which dominated the party between about 1972 to 1976, showed its approbation by installing the village leader, Wang Zuoshan, onto the standing committee of the national parliament, the National People's Congress, in 1975.

Dutiful, if dismayed, Yu Zuomin visited Xiaojin three times during the Cultural Revolution. On one occasion, he returned to Daqiu and organized a revolutionary song and dance troupe with eight hundred members, a third of the village. The singing wasn't bad, he remembered, and the drums and gongs actually enlivened things a little. "Kids were dancing, youths were singing, women were performing plays, even old men and women were mounting the stage to perform tricks. Everyone who performed earned ten extra work points," Yu recalled. But in the year of the troupe's existence, Daqiu's grain output plummeted by a third to 400,000 kilos. "Singing more was not going to produce more grain, and dancing another dance was not going to get us out of the poverty trap," he later recalled. "It was nothing but a mindless flurry."[10]

For a peasant like Yu brought up in the traditions of diligent labor and little pretense, the almost constant ideological campaigns of the 1950s and 1960s were an affront. Official party histories would stress the political problems of the period, the failure of "democratic supervision" during the Great Leap Forward and the "political chaos" of the Cultural Revolution. But peasant memories would remember different things: disruptions to harvest cycles, irrational planting policies, and, most of all, the invidious setting off of villagers against one another.[11] Yu's thoughts, later recounted, reflected a deep sense of frustration:

> Whenever the economy was doing well, a political movement
> would begin. Those doing enterprising work suffered. It was hard
> to pin any ideological problems on those who were not doing any-
> thing useful. But it was easy to find fault with those who worked
> hard. If you'd worked for ten years, making one mistake per year,
> by the time the political movement came you would be charged on
> ten counts. Once those charges were relayed all down the line of
> command and to the upper levels, you'd be history. It's hard to
> guess how many working people were ruined by these movements.
> The result was that those who just looked on, those who found
> fault with others, were always promoted afterward. If you were a
> leader, you had to learn to be impassive. When you encountered

frictions in society, you would try to avoid them, fearing to make a mistake, not daring to do any real work, not daring to take responsibility.[12]

It was not clear how China's peasants could become rich, but it *was* clear what was keeping them poor. The party's single-minded attention to the two "roots" of class struggle and grain production, Yu believed, were as pernicious to peasants as the old landlord system had been. "Unless those two roots are removed," he told villagers, "the seedlings of wealth will not survive."[13]

A half-serious joke that made the rounds of Daqiu in the early 1970s went as follows:[14]

QUESTION: What's the best way to kill someone in Daqiu without getting caught?

ANSWER: Bash in their head with a brick. No judge will ever believe that a person from Daqiu has enough money to own a brick. You are sure to be set free.

When the last embers of the Cultural Revolution died out after the arrest of the Gang of Four in 1976, Daqiu, like most villages, remained poor and miserable. Nobody was dying from starvation, of course. And life expectancy and literacy rates continued to rise. But the ways and means of the village had changed little in the past century. Most households, for example, maintained jealously guarded open latrine pits behind their homes to make fertilizer, producing a plague of flies and a stench that hung thickly in the air. Mud or adobe huts remained the norm. Perhaps most humiliating, given the scornful ditties that used to be heaped upon Daqiu, was the bachelor problem. Only three weddings were held in the village in the four years to 1977. By that time, it boasted an army of 250 bachelors out of a population of 2,800.

An old Chinese saying has it that "poverty creates a desire for change."[15] This desire was tearing across rural China in the wake of the Cultural Revolution. Although the country's famed economic reformer, Deng Xiaoping, remained in political limbo until 1978, it was clear as early as 1976 that attempts by Mao's chosen successor, Hua Guofeng, to uphold the collectivist policies associated with Dazhai and Uncle Chen were losing political support in Beijing. Many rural areas took the cue and began digging themselves out of poverty.

Among the national trailblazers, the central province of Anhui was the furthest ahead. Peasants there had been engaging in household-based farming on and off since the Great Leap Famine just to survive. In November 1977 provincial leaders led by Wan Li, later state premier, endorsed reforms in some prefectures that stripped the old communes of their might. Similar green lights for a return to private farming were soon given by provincial leaders in southern provinces like Sichuan and Guangdong.

Alongside farming reforms, some rural areas began to promote industrialization. This was arguably a more risky venture, since the party had long frowned upon farmers engaging in nonagricultural pursuits. After a brief rural industrial boom in the late 1950s caused by Mao's promotion of village steel production, farmers had been forced back to the fields to ensure that grain supplies remained ample. Throughout the 1960s, communes were prohibited from devoting more than 15 percent of their labor to so-called sideline activities, a stricture that forced village leaders to devise ever more ingenious ways to disguise the legions of peasants engaged at repair shops and brick kilns, hauling goods on wooden carts, or fashioning simple textile products at home.[16] Even when the villages erected wooden or brick sheds to process their harvests from the land, they had to abide by a strict policy of autarky known as the "three locals" (*san jiudi*), meaning that only local materials could be used and that they had to be processed and sold locally too.

But the loosening political atmosphere in the last days of the Cultural Revolution, coupled with a green revolution in the countryside and the neglect of rural industrial needs by state factories, prompted many rural leaders to set up factories.[17] Places like Jiangsu province were the quickest to realize the potential of crude factories to employ farmhands thrown out of work by farming reforms and to boost rural incomes. In 1974, Jiangsu leaders issued several new regulations to promote rural enterprises, still officially called "brigade enterprises" (*gongshe dadui qiye* or just *shedui qiye*). Henceforth southern Jiangsu, known as Su Nan, would be the testing ground and political debating point for the merits of rural factories. Soon the idea was catching on nationwide. In 1976, a National Rural Industry Administration was created by the central government, somewhat legitimizing the position of rural enterprises. By 1978, the country's 1.5 million rural enterprises employed twenty-eight million workers, or 10 percent of the rural workforce.[18] It was already an open secret that the farmers of Su Nan were building themselves two-story tiled houses with the profits from their factories.

Southern and western provinces dominated the early stages of rural reforms. This occurred for several reasons: their distance from Beijing allowed them to challenge central policies with greater impunity; they were wealthier and thus more willing to take risks; and they had an ingrained culture of resistance and initiative that the grim peasants of the northern plains did not seem to share. A place like Daqiu seemed the least likely place for a "breakthrough."

But other factors also influenced which villages made early dashes for wealth. Some scholars have found evidence to support the thesis that the more a place suffered during the Great Leap Famine, the greater was its impetus for change when economic reforms began in the mid-1970s.[19] By that standard, Daqiu would be expected to be among the earliest to change. Yu Zuomin put it like this: "We peasants have paid a stiff price for leftism. We still have nightmares about a return to the leftist persecutions and the poverty of the past. I have been poor and so has this village. We must never go back to that period!"[20]

Another critical factor was the role of local leaders. By taking initiatives, forging a consensus, and, in particular, ignoring, fighting, soothing, or simply co-opting the inevitable opposition of timid party cadres above, village leaders could make all the difference. In Daqiu, there was Yu Zuomin. Of all the people in Daqiu, he thirsted for change the most. He was quite literally fed up with the party and its political campaigns, which had brought nothing but woe to his village and to himself. Self-reliance and local initiative were a more promising road to recovery, he believed. The party's appeal to "rely on the party and the masses" was not enough. "We should rely on the party and the masses," he whispered to fellow villagers, "but above all, we should rely on ourselves."[21]

Daqiu's chance to do just that came in August 1977. That summer, the party launched yet another political campaign, this one to criticize the "left errors" of the past. Yu dutifully convened a three-day meeting of the village to discuss the campaign. But he got more than he bargained for. As news of rural reforms elsewhere had spread, villagers in Daqiu had grown restless for change. The same things that frustrated Yu frustrated them. Now there was a chance to act, to rely on themselves, to get rich. The people of Daqiu were not going to leave that meeting until they were satisfied.

The villagers mostly arrived at the dusty square in the center of the village before Yu himself on the first day. The elders carted heavy bamboo seats, while the young adults stood and the children played. When Yu arrived, he sat on a wooden stool in front of the assembled crowd. On his right was Liu Wanquan, a bald-headed man with a penetrating gaze who headed the village production brigade. An electrician by training, Liu was known in the village as Mr. Do-It-All. His family traced its roots in Daqiu further back than Yu's.

Yu began by asking for suggestions about how to "correct the leftist tendency" in the village. Then a torrent began. Some villagers accused him of having gone too far in "learning from Dazhai" during the Cultural Revolution. Others said he was no longer fit to rule and should stand aside in favor of a younger cadre who could lead the village to riches. The clamor had barely died down on the first day when the second day began, and then the third. The ponytailed Shi Jiaming, the rusticated youth who had stayed in the village as a production team leader, was among the critics. So too was Yu Zuoyao, Yu's own brother, who headed the village public safety committee. "Every person came to that meeting with an arrow," Yu Zuomin later recalled, "and my chest was the bull's eye."[22]

Each night during the three-day meeting, Yu stalked the banks of the Tuanpowa reservoir to the northeast of the village. Stepping slowly along the mud pathways, he smoked cheap cigarettes and pondered the future. There was a lot to consider. With the political situation in Beijing still parlous, another political movement could erupt. If so, he would be sure to suffer. On the other hand, news from around the country suggested that economic pioneers were being protected, and many were getting rich. If only he could pull his charges out of poverty, they would support him again.

The problem was that agriculture could never be a source of wealth for Daqiu. Unlike China's proverbial "lands of fish and grain" in the south and central regions, the soil and climate here were too unavailing. "This little village has nothing but alkaline soil. What kind of wealth could we get from the land? Who would ever buy it?" Yu thought as he wandered along the moonlit paths of the reservoir.[23]

Yu's mind drifted back to the village of his childhood. There had been two kinds of landlords then. One kind had relied solely on the land. The other had owned shops and small factories in Tianjin, the closest big city. When blight or bad weather came, the former suffered along with the rest of the peasants, eating chaff and hoping for a better tomorrow. But the latter survived, even prospered. If Daqiu owned factories like the landlord-capitalists of old, Yu reasoned, it would provide a stable and promising source of income. It was an ironic inspiration, given the antilandlord commitment of the Communist Party; but by this time, Yu had little time for the party's economic wisdom.

On the fourth day, Yu summoned the villagers back to the square. Most expected him to announce his resignation. The pale and haggard man who stood before them inspired little confidence at first sight.

"Fellow villagers," he began, his voice weak from a lack of sleep. "You have suffered along with me all these years. I don't blame anyone, either those above me or those below me. I take full responsibility. I am willing to resign."[24]

An uneasy stir went through the assembled crowd. While many had called for his resignation during the meeting, no one could really imagine Daqiu without Yu Zuomin at the helm. He had earned their trust during the tough times. Perhaps more to the point, no one else was in a position to lead the village. Liu Wanquan, the only serious alternative, stood firmly behind him. If they sacked Yu, the villagers worried, the county leadership might install an outsider as party chief. That would be a disaster. What's more, while decollectivization was bound to attenuate the influence of the central government, the need for a trusted and capable village leader would be that much stronger in the new and uncertain household-based economy of the countryside. Not only would good leaders be crucial to securing and allocating farming inputs, but they would also be needed to foster new jobs and opportunities outside of farming.[25] Certainly Yu had an obvious personal stake in preserving his position atop the village as the commune system fell apart, but it meshed nicely with the villagers' instinct to band together in the turbulent new market era.

"What other ideas do you have?" someone finally barked from the back of the crowd.

Yu had been waiting for this. "I have three goals," he began. "To make us rich, to build everyone a brick house, and to ensure that all our bachelors get married. If you won't trust me with this task, I'll step down. But if you give me just three more years, I'll change the face of Daqiu."

The villagers wanted to hear more. Yu then explained his plan. It was a critical time to experiment with the village economy, he said.

The village's history provided ample evidence of the need to make a living in new ways. Central government regulations would allow the village to keep most of the profits from its new sideline activities, after paying taxes. With the money earned from new ventures, he said, the village could build homes, erect a school, pave the roads, and construct a garden with a lotus pond and a pavilion. Daqiu could become self-reliant and pull itself out of poverty. Other villages were taking the road of family-based farming, but Daqiu should stick together as a single economic unit, pursuing industrial and sideline ventures and growing rich together. "And if I fail," Yu pledged, "you can desecrate the graves of my ancestors and throw me in the county jail."

"Good! Good!" the villagers hooted. It was not clear which they liked better, the economic plan or the prospect of jailing their failed leader and vandalizing his family graves. As a token of his promise, Yu returned home and placed a bedroll on his doorstep. If the day came to put him in jail, he would be ready. He had three years.

Only one Daqiu villager had ever worked in a factory. He was Liu Wanmin, the younger brother of Mr. Do-It-All, Liu Wanquan. As a worker in the Tianjin Cold-Rolled Steel Strip Mill beginning in 1960, Little Liu had earned the praise of factory leaders, climbing up to a managerial role by the early 1970s. But in early 1977, factory leaders discovered that he had served briefly as a soldier in the Nationalist forces before 1949. Little Liu was sent back to Daqiu in disgrace.

His reappearance in the village was timely. Desperate for help to get the newly endorsed factory program off the ground, Yu Zuomin gladly overlooked the historical blemish and took counsel from Little Liu. Naturally enough, Little Liu suggested building a small cold-rolled steel strip mill—the most basic of steel factories—in which precast steel slabs are rolled into coils of steel strip at room temperatures. Demand for steel was insatiable as construction and industry came to life across

China. The Tianjin mill Little Liu had left could not supply half the local market needs. Yu Zuomin readily accepted the idea.

The first problem was money. About Rmb 150,000 (U.S. $26,000) would be needed to build a strip mill, including the machinery. Yet the village brigade had just Rmb 50,000 in savings, and the villagers themselves could scrape together only Rmb 10,000. After some persuasion through the good offices of a relative, Yu convinced the county government to part with Rmb 37,000, claiming it was for irrigation works. Another Rmb 20,000 was borrowed from neighboring villages. About Rmb 20,000 was then saved by making bricks in the village's own kiln, which had been built in 1968 to make clay bricks for sale to construction teams in Tianjin. With another Rmb 13,000 borrowed from various sources, the money was finally collected. It was all they had.

A second question was who would run the factory. Mr. Do-It-All was the obvious candidate, given his handy reputation. But he would agree only on the condition that Little Liu, his brother, be hired as well. That caused a stir. Using the former Nationalist soldier for his bright ideas was one thing, but giving him a full-time job in the village's first factory was quite another. Some fretted that his background would cause political problems. Others worried that the factory would become "the Liu family shop."

Yu disagreed. Such suspicions had torn Chinese society apart in the previous two decades, he argued. Now they had to be put aside if the village economy was going to prosper. As he put it:

> If we judge everyone in terms of class struggle, we'll find everyone is an enemy because they have a bad family background, or their social relations are problematic. If we judge everyone in terms of the Cultural Revolution, we'll find everyone is a criminal because they have made historical errors. If we judge everyone in terms of factions, we'll find everyone is our enemy simply because they disagree with us. But if we judge people in light of the reform movement, we'll find that there are capable people everywhere.[26]

After much debate, Little Liu became the factory's first sales manager. Another 112 villagers were hired to man the mill. In early 1978, the village bought a second-hand cold-strip steel line from the Tianjin mill. Using it as a model, the diligent villagers crafted two more. The trial runs of the tiny factory were a frustrating process of trial and error. "We were really groping in the dark," Yu later recalled. "The moment we figured out one thing, we would be confused by another thing."[27] But after a few months, the three-line factory was put into full operation. Daqiu's industrialization had begun.

With a combination of uncanny timing, competent management by the Liu brothers, and a fair dose of good luck, the little steel mill exceeded everyone's expectations. The first rolls of steel strip were piled onto wagons and hauled into Tianjin by tractor. Sales were slow at first, and village leaders offered "gifts," meaning bribes, to secure some deals.[28] But that soon changed. China's economy was awakening, and Daqiu was ready and waiting. The steel was bought to make boilers, electrical appliances, vehicle parts, and a host of consumer products like band saws, razor blades, rakes, and kitchen knives. The more they produced, the more they sold. By the end of the first year, the factory had chalked up sales of Rmb 586,000. After paying back loans, deducting input costs and salaries, and paying Rmb 78,000 in taxes to the state, the plant was left with a net profit of Rmb 134,000.[29] It was more than the cumulative profits of the village since 1949.

In retrospect, it was a golden age for the establishment of rural enterprises. While a strict Stalinist planned economy continued to hamper city factories, most rural areas were either too timid or too poor to establish factories themselves. Daqiu was also under way a full two months *before* Deng Xiaoping maneuvered successfully to make economic development, not class struggle, the party's main task at a meeting in December 1978. "By the end of 1978, when other places were just beginning to realize they needed factories, Daqiu was already making its name. Who could compete with them?" the party's newspaper for intellectuals, the *Guangming Daily,* later asked.[30]

Yu, with modesty and necessary political correctness, later attributed the village's early success to the December 1978 party meeting. "Those who understood its meaning early got rich early, and those who understood it late got rich late. And of course, those who never understood it never got rich at all," he commented.[31] But it was clear that Daqiu, like many other Chinese villages, was way ahead of the glacial progress in Beijing.

The following year, 1979, Daqiu built a second factory, this one making steel pipes. Yu Zuoyao, the same man who had criticized Yu Zuomin, his brother, at the village meeting, was put in charge of the project. With his fuzzy pate, bushy eyebrows, and oversized ears, Yu Zuoyao bore more than a passing resemblance to his brother. With the Liu family in charge of one factory, there was no reason the Yu family could not run its successor. As in so many villages in rural China, traditional family and kinship ties were coming rapidly back into play as highly centralized state structures evaporated.

After several failed attempts to seek assistance from a steel pipes factory in suburban Tianjin, Brother Yu and his team went ahead on their own. A total of Rmb 900,000 was borrowed from various sources to purchase a secondhand production line. Using industrial manuals purchased in Tianjin bookstores, the budding peasant-industrialists learned how to operate the machines. They were "crossing the river by feeling for the stones," as the Chinese saying went, a phrase later used by Deng Xiaoping to characterize the whole process of China's economic reforms. Soon they were producing a decent pipe. And, as with the first factory, the products sold like hotcakes. Buyers who could not obtain pipes from sclerotic state factories happily turned to the little-known village in the southern reaches of Tianjin for their supplies. By the end of 1979, the pipes factory had racked up revenues of Rmb 1.7 million and profits before taxes of Rmb 350,000.

In 1980, the third factory in as many years opened, this one a printing plant. Although China was still several years from its consumer boom, simple products like packaged food and printed materials were already in serious shortage. The Daqiu Printing Plant was headed by Zhao Shuzhong, a former secretary of the village's Communist Youth League and the husband of one of Yu's daughters. With his close-set facial features, boyish smile, and wave of hair, son-in-law Zhao was a good-looking cadre. Aged barely twenty, he invested Rmb 100,000 of village money and took twenty-six people from the fields to start the plant, which began operations with a second-hand letterpress printing machine. The printing plant made notebooks for schoolchildren and contracted to print some government documents from surrounding towns and villages. Soon the letterpress machine was replaced with a better offset machine. Profits soared to Rmb 300,000 on revenues of Rmb 1 million.

Daqiu had made a good start. Combined profits from the three factories surpassed Rmb 2 million in 1981. With the proceeds, the village built its first brick school complete with wooden benches and tables, replacing a mud hut in which newspapers had been pasted on the walls to keep out drafts and add some color. Yu Zuomin had made good on his promise to give the village a new start. For now, at least, he was unlikely to go to jail and his ancestors could rest in peace.

But political risks remained. The rapid growth of rural factories in the early 1980s set off alarm bells within the left-wing faction of the Chinese Communist Party. Left-wing ideologues warned in articles in influential journals that the unbridled expansion of the nimble and low-cost rural enterprises would put state factories out of business, threatening the very heart of socialism in China. "At a time when the national economy is seriously out of order, we need to concentrate our rural efforts on agricultural production, not on building factories and commercial enterprises," warned two theorists in a typical outcry in the influential *Jiang Han Forum* magazine in early 1981.[32] Besides the likely deleterious effects on agricultural production and state industry, the writers warned, the diversion of profits out of the state sector could threaten Communist rule itself. "If industrial and commercial profits start flowing to rural areas, not only will it shake the basis of the entire state finances and affect the stability of state revenues, it will also affect economic stability and political peace and harmony."

Daqiu was one of the nearest examples to Beijing of rural enterprises threatening the big state factories on their doorstep. The village was cited in several left-wing journals as an example of the threat to socialism represented by rural enterprises. But Yu Zuomin, toughened by his ingrained disgust of the party's left wing, ignored the critics. "Some party theorists were attacking us directly and putting pressure on us to stop," he later recalled. "But we just put up with it and kept on going."[33]

Yu's confidence had been bolstered by events in Beijing. In 1979, the State Council and the party Central Committee had issued successive documents calling for an expansion of brigade enterprises.[34] Then the last shreds of doubt about the likely duration of rural reforms fell away when Hua Guofeng—who had appealed for a return to Dazhai-style rural development—was sacked as party chairman in late 1980. Deng Xiaoping became China's senior leader the following year, ending the five-year interregnum since Mao's death. Those like the villagers of Daqiu who had placed their bets on Deng were now uniquely positioned to benefit. Yu had guessed rightly that the outcry from the left against burgeoning village enterprises was merely the last gasp of a defeated bloc. As he later recalled:

> At the critical moment when we began our opening and reform,
> these supposedly clearheaded people suddenly became confused. . . .
> They ran everywhere asking whether something was capitalist or socialist. It seemed that the only thing that was socialist was themselves, while anything that did not accord with their views was capitalist.
> But I never believed this, and neither did the people of Daqiu.[35]

In 1982, Daqiu's fourth factory, the last of the "Four Mother Hens" as they were called, began operation inside seven disused horse stables with Rmb 100,000 worth of used metalworking equipment. If Yu Zuomin had taken political risks in hiring Little Liu for the first factory, he took plain business risks in making Zhang Yanjun the head of this fourth factory. Zhang, a heavyset cadre with a plain face and a scowl, was another former head of the village's Communist Youth League. He was also the son of Zhang Yupu, the closest that Daqiu had to a village patriarch. But mostly, Little Zhang was known for his scientific misadventures. As a young researcher in the village's feedstock operations in the mid-1970s he had single-handedly killed two hundred perfectly healthy pigs in just four months using experimental feeds. Most thought he was a quack. But Yu liked his enterprising character. Aged just twenty-one, he was hired to run the electrical factory.

As with the first two factories, the Jinhai Electrical Equipment Factory sought to quench the insatiable thirst for industrial materials in the country. The switches, breakers, car batteries, fuses, and small electric engines that came off its worktables sold quickly. As Little Zhang recalled of the early success, "In the initial stages, we relied on courage and friendships. At the same time, we relied on the fact that state enterprises were heavily constrained by the old state planning system. Rural enterprises took advantage of this head start, stepped in to fill the gap, and grew to be strong."[36]

It had been five years since that fateful village meeting. Daqiu was off to a good start, and Yu quietly removed his moth-eaten bedroll from the doorway. Although other rural areas of China were getting more attention in the national press for their farming reforms, Daqiu's industry made more money. To celebrate the lunar new year of 1982, Yu hired the finest traditional wooden-clapper opera troupes from Tianjin and Beijing to perform in the village. Gongs and drums had sounded in the village for political reasons during the Cultural Revolution. Now they were sounding to the beat of economic success.

A Chinese saying has it that "people are afraid of becoming famous for the same reason that pigs are afraid of becoming fat."[37] While Daqiu had successfully navigated the national political minefield of the early reform period, its modest wealth was soon the subject of local contention. Like a fattened pig in a sty, the village became the envy of everyone from the residents of neighboring villages like Little Qiu, its historical twin, to county leaders in Jinghai.

"There is jealousy on all sides," Yu warned. "It's like being surrounded by a raging fire that may consume us at any moment."[38]

While neighboring villages could be assuaged with small donations and opportunities to work in Daqiu factories, reconciling the county leadership to the village's new wealth was more tricky. The formal relationship between the county and Daqiu was clearly one of master and subordinate. The Jinghai party committee appointed the party chief of villages like Daqiu and maintained a "guiding relationship" (*zhidao guanxi*) over them. For nearly two decades the county had endorsed the village's own choice of Yu Zuomin, but that could change. The county could discipline and direct village chiefs, often by sending a deputy party secretary of the county to live in the village and "rectify" its policies. The county government, meanwhile, was responsible for crucial areas like infrastructure, taxation, and law enforcement. If they felt that the village's fealty to the county leadership was weakening, Jinghai officials could crush Daqiu.

Daqiu was not alone in finding its relations with higher-level local officials strained at this time, despite the fiscal benefits that the county reaped from the village's economic expansion. Throughout China, local officials were startled by the sudden irruption of peasant entrepreneurs in the countryside. After decades of being in complete control of their fiefs, county and township officials found the sleeping giant of rural China waking below them, and they were alarmed. One scholar described their reaction this way:

Local cadres were the first to vent their antagonism. When the new business class first appeared amid the policy confusion of the early reform period, cadres could not tell what was allowed and what was

not. Perceiving the new businesses as a vague threat to local authority, cadres felt compelled to interfere. They began to bully entrepreneurs by extending a hand (*shen shou*), or demanding a share.[39]

Daqiu's success had strained relations with the county on several
fronts. Jinghai leaders were afraid to endorse the still-maverick development path of the village, which was investing so much in factories to
the apparent neglect of agriculture. There were also growing allegations
of corruption in Daqiu. Some people said that village leaders had illegally diverted funds earmarked for irrigation projects into their factories, which was partly true. Others said the factory inputs were obtained
and the output sold through bribery, again not wholly inaccurate.
While such allegations were in the long run probably overblown, Yu
knew the damage they could cause. "Rumors will cast a shadow on you.
They are as fast as the wind and as sharp as a knife," he warned. "We'll
be unable to defend ourselves, and in the end we may be wiped out."[40]

Besides the factories, relations with the county were also tense over
Daqiu's involvement in two county work projects in 1980.[41] One of the
thrusts of Yu's economic revival plan for Daqiu had been to dispatch
villagers to work as contract laborers in the surrounding area. The two
projects involved digging oil wells in the Dagang oil field southeast of
Daqiu and cutting reeds around the Tuanpowa reservoir. Rather than
keep 70 percent of the contract payments for the village and paying 30
percent to the workers, as prescribed by the county, Yu gave 70 percent
to the workers and kept just 30 percent for the village. On both projects, the added incentives spurred the workers to do more, leaving the
village with more income in any case. But county leaders, already suspicious of the village's heedless attitude, were outraged when they
learned of the change. In theory, Yu had no business rearranging the
terms of compensation, especially when the changes favored individuals. "The oil well digging and reed cutting incidents were soon seen as
crimes I had committed," Yu would recall. "We were accused of prac-
ticing capitalism."[42]

One response engendered in Daqiu by the tensions with the county was a fortress mentality. Yu instructed villagers not to discuss Daqiu's affairs with people from neighboring villages. The school principal, Li Bingkai, was run out of town, accused of being a spy for the county.[43] As part of the same veil of secrecy, Yu began meting out rough justice in the village rather than reporting violent incidents to the county police. The fine for battery was set at Rmb 100 for each blow struck plus payment of all the victim's medical costs.[44]

Another response was an attempt to mollify county officials. Yu plied them with cartons of cigarettes or buckets of fresh fish when they visited, sometimes even an electric appliance. A few county officials became Yu's good friends. But there was one person he could not placate: Jinghai's longtime party secretary, Tong Zemin. A native of central Hebei province, the same area whose people had formerly disparaged Daqiu and its vicinity in song, Tong had good reason to feel miffed by the village's newfound wealth. As a veteran of the Communist Party who had served on and off as county party chief since 1964, he also felt aggrieved that the uppity farmer-entrepreneurs were suddenly living better than himself.

On the eve of lunar new year in early 1982, Tong summoned Yu to Jinghai for a talk. The celebration that begins on this night is the happiest day for Chinese people, especially in rural areas where the partying is a glimmer of light cast on an otherwise somber existence. Yu refused to come, and the two argued on the telephone.[45] At first they quarreled about the meeting. But soon, their dispute reached the heart of the matter.

"I've made revolution for forty years. Is it fair that you make more money than I do?" Tong stammered.

"What you earn is the people's money. What we earn is our own money," Yu retorted. Besides, he asked, "where is it written in the constitution that those who have been part of the revolution the longest should earn the most?"

Tong continued his assault: "There are serious reports of unhealthy tendencies in your village."

Yu easily volleyed this one, since county cadres were often seeking bribes in Daqiu: "If the county itself is unhealthy, how can we be healthy? If you blow from the northwest, how can we blow from the southeast?"

Tong became furious. "You're an arrogant fellow, Yu Zuomin!"

"Is it arrogance that's led us to increase production by a factor of five in four years?" Yu snapped back. "If so, then I've obviously not been arrogant enough. We should continue being arrogant for ten more years. If we did, you guys in Jinghai would surely die of jealousy."

For several weeks after that sharp exchange there was silence from Jinghai. Yu could only guess what was being planned. At best, he would be publicly criticized; at worst, sacked. But it was clear that there would be a confrontation, a tussle from which little Daqiu, despite its modest wealth, would be hard-pressed to emerge unscathed.

"This crossing of swords will not be an even match from any perspective," Brother Yu warned. "The county has the initiative. And they can strike at any time."[46]

When the strike against Daqiu finally came, it was at once less drastic and more ominous than expected. Tong Zemin declared that a twenty-person "inspection team" would descend on the village to investigate the allegations of corruption, "unhealthy tendencies," and policy irregularities. The team would be composed of officials from the four departments that handle law enforcement: the party discipline inspection department, the police, the prosecutor's office, and the judiciary.[47]

Yu's response was mixed. On the one hand, he welcomed the opportunity to set the record straight and clear the village's name. On the other hand, given the inability of the village to defend itself, he could only fear the worst. Surely an inspection team with a mandate to find problems would fabricate them if necessary. Who would ever do business with the village again if it was accused of being a sham, the Dazhai of the east?

"I don't mind if some people try to compete against us through fair economic competition," Yu told a visitor. "But it's wrong for them to use political methods to discipline us."[48]

When the inspection team members arrived in mid-March, led by the head of the county's rural work department, they were billeted in a simple adobe hut rather than at the village guesthouse.[49] When Yu paid the team a visit on the night of its arrival, he immediately found himself under intense scrutiny.

"Do you think you can pass the test?" the team leader asked.

"Why do I have to pass a test in the first place?" he replied.

"If you haven't done anything wrong, then why be afraid of ghosts at the door?" (Losing sleep over a fear of ghosts was a way of saying you had a guilty conscience.)

"Even though I haven't done anything wrong, the ghosts still come to the door and demand I open up," Yu protested. "Isn't this just like a plot to make me lose sleep anyway?"

The people of Daqiu did not take kindly to this invasion of their hamlet, and Yu did nothing to douse their feelings. Everywhere they went, team members were surrounded by jeering villagers. Some even wielded bricks, a poignant symbol of Daqiu's new wealth given the old joke about how to kill someone without getting caught.[50] When one team member complained about the close company, Yu riposted by reminding him of the party's appeal to cadres to "stick close by the masses." "How can a member of the Chinese Communist Party be afraid of the masses? If you don't stick close to the masses, how will you ever conduct your inspection?"[51]

Spring wore into summer. By day, the team would tramp from office to office, poring over perfectly kept account books and interrogating reticent factory staff. By night, they would twist and turn uncomfortably on the hot brick beds in their hut. The beds, known as *kang,* were wonderful in winter when they were warmed by twin flues from below, but in summer they made you hot and nauseous, like a river fish being cooked in a bamboo steamer.

Yu remained at home with his wife for most of the time, brooding on the future. Although the factories, the Four Hens, continued to operate as usual, everything Yu had built seemed in danger of unraveling before his eyes. It was as if another hated political movement had swept into town. "The senior leadership has promised there will be no more political campaigns. So why do we still need campaigns to rectify individuals, especially campaigns that are not officially sanctioned?" he complained to friends.[52]

The inspection team remained in Daqiu for seven months, until October. In the end, though, the members could find no solid evidence of wrongdoing, not even enough to prove Yu had overpaid the contract workers. Attempts to draw Yu into squealing on county officials who had accepted bribes also failed. By the time the team left, it had dwindled to just one person.

"This leader [Tong] was always rectifying people during the Cultural Revolution and so he used his power to send a team into our village to do the same," Yu recalled later. "But after seven months, they did not find even half a problem. How about that!"[53]

Although it was a relief when the team left, the experience had a profound effect on the way Yu Zuomin ran his village. Within the village, the harrowing episode resulted in Yu becoming more assertive of his rule. The alleged role of Li Bingkai, the county's supposed mole, in undermining his authority made Yu more wary than ever of dissent. If the majority of the village wanted him as their chief, he reasoned, then the minority should shut up or ship out. It was hard enough to protect the village without having to worry about an exposed flank. Just five years earlier, Yu had accepted a hail of criticism and begged to remain the village leader. Now he attacked those who brayed at his rule. "I am the leader and everyone should sing my tune," he told villagers. "I don't want a single person who does not sing my tune."[54]

As for those on the outside who would undermine his rule, Yu adopted an ever more fierce and unflinching attitude. His early attempts to coddle county leaders had failed. Now was the time, he believed, to form a cordon around Daqiu and defend it to the death. "I don't want to be an official. But nor do I want to be bullied," he explained.[55] "It's that kind of attitude," one Chinese newspaper noted later, "that has enabled Yu Zuomin to overcome bureaucratic interference from above."[56]

Thus the real legacy of the 1982 inspection team was its effect on Yu Zuomin and his rule in Daqiu. The village was off and running along the road to riches in early reform China. But roadblocks appeared early on. If it wanted to continue, the village would have to be both strong and united.

Like Uncle Chen of Dazhai before him, Yu Zuomin was barely literate. But, also like Uncle Chen, he had no doubts about the power of the written word in Communist China. A mention in the heavily controlled official press usually brought with it the stamp of party approval. Yu reasoned that if Daqiu were to be celebrated by the national propaganda system as Dazhai had been before it, the repute would bring rich rewards.

Tianjin was the home to one of China's most celebrated party-approved writers, Jiang Zilong. A jovial man with a set of thick black glasses, Jiang had gained early success with a 1979 short story called "Factory Manager Qiao Assumes Office." Written in typical socialist-realist prose, the story portrayed a bold and upright cadre who rights the fortunes of his struggling heavy machinery plant, winning praise for himself and the party in the process. In the spring of 1983, Yu dictated a letter to Jiang Zilong inviting him to visit the village. "I have read your short story about factory manager Qiao, but I am even more daring than he," the letter said. Using his finest flattery, Yu insisted that only a great writer like Jiang could grasp the complexities of the Daqiu tale. Jiang knew he was being used. "Yu Zuomin called me when he was in a very difficult position politically," he recalled in an interview. "They were rich, but they were not yet famous."[57] Still, that was no reason to refuse. Bogged down in a short story that was going nowhere, Jiang readily took the bait and headed for Daqiu.

In his two-week rustication, Jiang visited factories, chatted with village elders, and generally enjoyed himself. The factory buildings, lotus ponds, irrigation ditches, and fruit orchards were quite a sight in this once famously poor village. The village meeting room where he talked to people like Little Liu, Brother Yu, and Mr. Do-It-All was newly outfitted with furniture made in a workshop attached to the printing plant. Yu and his villagers smoked factory-made rather than handrolled cigarettes. Several cadres had new black leather shoes in place of their old army-issue green rubber footwear. Most men wore fetching new tunics of the sort worn by Mao Zedong. About the only thing that still distinguished Yu as a peasant, Jiang remarked oddly, "is his short, flat head."[58]

The modest wealth that Jiang saw in Daqiu was real. Output from the original four factories, the Four Hens, would double in 1983 to Rmb 30 million, while pretax profits would rise by half to Rmb 6 million. In that year, according to the official annals of Tianjin, Daqiu was already one of the richest villages in China, with an income per capita of Rmb 1,266.[59] Jiang was intrigued by the difficulties of adjusting to this wealth after years of deprivation. He noticed, for example, that the thousand-odd new brick houses in the village were identical, right down to the knockers on the wooden doors. Daqiu people, he concluded, hoped to find safety in numbers in case a new political campaign erupted. "The aesthetics of peasants here are controlled by political sensibilities," he wrote.[60]

In the evenings, Jiang sat listening to Yu tell the village's story, from the bad old days of poverty, to the crucial meeting in 1977, the first factories, and finally to the county inspection team. The tumultuous story and Yu's cocky attitude gave Jiang pause. "This is a dangerous person," he wrote. "If my pen gets mixed up with him, who knows what trouble I'll have."[61] Despite the dangers, Jiang was attracted by Yu's simple and frank personality. In any case, the party would probably be happy to read this heartening tale of rags-to-riches success, especially if it was attributed to party policies. "At that time, Yu was just a simple peasant with a good story to tell," he recalled in an interview. "He had found a way to develop his village, and that was quite an achievement."[62]

Jiang returned to Tianjin carrying several crammed notebooks. After a few short months, he produced a short story called "Yanzhao Elegy" (*Yanzhao beige*), Yanzhao being the ancient name for the northern China plains containing Daqiu. The story was published in the spring 1984 issue of the China Writers Association's mass-circulation magazine *People's Literature*. Though the names were changed, the story was a barely concealed account of Daqiu's rise from poverty, ending with the county inspection team's attempt at intimidation. In the story, the village was called Dazhao and their leader was named Wu Gengxin, the surname meaning "battle" and the given name "plow up the new." Jiang knew that the novel would be read as a more or less faithful depiction of the Daqiu story. "I don't want to write an unintentionally revealing statement to the effect that the characters and places in this novel are entirely fictional and readers should not compare them to the real place," he declared in the preface;[63] it would be like the thief of Chinese legend who puts a sign reading "no gold buried here" above his concealed stash.

Given that the fictional veil was thin, the candidness of the story was surprising. Many of Yu's comments about the party's misguided policies of the past were printed word for word, and the resentment felt by many county and city cadres toward rich peasants was amply described. Jinghai leaders were portrayed as thugs and crooks.

The appearance of "Yanzhao Elegy" caused an immediate sensation in China. Almost overnight, Daqiu's fame skyrocketed. What had been a well-known village in the Tianjin area suddenly became a national icon. Jiang's use of earthy rural phrases and words gave the story an immediacy often lacking in the prose of other official propaganda. His veiled criticisms of leftist ideologues and imperious local cadres also seemed to strike a sympathetic chord among readers. Among the many decisions Yu Zuomin took in developing Daqiu, his choice of Jiang Zilong as a portraitist was among the most clever. "Not many people need an introduction to this wonder person of the 1980s," one Chinese author would write of Yu years later. "People were long ago introduced to him by Jiang Zilong's short story."[64]

With the publication of "Yanzhao Elegy," Daqiu became a place of pilgrimage as a steady procession of village cadres and state leaders visited to "obtain its holy scriptures" (*qu jing*). In September 1984, Vice Premier Wan Li, the one-time reformer of Anhui province, became the first-ever central government leader to pay a visit. Months later, in January 1985, Wan returned at the head of a central government study group that included party secretariat member Hu Qili and the recently elected liberal mayor of Tianjin, Li Ruihuan. Even more dust was kicked up by lesser mortals, 88,000 of whom tramped to the village in buses and cars in 1984 seeking clues to its success. That worked out to 241 people per day.

The attitudes of the Jinghai leadership soon swung into line. Tong Zemin was sacked as party chief in late 1984 for unknown reasons and replaced by a younger and better-educated cadre from Tianjin named Zhang Kejun. In June 1984, the county held a first-ever conference in Daqiu on "developing industry to achieve wealth," attended by a Tianjin deputy party secretary, Wu Zhen. In the flash created by one short story, the county government swung from being a sworn enemy to a grudging cheerleader of this upstart village.

The higher profile of the village also brought about its first mention in the foreign press. In a story on rural factories in February 1985, the Associated Press noted: "The industrialized village of Daqiu, specializing in food processing plants, has a per capita income of $714 (Rmb 4,100) a year, more than six times the national average."[65] The report was mistaken, of course; steel, not food, was the driving force of the village economy. But that mattered little. Journalists and officials alike were lighting on this village as a symbol of the economic and social changes sweeping the countryside. Daqiu was well on its way to becoming China's model village of the reform era.

TWO

Four Hens and a Slogan

If we look up, we can concentrate on the future. If we look down,
we can concentrate on money. But only by concentrating on money
can we concentrate on the future.

Yu Zuomin, 1986

Daqiu was not alone in succumbing to the allure of industry in the
1980s. Across China, farmers everywhere were dropping their scythes
and heading for factories. By 1986, seventy-nine million people, or 20
percent of the rural labor force, were working in rural factories and
producing a quarter of the country's industrial output. From making
simple items like footwear, clothing, paper, bricks, ceramics, household
goods, and plastics in the early 1980s, rural concerns were soon moving
into more advanced sectors, like vehicles, electrical machinery, and
home appliances.

"What took us by complete surprise was the development of rural
industries," senior leader Deng Xiaoping would later recall. "A diversity of production, commodities, and all sorts of small enterprises
boomed in the countryside, as if a strange army appeared out of nowhere."[1]

The rural industrial boom was a surprise because the odds were so heavily stacked against the firms. Operating outside of the formal state planning system, their access to credit and materials was severely constrained. Even when they could get loans from state banks, they paid higher interest rates and had to repay principal on time. Another apparent handicap concerned ownership—meaning the right to sell the assets, the right to manage them, and the right to keep the income they generated.[2] Since the townships and villages, which were the successors to the communes and brigades of the Maoist period, owned the right to sell and retain profits from the enterprises, it seemed unlikely that enterprise managers would go all out to make the firms successful.

So why did they flourish? Partly because these same factors proved to be blessings in disguise. Although the procurement of materials and credit was difficult, operating outside the state plan gave the firms a flexibility that often proved to be of greater value. They could make decisions on production and marketing with a speed that state firms could only dream of. The incentive problem for managers, meanwhile, was easily remedied by the adoption of the "contracting" (*chengbao*) system. While the townships and villages retained the right to sell the assets and keep the profits, they could delegate the management rights to local entrepreneurs with built-in incentives. In Daqiu, for example, the heads of each of the Four Hens was entitled to a basic salary plus 1 percent of net profits.

Left-wing commentators often accused rural firms of being no different from "fake collectives" (*jia jiti*), private firms in the countryside that called themselves collectives for political protection. But the system also worked wonders. Suddenly, everyone had a stake in better performance from the factories: the managers, who earned incentive pay; the villages, which retained the post-tax profits; and the township and county governments above them, which had been allowed to keep a greater share of the tax revenues generated in their localities under fiscal reforms in the early 1980s.[3] Applying their personal influence to business and tapping the deeply felt desire of peasants to cast off the poverty of the past, an emergent class of cadre-businessmen in the countryside made miracles.[4]

The rural firms also had an amenable external environment for growth. For one, China's economy was enjoying huge one-time gains from the decollectivization of agriculture, which made GDP soar at double-digit rates. In addition, the moribund state industrial sector lay like a great fallen tree on the forest floor on which the rural firms grew like fungus. The inputs that state firms could not get through the inefficient state planning system—like the steel products made in Daqiu—were happily supplied, at a price, by the rural firms. The inputs they had in abundance, meanwhile—like cement, chemicals, and factory space—could be sold at reduced prices to rural firms able to put them to better use.[5] In the countryside itself, decollectivization had created a deep pool of surplus labor that the factories could tap. As one scholar wrote, "Entrepreneurs put the countryside's resources to work: discovering unappreciated productive assets, buying surplus labor, and investing countless bits of idle capital, and doing all of this more creatively and efficiently than the old collectives."[6]

One thing was for sure: the growth of rural firms owed little to central policies, excepting the fiscal reforms that gave counties and townships an incentive to promote rural factories. "This was not an achievement of the central government," Deng admitted later. "It is not something I had thought about, nor had other comrades. It took us by complete surprise."[7]

It was a pleasant surprise for Beijing, too. The rural firms allowed the central government to reduce its transfer payments to local governments for infrastructure. Grain output declined less than expected even as villages like Daqiu invested heavily in industry, quieting those who had worried about a huge decline in agricultural production. And given the deprivations peasants had suffered in the first three decades of Communist rule in China, the wealth and jobs generated by the rural firms significantly eased the transition from collective agriculture, averting potential unrest.

Attitudes within the party soon began to shift from muted hostility to grudging enthusiasm. In 1984, the State Council issued Document Number Four, on the issue of rural industry. Although it contained little in the way of new initiatives, the document, like a papal bull, fully legitimized rural firms. The old term for the firms, "brigade enterprises" (*shedui qiye*), was replaced with a new one, "township and town enterprises" (*xiangzhen qiye*), later translated as "township and village enterprises" or TVEs. This gave the firms a legitimacy in their own right no longer linked to the crumbling commune system. Suddenly they could get loans from state banks and forge formal links with urban state factories, giving them more secure sources of supplies and markets for outputs. The *People's Daily,* in 1986, called the creation of TVEs "a vital second step" (after the breakup of collective farming) in rural reforms. "Restricting and attacking rural enterprises will inevitably mean doing so to agriculture and ultimately to the peasants themselves," the newspaper warned. "The peasants cannot grow rich without engaging in industry."[8] It was as if Yu Zuomin himself were speaking.

As in the early 1970s, Daqiu was well ahead of the official curve in the 1980s. Most rural areas only latched onto the idea of investing in TVEs in the mid-1980s. By then, Daqiu was already transforming its crude start-ups into respectable enterprises. Each of the factories was incorporated in the early 1980s and put under a newly formed village holding company, the Daqiu Village Agriculture, Industry, and Commerce United Company.[9] Many villages were establishing such conglomerates at this time in an effort to add more value to their agricultural production with processing and packaging activities. Daqiu, however, was different: its conglomerate was established as part of efforts to abandon agriculture, not to make it more lucrative. In addition, the conglomerate became more than just a corporate entity. All the government powers of the production brigade (the essential commune structure) were transferred to the conglomerate. Secretary Yu—now better known as Boss Yu (*Yu laozong,* or sometimes *Yu laoban*)—became the conglomerate's president. Daqiu was now a sort of Daqiu, Inc.

Politically, the creation of the village conglomerate further accelerated Daqiu's already quickening pace toward authoritarian and hierarchical rule. As leaders of the old village production brigade, people like Yu and Mr. Do-It-All had been subject to some degree of popular supervision. Not so for company presidents, who appointed themselves and enjoyed virtually unfettered powers. China's parliament was at this time debating a new law (passed finally in 1987) that would empower the country's nearly one million villages to elect the heads of their own governments, called "villager committees" (*cunmin weiyuanhui*), through popular, direct elections. Such committees would be in charge of important aspects of local government, including welfare, public order, education, tax collection, public investment, and birth control. But in Daqiu, the villager committee would never exist except on paper. Daqiu was going the way not of popular democracy, but of authoritarianism by consent.

The incorporation of Daqiu was also a perfect example of the role of the "local state" in China's reform-era rural boom.[10] Local cadres, not private entrepreneurs, were the main agents of economic development in this era. They set up the rural factories and ensured they turned a profit. In the case of Daqiu, the local state leaders formally entrenched their role by setting up a village conglomerate. Put another way, the rural factories in Daqiu did more than work closely with the state; they became the state.

Socially, the creation of the village conglomerate in a sense made Daqiu a true collective for the first time. That is, for the first time, the village's economic and political institutions were a collective oriented solely toward serving the interests of villagers and largely autonomous of outside interference. The old communes, by contrast, had been run along lines dictated by the central government and had been overseen by the county. Different parts of rural China were adopting different systems to replace communes at this time. Many southern and coastal places—with more savings and arguably more individualist urges—were replacing the communes with household-based farming and privately owned as well as collectively owned rural enterprises. But elsewhere, especially in the north, many villages chose to stick together by maintaining almost total collective control over economic activities.[11] It was not so much decollectivization as the replacement of one kind of collective with another. Socialism had finally come to Daqiu.

The village collective was in many ways a family-based collective too. Certain leading village families—including those of Yu Zuomin, Liu Wanquan, and patriarch Zhang Yupu—held many of the top positions in both administration and business. A Chinese sociologist who spent several lengthy periods rusticating in the village noted that these few families held "all key positions in the economic, political, and social spheres" as well as "the wealth, power, and status in the system."[12] This stark reassertion of family and clan networks that had to a large extent been suppressed in the first three decades of Communist rule in China should not come as a surprise. Peasants in China had always organized themselves according to family-based clans, and once the intrusive state withdrew from rural life it was natural for them to step back in. In the case of Daqiu, the role of the tight-knit families was an important reason for the maintenance of a spirit of cooperation among the Four Hens despite growing competition. Yu argued that families were perfectly suited to running TVEs. "In a rural factory, a husband may be the manager, the wife may be the controller, and the son may be the marketing manager. Whenever an idea is proposed, it is easier to achieve unity. . . . From this perspective, there is nothing wrong with having a family manage an enterprise," he said.[13] The same logic was extended to the management of Daqiu itself.

The economic impact of Daqiu's village conglomerate was the most far-reaching, however. Under arrangements worked out when the conglomerate was founded in 1983, each of the Four Hens was obliged to remit 70 percent of its annual net profits to the conglomerate. Of the remainder, something like 10 to 40 percent was distributed as manager and worker bonuses, and the rest was reinvested.[14] The Four Hens in turn employed the same simple contractual relationship with their own subsidiaries. With this structure in place, Daqiu's industrial activities expanded with a speed and range that is startling. By 1987, the Four Hens had hatched 107 subsidiaries, and Daqiu had vaulted into the number-one position among villages in China in terms of output, taxes paid, and net profits earned. The brood expanded to a total of 200 chicks by 1990.[15] By then, the Four Hens jointly employed six thousand workers (including migrant workers) and had total revenues (excluding intercompany sales) of Rmb 639 million (U.S. $110 million), accounting for 18 percent of the entire industrial output of Jinghai county. Boss Yu was hailed as the "Lord of the East" in the old eastern townships.

Under the Liu brothers, the original cold-rolled steel strip factory expanded gainfully into areas like specialized copper materials for tubes and wiring, hot-rolled alloys for gates and windows, electrical welding rods, electric cable reels, and all sorts of new steel tubes, blanks, pipes, and bars. By the late 1980s it was entering new fields like bicycle parts, furniture, and chemicals. Mr. Do-It-All, Liu Wanquan, now company chairman, was named an "outstanding peasant entrepreneur" by the Tianjin government in 1987. Liu appointed Zhang Yuyin, a cousin of village patriarch Zhang Yupu, as company president in 1988, dispelling once and for all fears that the company, now called Wanquan Industrial Company, would become the "Liu family store."

The second hen, headed by Yu Zuomin's brother Yu Zuoyao, ventured even further from its roots and soon became the biggest and most profitable company of the four. The original pipes factory was followed by new concerns making paints, furniture, electrical transformers, foam board, and auto parts. In a clear sign of the capitalist spirit guiding the village businesses, it also expanded directly into the same product areas as Wanquan Industrial Company: steel products like pipes, bars, and strip, as well as welding rods and copper tubes and wire. The Daqiu factories were not only competing against the rest of the country, they were also competing against each other. The result was that Daqiu was soon China's biggest producer of cold-rolled steel strip and of welded steel pipes. Brother Yu, who remained both chairman and president of the newly renamed Daqiu Industrial Company, was named a "national outstanding young factory manager" in 1988.

After a halting start, the third hen, initially engaged in printing, soon shifted into new areas like printing machinery, aluminum and wood products for construction, cement blocks, tin cans, hard plastic materials, and chemicals like paints and dyes. Its aluminum doors and windows were installed in such prestigious buildings as the Great Hall of the People in Beijing, the stern Soviet-style building on the west side of Tiananmen Square that is the home of the national parliament, and the Beijing World Trade Center. As with the second hen, the newly renamed Jinmei Industrial Company also diversified into steel products: pipes, bars, tubes, cold and hot-rolled strip, and welding rods, as well as a few specialty products like galvanized and zinc-plated steel tubes. Its successful line of Faraday-brand car batteries, no longer the sole preserve of the fourth factory, was quaintly named after the nineteenth-century English physicist. The handsome Zhao Shuzhong, chairman and president of the company, was also named an "outstanding peasant entrepreneur" by the Tianjin government in 1987.

The ironic fate of the fourth hen, led by the former mad scientist from the pig lot, Zhang Yanjun, was that it became the most innovative and technologically advanced of the four. Beginning with the electrical machinery and equipment factory in 1982, the company soon expanded into switch gear equipment, welding torches and rods, electronic ballasts, and even motorcycles, small tractors, and three-wheeled motorized buggies. Its agricultural products included chicken and pig feeds, this time both nonlethal and profitable. Zhang hired technical instructors from the nearby Tianjin Polytechnic University

TABLE I   CUMULATIVE NET PROFITS AND TAXES OF
THE FOUR COMPANIES TO 1990 (IN MILLIONS OF RMB)

	Net Profits	Taxes Paid
Wanquan Industrial	90	43
Daqiu Village Industrial	130	25
Jinmei Industrial	56	34
Jinhai Industrial	75*	NA

*Figure includes tax.

TABLE 2   REVENUES AND STAFF
OF THE FOUR COMPANIES IN 1990

	Revenues (in millions of Rmb)	Staff
Wanquan Industrial	165	1,538
Daqiu Village Industrial	286	1,500
Jinmei Industrial	117	1,685
Jinhai Industrial	156	1,359

NOTE: Includes intercompany sales. Rmb 100 = U.S. $17.

SOURCE: Jinghai annals, "Daqiuzhuang."

and from the Tianjin Electrical Goods Factory to conduct research and teach in Daqiu. A formal extension campus of the Tianjin Polytechnic University was opened in the village in 1984, and joint research projects were established with thirty institutes and state companies around the country. Like the other hens, the newly renamed Jinhai Industrial Company found it hard to resist the allure of metal products, for which national demand was insatiable. Factories were set up to produce zinc-coated steel pipes, copper bar and wire, and angle steel. (See tables 1 and 2.)

The Daqiu economic miracle of the 1980s was a textbook example of the growth of rural industry in reform China. The strategies used by the village were born of the changed political and economic circumstances of the era, which allowed places like Daqiu to organize and produce like never before. As Yu was fond of saying, "Anyone who visits with a feudal mentality will not understand us. Anyone who visits with a small-scale rural subsistence mentality will not grasp our essence. Anyone who visits bearing a traditional outlook will find us a mystery. But anyone who visits with the outlook of opening and reform will find us blindingly obvious."[16] A few general points are worth noting about how the village companies prospered:

Expansion: Investments were made with a one-year payback in mind. Given the strong demand for most products, this was not unreasonable. The companies diversified by identifying products for which there was significant undersupply. The movement of all four companies into steel products and other building materials was driven by this motive. The short time horizon also owed to the high costs of borrowing for TVEs. Daqiu companies avoided debt and expanded mainly through retained profits. The total outstanding bank loans of all Daqiu companies was just Rmb 69 million in 1990, compared to total profits of Rmb 42 million in that year. As Yu said about the danger of relying on fickle state bankers: "It's like farming. You never know when it might not rain."

Scale: Each individual factory was kept small and nimble, rarely exceeding a total staff of one hundred. This was typical for village-owned TVEs across the country, which averaged between ten and twenty employees each in the 1980s.[17] Top-level managers in the Four Hens, of which there were just thirteen in the mid-1980s, were also kept to a minimum. The lean structure meant that companies could move in and out of different sectors as market conditions changed. As the Chinese saying went: "A small boat is easy to turn around" (*Chuan xiao, hao diao tou*).

Marketing: Sales were bolstered by a national network of sales offices that sold some or all Daqiu products. Staffed usually by outsiders working on commission, the offices provided simple, one-stop shops for village products. They also provided critical sources of information on potential new products. In the mid-1980s, there were forty Daqiu sales offices around the country. By 1990, Jinmei Industrial had forty-two sales offices, Wanquan Industrial had thirty, and Daqiu Industrial had another dozen.[18]

Corporate structure: Companies competed against each other in product markets, especially steel products, and for top managerial talent. But they cooperated in other ways, such as through intercompany sales of inputs, which were equivalent to around a tenth of annual revenues. The corporate structure, with one common holding company divided into four separate "profit centers," as they would be called in modern-day business jargon, evolved naturally and proved efficient. "This system helps the Daqiu factories to compete with state firms even as the state firms are becoming more competitive," the Jinghai government said in a 1987 article.[19]

Remuneration: Performance pay was significant. Factory managers could keep 1 percent of their factory's profits, and Yu Zuomin promised that this system would not change "in two thousand years." Brother Yu earned Rmb 1.5 million in 1991 for his efforts at Daqiu Industrial, the biggest-ever salary recorded in the village. Younger managers from the village (twenty were still in their twenties in 1987) were chosen for their aggressive approach to business. Sales agents could not claim business expenses but would share in profits.

Outside management: Outside experts in certain technologies, or, increasingly, talented young managers and marketers from outside, took on a bigger and bigger role. The number of "outside experts" in the village rose from 127 in 1984 to over 300 by 1986, and to 700 by 1990. The so-called Sunday engineers, who moonlighted for Daqiu from their state factory jobs on the weekends, soon became weeklong engineers and were given fancy new houses in the village. Former schoolteachers came to Daqiu and became wealthy managers. These experts were paid the same as locals, but did not enjoy permanent residency rights.

Workers: Like any booming industrial area, Daqiu made increasing use of migrant peasant workers. Having begun as migrants themselves,

the Daqiu people were now in a position to employ others. The first official count of migrant workers in the village was 4,905 in 1988 (compared to the village's own workforce of 1,569). By 1990, that figure had
grown to 7,000. Daqiu soon came to resemble any other booming
coastal city, or special economic zone, except that it was smack in the
middle of the north China plains. The migrants were paid about a
quarter what locals were, on average.[20] Mobility across companies was
high, however, so they could not be underpaid.

One other factor frequently cited to explain the rural industrial
boom in China is corruption, and it is worth considering here. The
vice premier in charge of agriculture for most of the 1980s, Tian Jiyun,
once remarked that "if there was no such thing as corruption, there
would be no such thing as a TVE."[21] That comment reflected a general presumption that rural firms were resorting to corruption to survive since they faced such a daunting array of obstacles. Most important was their limited access to key raw materials, like cement and
chemicals, and to other inputs like bank credit; they also faced a complete ban on buying steel, coal, and petroleum. Rural firms were expected to obtain materials locally, but that was often impossible. Corruption, meaning business practices based on dishonesty or illegality,
became the only alternative.

Corruption by rural firms came in two major forms, known by their
Chinese names *zhanwu* and *daomai*. The former, literally "getting hold
of materials," referred to the armies of purchasing agents employed by
rural firms whose role was to secure supplies to keep their factories
ticking. That often meant convincing cadres at state factories to part
with their allocations of scarce materials. The pain of separation was
inevitably eased with under-the-table bribes in red laisee packets, or
sometimes just a night on the town. "What's a bribe? I don't have a
clear idea," an unidentified TVE manager once told the official *China
Peasant* magazine. "The development of any TVE is filled with many
man-made obstacles. The reality is that you may know what you're

doing is wrong, but there is no other way. If you don't do it this way, the enterprise will never develop."[22]

The other form of business corruption arose from the opportunities to arbitrage in various product markets. The introduction of a dual-price system for many commodities in 1984 opened vistas for rural firms to exploit the differences between the free and controlled prices. This practice of obtaining goods at state prices and reselling them at market prices was known simply as "reselling," or *daomai*. It was practiced by anyone with the necessary connections, including the relatives of senior officials.

The growth of such transactions caused more and more resources to flow out of the state sector, thus choking off the supplies of many state firms. Many state factories, especially in the tobacco and steel sectors, were forced to close down for lack of supplies when inflation began raging in the late 1980s and *zhanwu* and *daomai* by rural firms became rampant. Beijing made several fruitless efforts to stop the trade by allowing more market pricing and by reducing the number of products under price control. By the early 1990s, however, Beijing had conceded defeat and most goods were sold at market prices. In this as in so many other ways, the rural firms had a major impact on transforming the Chinese economy, from planning to markets.

Both *zhanwu* and *daomai* were almost certainly a small but contributing factor to Daqiu's early success. As far back as 1977, as we saw, village officials had diverted funds earmarked for irrigation in order to build their first factory, a kind of *zhanwu* involving credit. Later, as Daqiu factories plunged into the metal products sector, where the input shortages faced by rural firms were acute, the village's purchasing agents almost certainly engaged in extensive *zhanwu*. "In the past, we peasants only understood the concept of joint purchasing and joint selling of manufactured goods. We thought that any kind of business deal was suspicious," Yu said in 1987. "But now we have to develop a mentality of commodity production and alongside that develop the mentality of markets, information, and competition."[23]

The extent of *daomai* of course related closely to the nature and extent of *zhanwu*. The greater and more valuable were the materials obtained by *zhanwu,* the greater was the incentive to engage in *daomai.* One incident, explained to this author, shows how both practices were used in Daqiu. In 1988, village managers secured an order for five thousand tons of steel from the giant state mill midway along the Yangtze River, the Wuhan Iron and Steel Corporation.[24] In this year, the average free market price of steel, Rmb 1,680 per ton, was 60 percent higher than the state price of Rmb 1,050.[25] This meant the village and the Wuhan factory stood to split a quick profit of Rmb 3.2 million (Rmb 1.6 million each) simply by reselling the steel on the free market. The steel was loaded onto trucks in Wuhan and moved north to Daqiu. There, it was given a polish and new plating in a village mill. When the steel was resold on the free market, the windfall to Daqiu alone reportedly amounted to Rmb 4.5 million. The one-off gain was the equivalent of 5 percent of the village's entire net profits for the year.

So was Daqiu a fake? Was its soaring income the result of smoke-filled rooms rather than smoke-filled air? Hardly, and for two reasons. For one, Daqiu was mostly adding value to the materials it obtained through *zhanwu,* not just collecting quick profits from *daomai.* Those engaged in nothing but *daomai,* such as well-connected political figures, were not adding value, even if they helped steer resources to the most efficient use. But in Daqiu, the rows of belching smokestacks and warehouses stuffed with goods were proof enough that the village was adding value to, not just reselling, scarce commodities. Second, after peaking in the years 1986 to 1988, the opportunities for making profits from *zhanwu* and *daomai* steadily lessened. Not only was the competition stiffer as rural firms mushroomed, but the opportunities lessened as state prices were abolished and inflation eased.

Yu admitted in 1989 that the village had enjoyed "a few special opportunities" on its road to riches. But, he said, "it is wrong to say that across the board all TVEs rely on unhealthy practices to get started."[26] More important, sustained economic growth in Daqiu, as elsewhere, increasingly depended on old-fashioned factors like leadership, timing, efficiency, hard work, and entrepreneurial energy. Daqiu was no bogus model. While it could be argued that the village's good name gave it an advantage over other more obscure villages, these were the rewards of its entrepreneurial sense, which included developing value in the Daqiu brand name. As the *China Youth Daily* newspaper would later comment, "Many people wondered if Daqiu was relying on improper methods, earning dirty money. But Daqiu has performed well for so many years. Who would dare say it has relied on nothing but laisee packets?"[27] Or as the *China Business Times* noted: "No one says Daqiu rose to wealth using special privileges."[28]

So how do we sum up the factors that made Daqiu tick, that propelled it to the top spot as China's richest village? The village operated like a giant company with four profit centers. It boasted a market sense that ensured products were produced well and sold widely. It was adept at *zhanwu* and *daomai*. Incentive systems were used for management and staff. And large numbers of migrant workers were employed. Atop all this was a family-based system of rule led by Yu Zuomin himself. Yu put the system together and made it work wonders. The importance of a charismatic leader was mentioned above in relation to early reforms in rural areas. But it was no less important in determining the success of those reforms once under way. Like a ship's captain, Yu set the village to sea, kept the sails full, steered a steady course, and ensured the crew was coordinated. He was the Great Helmsman of Daqiu. As the *China Youth Daily* said of Daqiu's success, "In a word, it has to do with Yu Zuomin himself. His role is all-important. He is the big secret of Daqiu."

In 1985, a Japanese steel company from which Daqiu was planning to buy equipment invited Yu Zuomin for a fifteen-day excursion to Japan. Donning an undersized ash gray suit and toting a black nylon suitcase, Yu flew to Tokyo from Beijing in mid-March. It was the first time he had left China.

Like so many Chinese modernizers before him, including the founder of the Chinese republic, Sun Yat-sen, and the writer Lu Xun, Yu found inspiration in Japan, an Oriental land that was in many ways more Chinese than China itself. While marveling at the skyscrapers, multideck freeways, and private cars in the booming country, Yu began to recalibrate his sense of what it meant to be well off. "I used to think that living in a brick house was the greatest thing in the world. But when I came back from Japan, our village suddenly looked very rustic," he wrote in the national magazine *New Observer* after returning. "Of course, brick is better than straw, but it is still far short of those exquisite houses in Japan. It made me realize how backward we still are in China."[29]

Alongside the material wealth, Yu was impressed by the social achievements of Japan. The polite and well-educated Japanese were a far cry from the boorish and illiterate peasants of China, he believed. Not everything in Japan was admirable, of course. Yu professed himself shocked by the "very uncivilized television programs" on view in his hotel room, and by all the "drinking and groping" at the hands of kimono-clad Japanese hostesses at one beachside banquet he was taken to. But in general, he was greatly impressed with the country. It prompted him to think deeply about the purposes to which Daqiu's wealth might be used. "I was struck by the extent to which ignorance, conservatism, and backwardness have been left behind by China's history, and how these things are closely related to the question of poverty," he wrote. "We want peasants to be rich, but being rich is not the final goal. The goal is to raise their cultural levels."[30]

The average income of native villagers in Daqiu grew quickly on the back of factory expansion in the 1980s. From around Rmb 4,000 per person in 1984, it bounded upward to Rmb 10,000 in 1986 and about Rmb 20,000 by 1990. Somewhere along the way, Daqiu was crowned "China's First Village" (*zhongguo diyi cun*) in terms of total output as well as income per capita. As in Japan, that wealth supported an array of visible improvements in material life. Free education for all village natives was offered from 1984, and a new kindergarten and primary school were built. The first hospital was built in 1986 and furnished with imported Japanese medical equipment and a brand-new ambulance.[31] New brick houses with central heating and electric ovens were allocated and built for every village native's household throughout the 1980s. The houses were furnished with swish leather goods from the village furniture factory. Anyone who bought a color TV was given free electricity. When a delivery truck from the Tianjin Color Television Factory set off for the village with a full load, it made national headlines.

But for Yu, growing wealth needed to do more than just provide conspicuous material comforts. It needed to translate into a more dignified culture as well. Yu believed that China's peasants had suffered from their rustic image. Chen Yonggui, "Uncle Chen" of Dazhai with his *yangduzi* white head wrap and grass belt, had been beloved by urban intellectuals. But his demeanor, Yu believed, only reinforced the stereotype of rural residents as bumpkins. The results were baleful. Locked into their reputation as poor country cousins, places like Daqiu could never muster the resources to stand up to wanton interference from upper levels. The Uncle Chen stereotype, Yu thought, was preventing China's peasants from achieving the broad equality that might have spared them from disasters like the Great Leap Famine; it was still constraining their lives. "If we allow the force of habit to lead us, it will be a continuous death," he told villagers. "We have the power to remake our own lives. What are you afraid of?"[32]

These were the earliest stirrings of what would later emerge as Yu's quest for what he perceived as political, social, and economic equality for China's peasants. Before advocating that vision on the national stage, however, he sought to initiate it at home. To that end, he imposed one regulation after another on daily life in Daqiu, aimed at making his villagers dignified as well as rich. The construction of adobe huts was forbidden, for example, as was the raising of chickens in courtyards. Every adult male in the village was instructed to purchase a Western-style suit and a pair of leather shoes, for which the village gave him money. Anyone failing to wear the suit on a regular basis had to repay the money. Those wearing traditional garb would be fined.[33] It was as if Yu had launched a Cultural Revolution in Daqiu.

Yu's efforts to remake his village even extended to a modest attempt at brainwashing. The Brave New World of Daqiu included a Rmb 600,000 closed-circuit television system, complete with a studio for making shows and a cable network to connect every household. Through this system, villagers were obliged to tune in to Yu's speeches once a week, just as they had been forced to listen to speeches blaring from loudspeakers in the days of the commune. Whenever an issue was causing problems, Yu would come on screen to warn, cajole, and instruct. "Being poor was difficult enough," he was fond of saying. "But being rich is even more difficult. It's just one trouble after another."[34]

It did not escape his attention that villagers often resisted the edicts. The problem, of course, was that his definition of cultural advance was arbitrary and often rubbed villagers the wrong way. The most recalcitrant bunch, predictably, were the village's four hundred–odd elderly. Their habits had been formed during the tumult of China's early twentieth century and were not easily changed. They hid their money under mattresses, wore old clothes, longed to sit on fire-heated brick *kang*s, and generally failed to show any flair. Yu's fight against the ingrained habits of the hoary brigade would have been comical were it not so pitiful. Those who discarded their traditional blue cotton-padded silk jackets, or *mianao,* and wool-lined cloth shoes were given a Rmb 5 supplement to their Rmb 50 monthly pension, but only half accepted the inducement. On another occasion, just a dozen elders signed up for an all-expenses-paid summer vacation to the swank northern coastal resort of Beidaihe. Yu was furious. "The old people are too modest," he barked. "They don't understand opening or reforms. They still think they're living in bare subsistence."[35]

Yu's ways were like a gentle tyranny. Perhaps it was inevitable that a village leader with such a burning inner desire to see his people become respected citizens would veer in this direction. Indeed, many official commentators praised his strong-arm tactics, arguing that without them the village would never have progressed beyond higher incomes. "His courage has changed a thousand years of peasant thinking," Jiang Zilong wrote in "Yanzhao Elegy." "He has opened up the rural consumer market, opened up a world of culture to the peasants, and destroyed the differences between city and countryside."[36] Or, as the *China Youth Daily* commented:

> Its not easy to ensure that material betterment causes cultural betterment. But Daqiu is lucky to have Yu Zuomin. He is at once both modern and traditional, political and economic, democratic and dictatorial, persuasive and threatening. And there is but one purpose: to thoroughly change the thousand-year-old narrow outlook of the peasantry. . . . Only when you understand Daqiu can you understand why Yu Zuomin's "tribal elder"–style leadership is so effective.[37]

Only with the villagers marching in serried rows with their Western suits and modern appliances, Yu Zuomin believed, would his village be respected by foreign investors and upper-level officials alike. Then, it could be assured of safety. And marching at the front would be Yu himself, the "Lord of the East."

Daqiu's growing wealth and its attendant fame furnished Yu Zuomin with increased opportunities to articulate his new vision of equality for rural China as the 1980s wore on. In September 1986, Daqiu held its annual economic planning meeting at the huge, Soviet-style Minorities Cultural Palace exhibition hall in the center of Beijing, a bold move that reflected the village's growing confidence. More than six hundred of the country's top rural economists accepted invitations to join the deliberations. Yu, who presided during the three-day affair, declaimed frequently on the virtues of capitalist-style development. On the last day, he amused the gathering with a memorable phrase that contrasted the old-style communist appeal for the people to concentrate on the socialist "future" with his own belief that people should concentrate on the single-minded pursuit of wealth, as represented by "money." "If we look up," Yu said, "we can concentrate on the future. If we look down, we can concentrate on money. But only by concentrating on money can we concentrate on the future."[38] Only with the wealth generated by a singular attention to economic development, Yu seemed to be saying, could a society accumulate sufficient resources for other goals, political, cultural, and social. Indeed, those things would flow naturally from the increased generation of wealth. "His point was that the beautiful flowers of economic efficiency are bound to produce plentiful political fruits," the *China Youth Daily* later explained.[39] It was a belief that Yu had put into practice at home, and now he passed it on to the country at large. The fact that the words for "future" and "money" were homonyms in Chinese—both pronounced as an upward-inflected *qian* ("chee-en")—made the twenty-character slogan both funny and trenchant.[40]

After the conference, one of the famous economists who had attended, a former vice minister of science and technology and vice president of the prestigious Chinese Academy of Social Sciences, Yu Guangyuan, wrote a newspaper article praising the "money slogan." But the endorsement proved to be a great moment in bad timing. A few months later, China's cities were rocked by the worst bout of student protest in a decade. The riots, with their calls for democratization and more freedoms, led to the removal of the liberal party general secretary, Hu Yaobang, and to the launch of a new campaign against "bourgeois liberalization," code for Western thoughts and values. Yu's slogan had raised few eyebrows at first; but its clarion appeal to money worship now ran headlong into the oncoming train of an anti-Western political campaign.

In early 1987 an unnamed "senior party leader," possibly the conservative vice premier Yao Yilin, criticized Yu's money slogan in an internal party document. The slogan was just the sort of defiant appeal to supposedly Western values that the party was then attacking. Yu was singled out as the prophet of a dangerous trend.[41] "The nub of this great criticism," the newspaper *TVE News* later commented, "was that Yu's statement was interpreted as meaning 'concentrate only on money,' which was a sign of bourgeois liberalization and political problems."[42]

Daqiu and Yu Zuomin were suddenly caught in the middle as the tectonic plates of reform China shifted uneasily. That had been the case in the early 1980s, when the village's first factories ran right into a national debate on rural industry. Now the village was at the center of a national debate on ideology. The village had escaped the first time, but not before a taxing and dangerous confrontation with the Jinghai county leadership. This time the challenge came from Beijing itself, which could blow the village over with a single puff.

Once the "senior leader" decided to attack Yu, national newspapers and journals swarmed like a wolf pack. "This concept of concentrating only on money is the tumor that will spread corruption and mistaken thinking in our society," the party journal *Academic Exchange* warned. "Eventually it will lead to calls for complete Westernization."[43]

Yu was at first stupefied by the attacks. "Money is the result of hard work," he said. "How can the country develop without money?"[44] But as the weeks dragged on, his reaction changed to one of defiance. Yu was unabashedly proud of his village and its achievements, and he was not about to see them despoiled by Beijing leftists. He also seemed to relish the head-butting with ideologues, a new motivation for his struggle that would loom larger as time passed. For both reasons, he stood his ground as the storm raged. "Some well-intentioned old leaders came to me and said that I should be a little more modest and just

admit my mistake," he recalled later. "But I responded: 'I am responsible for making Daqiu rich. What have I done wrong? Why should I be
modest? I should be more proud!'"[45]

When that first attempt at friendly persuasion failed, other supporters of Yu and his village in Beijing tried another tack. One sympathetic senior leader suggested that Yu simply restate the slogan, but
replace the word "money" with "economic efficiency" and the word
"future" with "communism." Then the slogan would have a pleasing
ring to leftists, even if it made a pro-reform point: "Only by concentrating on economic efficiency can we concentrate on communism."
But Yu was a peasant reared in the traditions of plain talk, not verbal
pirouettes. "When you go to the store, you don't ask the shopkeeper:
'How many economic efficiencies for this item?'" he reasoned with un-
assailable logic. "You ask: 'How much money?'"

Yu's unflinching attitude spurred further attacks on the money slogan, which might have eventually brought real harm to Daqiu. But
fortune smiled on the village. In late 1986, the *TVE News* had launched
a contest to select the one hundred "most outstanding peasant entrepreneurs" in the country, a contest that seemed to symbolize the growing acceptance of rural industrialists within the socialist state. Yu
Zuomin's name was naturally included among the 1,500-odd candi-
dates, and when the winners were selected in early 1987, he was of
course among them.

The awards ceremony was to be held in Beijing in late April. Despite
the ongoing public criticism of the money slogan, Yu made his way to the
capital for the event, and on April 29 he was duly presented before the
party elder Bo Yibo to receive the award. Climbing onto the podium, Yu
was unsure what to expect. Bo was certain to raise the issue of the money
slogan. But the wily party elder's attitude was unpredictable. Perhaps the
best Yu could hope for would be a mild reproach.

"Who invented this slogan?" Bo asked the moment he handed Yu a
plaque.[46]

"It was me," Yu replied immediately, hoping to take the blame. "It had nothing to do with anyone else."

"And what did you mean by it?" Bo pursued.

"By 'concentrate on the future' I meant concentrate on communist ideals and on the socialist outlook, leading a comfortable lifestyle in our village . . . and implementing our long-term village plan," Yu explained. "By 'concentrate on money,' I meant raising economic efficiency. My point was that the two should not be linked."

Bo nodded his head and looked up at the two journalists standing nearby listening to the conversation. Then he turned back to Yu: "What you say is right. There's nothing wrong with it," he declared solemnly. "Your words have been misinterpreted by others."

With the wave of his wand, Bo had dispelled the ominous cloud hanging over Yu Zuomin and Daqiu Village. Bo, a former vice premier and vice minister of the State Economic Reform Commission, was an avid supporter of rural enterprises. Still, he had needed some concession from Yu in order to rehabilitate this favored peasant. Yu had at first balked at replacing the word "money" with "economic efficiency." But face to face with Bo Yibo, he met the state leader halfway, admitting that money *represented* economic efficiency. It was all Bo needed. Yu breathed a sigh of relief, smiled, and walked off the stage.

In a flash, the sun appeared again on Daqiu. The criticism campaign in the media ended and the newly honored Yu was again praised in several newspapers as one of the nation's foremost peasant entrepreneurs. Bo Yibo's absolution brought Daqiu back into favor and cleared the road for the village's emergence as the most celebrated model of China's rural reforms. Still, Yu would remember the incident for many years. "I'm just a coarse old peasant," he later observed, "and there was nothing wrong with what I said. But some people found it unpleasant to hear, so they criticized me for months. How can it be acceptable to expend such efforts against a single old peasant?"[47]

A few months later, the organizers of the first outstanding peasant entrepreneur contest decided to hold a runoff to choose the country's ten "very best" peasant entrepreneurs. This time, the contest was cosponsored by the national radio and television stations and plans were made for a gala awards ceremony in Beijing. Yu's name, now politically rehabilitated, was entered in the follow-up contest, and again he came up a winner.

On 2 September 1987 the ten winners—nine men and one woman, three from inland provinces and seven from coastal provinces—were honored at an even more elaborate awards ceremony in Beijing. The ninety other winners from the first contest and an added complement of fifteen hundred more top peasant entrepreneurs from around the country were also honored. Vice Premier Tian Jiyun, he of the devious aside about the inextricability of corruption and rural enterprises, presided. The ten top winners were all interviewed on national television and radio and profiled in the *TVE News.* The official English-language newspaper, the *China Daily,* in a commentary on the event, hailed the winners for "playing a crucial role in boosting rural reforms by pioneering a market-oriented economy."[48]

Four days after the ceremony, the country's new party general secretary, Zhao Ziyang, met the ten winners in a small gathering at the sequestered Zhongnanhai leadership complex, once part of the imperial Forbidden City in the heart of Beijing. Zhao was a liberal whose policies as party secretary of inland Sichuan province had helped spark rural reforms nationwide in the late 1970s. Now he was in a position to commend the determined peasants who had given life to such reforms. "Unless large numbers of rural residents move into fields like forestry, husbandry, processing, industry, trade, and transport," Zhao told the gathering, "the countryside will never prosper." He also brushed aside ideological worries about creeping capitalism in the countryside. "It does not matter whether these enterprises are privately or collectively owned," he said. "They play their role in developing our socialist commodity production. They are both permitted and legal."[49]

Yu's selection as one of China's top ten peasant entrepreneurs provided him with yet another opportunity to articulate his vision of equality for rural China. Until now, he had been just a rising and brash village leader with a lot to show. But this honor elevated him to the status of a spokesman for rural enterprises as a whole. That is, it made Yu representative of more than just his own village.

While the other top ten winners graciously accepted their honors and praised the party, Yu made immediate use of his new status to speak out. In his acceptance speech on 2 September, and in several subsequent media interviews, he launched headlong into several controversial subjects close to his heart. One issue he tackled was the constitutional status of rural enterprises. While Zhao Ziyang had admitted that TVEs were both "permitted and legal" (*yunxude, hefade*), they still remained stuck in the penumbra of socialist China. The official policy of the state, which would be incorporated into the constitution in 1988, said that such nonstate (*fei guoyou*) companies were a "necessary supplement" (*biyao buchong*) to the dominant state sector. But by the late 1980s, rural industries were already accounting for a quarter of national industrial output—far more than a "supplement"—and dominating many sectors, especially in light consumer products. Besides being inaccurate, the characterization of rural firms as a "supplement" meant that they were permanently at a disadvantage to state firms. They played second fiddle in everything from obtaining credit and materials to access to markets. The necessity of engaging in *zhanwu* and *daomai* galled peasants like Yu Zuomin, as he made clear in his speech:

> Even though the party center has clearly supported the development of TVEs, there are still many people who remain suspicious of the role they play in economic development in China. These people feel there is something not quite right about developing TVEs. So it's all the more important that we clearly recognize the

important role played by TVEs and that everybody earnestly and honestly supports them. . . . As for the important use and meaning of TVEs, I think we have to study the issue of whether TVEs are really just a "supplement" to the state sector. Last year [1986] they accounted for 23 percent of national industrial production. Is this just a supplement? The first universal couplings for vehicles ever exported from China were made by a TVE led by Lu Guanqiu [head of the Hangzhou Universal Coupling Factory and one of the ten winners]. Is his factory just a supplement? Experience shows that TVEs are playing a pillar [*zhizhu*] role in the national economy. They are competitive rivals as well as partners of state industry. It is normal to have competitive rivals. Through competition, we propel each other and advance together. We need to have fair competition. In the course of competition, we should not put the squeeze on TVEs. That would not be right.[50]

The second issue Yu tackled at the awards ceremony would loom larger in his later discourse: the meaning of socialism. As we have seen, Yu was among the most vocal peasants openly decrying the shortcomings of the party's past economic policies. The whole story of Daqiu since 1977 was one of defying the cavils of leftist party cadres and redefining the meaning of socialism. Socialism, Yu believed, should be defined as a system bringing common welfare to the people, not one in which the state owned all the means of production. Speaking from the podium at the awards ceremony, he said:

We really have to look at this issue of what is socialism: poverty or wealth? In the past, we said that socialism was good, but the people's stomachs were empty, they wore ragged clothes, and nobody could get married. How could we honestly say socialism was good? Now we peasants have relied on TVEs to get rich, grain output is rising, and the people can honestly say from their hearts that socialism is good. Looking at the arresting growth in Daqiu, how can people not see that this kind of socialism has a real attraction?[51]

On both of these issues—the status of TVEs and the meaning of so-cialism—Yu was making points that did not have an immediate bear-ing on his village. In that sense, he was beginning to wage a political struggle that differed markedly from the past. In the first decade of Daqiu's growth, Yu and other village leaders had pursued simple is-sues of immediate interest to Daqiu. Now Yu was branching off into complex issues with a longer-term and broader significance to rural China as a whole. Yu's new struggle—born of his village's wealth and his personal status—also became less conciliatory and more confronta-tional in its rhetoric.

This emerging political discourse was given a further leg-up in late 1987 when Yu was selected as a delegate to the 1,900-member na-tional committee of the country's political advisory body, the Chinese People's Political Consultative Congress, or CPPCC. Yu was named as a representative of the "agricultural sector," an ironic laurel given his village's repudiation of agriculture. To be sure, the promotion fell far short of the vice premiership that had been lavished on Uncle Chen: China's peasant heroes could no longer expect to stand atop the ram-parts of the state. Still, it was a valuable post for Yu. National CPPCC delegates convened once a year for a grand meeting in Beijing in which they discussed national policies, often within earshot of the media. That gave delegates a ready-made platform for their personal agendas, as well as an entree into the complex mesh of personal networks in Bei-jing that run the country. The position also gave Yu greater sway to question and seek to change policies that directly affected Daqiu.

Given the emergence of his political struggle on the national stage, the first official profile of Yu as a CPPCC delegate by the Xinhua news agency was especially ironic. Yu, the agency wrote, "blamed the past" for the village's deprivations during the Mao era but "thanked the party for making things a little better" all the same. Even today, the agency wrote, Yu could not read or write much, but his village had grown wealthy "thanks to the party's policies."[52] Those statements were at best distorted. Yu squarely blamed Mao and his sycophants in the CCP for the three decades of deprivation before 1977. After that, Daqiu had grown rich mainly by casting off the dictates of the party, not by relying on them.

Beijing may have expected Yu Zuomin and his village to happily adopt the role of all model villages as tools of the party's self-serving propaganda, but the seeds of rebellion lay buried in Daqiu, waiting to sprout. The only question was when.

The laurels bestowed upon Yu Zuomin in 1987 brought Daqiu fully into the role of a model village in the sense traditionally associated with others in Communist China. State leaders began to troop to the village for photo-ops, while the propaganda system rooted through the village searching for miracles and miracle-makers.

Zhao Ziyang became the first top Chinese leader to visit Daqiu when he spent a day in the village on 21 May 1988. After touring the middle school and some factories, he held court along with Yu in the recently refurbished village meeting room. Zhao was "extremely pleased" with the development of the village enterprises, he said. "It's possible for our city factories to learn from the good experiences of such TVEs," he noted, reversing the conventional wisdom that TVEs needed to learn from their state-sector counterparts in areas like management and technology. "Capable peasant entrepreneurs should even be allowed to enter the cities and run factories," he added.[53]

Zhao's visit brought tangible rewards. A month later, the Ministry of Construction declared Daqiu one of the first "town and village architecture experimental zones" in the country. Under the plan, the central and county governments would invest Rmb 22 million to rebuild roads and buildings and spruce up public areas in the village—a not inconsiderable figure given that the village's own investment in infrastructure for the entire 1980s had been Rmb 138 million.[54]

In Zhao's footsteps came a clutch of other senior leaders and a stream of lesser mortals from the media, business organizations, universities, and the military.[55] One important visitor, in light of later events, was Tianjin mayor and party chief Li Ruihuan, who came in late 1988. Li had been Tianjin mayor since 1982 and the city's party chief since joining the party politburo in 1987. As the son of an itinerant carpenter from the city's poor northern county of Baodi, he had a natural compassion for the likes of Yu Zuomin. He had sent his deputies to the village on several occasions in the mid-1980s and enjoined rural cadres to learn from its rapid growth. He was also a known advocate of TVEs, having made several symbolic trips to the hotbed of rural industry in southern Jiangsu province.[56]

The visits to Daqiu by high-level leaders were valuable for many reasons, not least of which was that Daqiu's position was strengthened vis-à-vis the Jinghai county leadership. While the county's attitude toward Daqiu had improved markedly since the low point of the 1982 inspection team—encouraged no doubt by the bulging tax revenues it was reaping from the village—there remained a distinct lack of comradely warmth between the two places. As the stream of top officials continued, Yu openly criticized the Jinghai party secretary, Zhang Kejun, for his notable failure to visit the village since coming into office in 1984:

> Is our chosen road to riches correct or not? Don't pay attention only
> to the number of people coming here from all over the country. In
> the past three years, the top leader of the Jinghai party committee
> [Zhang] has not come here even once. Why don't these leaders
> come and see us? Are we right or wrong? Why do they remain
> silent?[57]

Paralleling the stream of high-level visitors to Daqiu was a growing wave of national publicity. Much of the publicity, of course, centered on Daqiu's remarkable industrial growth and its attendant social changes. For example, the *People's Daily* in mid-1988 praised the large numbers of Daqiu women—half of all the females of working age—who had chosen to remain housewives given the large incomes of their husbands and sons.[58] "In the past we learned from the women of Dazhai who all worked. But they only earned eight cents [less than men] for every work point. What kind of liberation was that?" Yu said.[59] Yu also achieved an important first by penning an article for the *People's Daily* in early 1989. As ever, he did not allow such a perquisite to blunt his sharp criticisms of the party's misguided policies of the past: "Poverty was glorious, while wealth was a disgrace," he wrote, describing the political constraints on Daqiu's early development. "It reached ridiculous proportions!"[60]

While rural industry and peasant "modernization" were the main themes of the reports on Daqiu, propagandists never allowed facts to get in the way of a good emulation campaign. Nowhere was this more true than in the official promotion of Daqiu's agricultural sector. This was in fact one of the supreme ironies of the Daqiu emulation campaign because the village had grown rich specifically by moving labor and resources out of agriculture. By the late 1980s only a handful of locals were still working the fields, and agricultural output continued to plummet as a proportion of village income. Nevertheless, encouraged by a national press eager to report details of its agricultural as well as industrial success, Daqiu leaders invested modest sums in showcase agricultural projects. "Upholding agriculture" was an important tenet of party policy for rural areas, and it was worthwhile for Daqiu to spend a little money to insure itself against being accused of violating this sacred creed. "Daqiu focused on building rural factories from the late 1970s, until it had the means to invest in agriculture. In many ways, its farmers have returned from the dead," the *China Youth Daily* proclaimed. "Everyone from the central government to the local leaders want rural areas to be like Daqiu, which has not forgotten agriculture despite getting rich."[61]

The political value of maintaining a robust agricultural sector had been first apparent in the early 1980s. When the village belatedly adopted the household-based farming system in 1984, one of the few natives who opted to remain in the fields rather than sign on with a factory was Ma Deliang, a small, square-jawed man who had headed a production team in the old village brigade. Ma and his wife contracted to farm nine hectares of village land. The village then paid all the costs of seeds, fertilizer, and other inputs and provided new infrastructure in the form of irrigation and pumping systems, tractors, planters, and harvesters. As a result, Ma harvested a remarkable fifty tons of wheat from his small plot that year, pocketing a tidy profit of Rmb 20,000 in the process. When the national media uncovered the stirring feat, Ma and his wife were declared to be "the richest household specializing in grain production in China."[62] A French television station later reported the story, and Ma and his wife were invited to Paris in 1985 to receive medals of honor from the French Ministry of Agriculture.

Flush with the knowledge of the political benefits of a miraculous agricultural sector, Yu Zuomin invited one of the country's most famous and powerful scientists, Qian Xuesen, to be the village's chief agricultural adviser in 1985. Qian, then a vice chairman of the CPPCC, readily agreed (and Yu's elevation to that body two years later may have owed to this relationship). The appearance of Qian at the helm of the village's agricultural sector was fitting. A former California Institute of Technology professor, Qian had been deported from the United States in 1955 as a Communist spy. He went on to join the ranks of the party elite as an alternate member of the Central Committee and as the father of the country's nuclear missiles program. But he was best remembered in intellectual circles for having tragically abandoned his scientific objectivity and written glowing articles about the miracles of the communes just as Mao was pushing China into the Great Leap Famine in 1958. Now this discredited scientist was lending his name to the agricultural activities in the party's latest model village. Henceforth, news from Daqiu's farms would be viewed with skepticism.

Under the direction of Qian, who drove himself to the village once a month, Daqiu began investing considerable sums in grain production, about Rmb 1 million in both 1986 and 1987, for example. The investments boosted grain output to 2.4 million kilograms in 1987, almost double the figure of 1978 and accounting for one-fifth of all Jinghai county's grain remittances to the central government. In 1988, a further Rmb 30 million was spent leaching the alkalines from the top meter of the soil, a curious attempt to literally wash away the village's historical disadvantage in agriculture. More than two hundred agricultural scientists took part in the project and guided the planting of new wheat and corn crops. Grain output would reach 3.5 million kilograms in 1990, the equivalent of 53 kilograms per hectare, which was declared to be a record for alkaline soils. By not counting the fifty migrant workers in the fields and the twenty outside agronomists, Daqiu also claimed that its grain yields per person employed—fifteen natives in all—were records.[63] The sham propaganda of Daqiu's agricultural sector was coming fast and furious.

Another aspect of Daqiu's agricultural showcase was an array of government-supported high-tech farming experiments, most of them paid for by the State Science and Technology Commission. These included the Daqiu Biotechnology Research Institute, established in 1988 to develop and produce new feed yeasts, and a much-televised "advanced mechanized" pig-feeding station on the eastern edge of the village, where the feasting swine were kept in air-conditioned comfort and monitored via closed-circuit televisions.

Despite all this, it is clear from official figures that agriculture never came close to becoming a mainstay of the village economy. By 1991, the village's total agricultural output—by then consolidated under a single new company, Huada Group—was worth Rmb 150 million and profits were Rmb 15 million. Those figures represented just 8 percent and 15 percent of the village totals in that year. While this suggested that returns were higher for agriculture than for industry, much of the high returns can be attributed to the state aid the village received for agriculture. More important, Daqiu's wealth still came overwhelmingly from its own factories. This was a key difference between Daqiu and Dazhai before it. Being a model brought the propagandists to both, but Dazhai became reliant on the propaganda, whereas Daqiu, even if it put on a farming exhibition for the press, retained the autonomy provided by its factories. For Yu Zuomin, increasingly determined to shake the foundations of Communist China's rural order, that was an important advantage.

Under the twin influences of sudden economic reforms and a government spending spree on fixed investment, China's economy overheated wildly in 1988. Retail price inflation soared to a post-1949 high of 19 percent, and official corruption relating to the reselling of scarce commodities proliferated. The atmosphere of economic uncertainty and political resentment led to a groundswell of popular discontent which reached its zenith during the Tiananmen Square demonstrations of April and May 1989.

While the Tiananmen demonstrations were largely an urban phenomenon with little resonance in the countryside, the bloody army crackdown in Beijing that ended them on 4 June brought several changes that affected rural areas. For one, the ouster of Zhao Ziyang as party general secretary meant that rural areas which had flourished under his protection, including Daqiu, suddenly became vulnerable to attack. In addition, township and village enterprises, TVEs, were blamed for contributing to much of the inflation and economic disorder that had stoked the social fires preceding Tiananmen. Mostly, such criticisms were couched in friendly terms about management and efficiency. But many party leaders believed that TVEs were to blame for the spread of *daomai* and *zhanwu,* which had fueled corruption, driven up prices, and undercut state firms. As the 1990 TVE Yearbook put it: "When the national economy ran into problems in 1989, the long-standing censure and reproach of TVEs suddenly intensified. Some comrades even raised the slogan 'Overthrow TVEs, save our national enterprises' or 'Economic rectification means chopping down TVEs.'"[64]

Adding to the opprobrium was politics. Leftists in the leadership, recalling the "false collectives" jibe leveled at some TVEs, began to argue again that the firms were a beachhead for capitalism in the country. "People said that TVEs were the source of all unhealthy tendencies in the country. And that their system of management was capitalist in nature," one official history of the period has noted.[65]

At party plenums in June and November 1989, the new party general secretary, Jiang Zemin, the former party chief of Shanghai and a longtime state enterprise fan, announced the onset of a three-year economic "rectification" program to correct the excesses that had preceded Tiananmen. Inflation was to be brought under control by strict new credit guidelines for banks, while fixed investment was to be steered away from hotels and seaside villas and into agriculture and infrastructure. Under the wrenching new policies, retail price inflation fell to just 2 percent in 1990. More than one hundred thousand companies, mostly run by party and government departments, were closed down for involvement in *daomai* and *zhanwu*. Economic growth plummeted from double-digit rates to 4 percent in 1989 and then 5 percent in 1990.

For the TVEs, the economic rectification plans were summed up in a four-word slogan: "Adjust, rectify, renovate, and improve." Official figures suggested a steep decline in the number of TVEs as a result of the shakeout: in 1989 alone, more than 75,000 TVEs nationwide were forcibly closed. A third of them were said to be short of capital or materials (possibly code for involvement in *zhanwu* and *daomai*), while another third were said to be in need of better management.[66] Overall, the number of TVEs fell in that year by two hundred thousand from 18.9 million to 18.7 million.

It was a wrenching slowdown on paper. But the real effects on rural enterprises, most of which operated beyond the ken of central officials, appeared to be more attenuated. In the case of Daqiu, the economic effects were even less noticed. Just four subsidiaries of the Four Hens were closed in deference to the program, a small fraction of the two hundred–odd companies in the village by 1990. Nor did credit flows to the Four Hens show any signs of abating. As village official Li Fengzhuang, Yu's nephew, later said: "During the austerity program, we could always get bank loans because our enterprises were so profitable."[67]

Indeed, while caution was the byword for most TVEs during the 1989–91 period, Yu Zuomin actually launched an expansion plan at this time, sensing that the moment the economic brakes were lifted the national economy would accelerate quickly. "The tiger is coming down the mountain, the monkey is climbing into the tree," he told village cadres during an economic planning meeting in late 1990. Translation: it was a critical time of opportunity, and those who seized it would be handsomely rewarded. "The market slump caused us some problems, that's for sure," Yu would later recall. "But it also presented a great development opportunity."[68]

If the direct economic effects of the post-Tiananmen backlash in Daqiu were limited, the direct political effects may actually have been beneficial. For one, the loss of Zhao Ziyang as a high-level patron was partly if not more than compensated for by the elevation of Tianjin mayor Li Ruihuan to the politburo standing committee (and chairman of the CPPCC), putting him in the center of power in Beijing. The rectification campaign also provided Yu Zuomin with a chance to burnish his image by stoutly defending the new policies nationally, even if they were being flouted at home. Yu was frequently quoted in the national media affirming the merits of the drive. "It will give great impetus to the development of rural industry," he said in one interview with the *People's Daily.* "The more we rectify, the more we will improve."[69]

Those exertions paid off immediately for Yu in the form of new laurels. In late 1989 he was honored in Beijing as a "national model worker" (*quanguo laodong mofan*), an honorific that put him into the elite class of spokesmen for rural industry. A few months later he was named as one of six vice chairmen of the newly formed China Township Enterprise Association, created by Beijing to get a firmer grip on the widely dispersed and little-understood rural firms. He Kang, the outgoing minister of agriculture, headed the new association. The honorary chairman, meanwhile, was none other than Yu's savior from the money slogan crisis, party elder Bo Yibo.

One might have expected that Yu, now honored as a CPPCC delegate, a national model worker, and a leader of a government-run industry group, would become a docile member of the ruling structure in China. His village was rich, he was winning accolades, and there appeared nothing to be gained by going against the grain.

But Yu was a peasant leader with a difference. His struggle was for more than wealth and power. It was for equality. And it was for personal satisfaction. When he had returned from Japan in 1985, his vision of a peasant China living on equal terms—not just economically but also socially and politically—with those in the cities had began to crystallize. When he won his award in 1987, he had used the opportunity to articulate his concerns to a national audience. Now he was gaining the means to advance his agenda even further.

No one in Beijing expected Yu Zuomin and his village to become anything more than a happy model of the party. The coming years would show how wrong they were.

THREE

Long Live Understanding!

I have enough money, the village is rich, I have plenty of accolades, and a lot of face. I could easily retire right now and enjoy all of this. But that would not be the real Yu Zuomin. I would rather be overthrown than just lie down, myself.

Yu Zuomin, 1992

In all the years he had ruled Daqiu, Yu Zuomin had been openly challenged by just one family in the village. The sixty-four-year-old patriarch of this family was named Liu Yutian (not related to the family of Mr. Do-It-All, Liu Wanquan) and was known by his given name, Jade Field. Though he was Yu's senior by just a few years, and the two had played together as children, Jade Field considered himself a village elder. That meant he could second-guess Yu's decisions and criticize his rule. There was nothing wrong with that, of course. Indeed, Yu's autocratic tendencies and his unfettered powers were sorely in need of restraint. But as the village emerged into the full glare of modeldom in the early 1990s, Yu's tolerance for any form of dissent wore thin. It seemed inevitable that Jade Field and his children, who held senior positions in village companies, would be forced into silence.

While sitting at lunch one day in March 1990 in a crowded village canteen, Jade Field's eldest son, Liu Jingang, a vice president of the Daqiu Industrial Company, began to grumble to his driver about Boss Yu.[1] The village leader was using several million yuan of village money to build luxury villas for his two daughters in the county capital, he charged, and his sons were lazy idlers living high off the village's wealth. What's more, it was an open secret that this supposedly virtuous leader was having affairs with several women in the village. How could he be trusted?

It did not take long before those casually uttered remarks found their way back to Yu himself. Predictably, the village leader was furious. The talk of his sexual affairs was true enough, as everyone knew. Yu by this time had developed an intimacy with Shi Jiaming, for example, the rusticated youth twenty-five years his junior who had remained in the village after the Cultural Revolution. That affair had already produced one son.[2] Mistress Shi, as she was known, had divorced her husband in Tianjin and moved her extended family to the village in the 1980s, becoming an ear for Yu's troubles when things went wrong and a source of sexual favors despite his advancing years. If Mao had lain with peasant girls, Yu reckoned, why couldn't the country's most famous peasant leader do likewise?

Most of Yu's anger concerned the allegations of corruption, though. People had called him rough, arrogant, even dictatorial in the past, but no one had called him corrupt. The people of Daqiu supported him because they believed he was working in their interests. Now a scurrilous rumor threatened to undermine that trust.

Liu Jingang was summoned to the village office in early April to explain himself. After a testy exchange, Yu sent him away and ordered all twelve members of the Liu family detained in various village offices. They were accused of hooliganism, corruption, cheating, and, most serious of all, forming a clique. Yu was resolved to extinguish this challenge once and for all.

A week later, a seven-member group of village thugs, several of them cadres, marched to the Liu family home and dragged Jade Field into the streets. The proud family patriarch was forced to stand in the open, strip to the waist, and bow his head as criticisms of his failure to "discipline" his family were read aloud. Then things got out of control. One onlooker spat on the defenseless man. Another pushed him. Within seconds, bystanders descended in an orgy of violence. Belts, clubs, and steel bars rained down on the fallen figure. When they stood back, Jade Field lay unconscious in the dust. He had eight broken bones and massive internal injuries and was bleeding from a deep gash on his chest. By the time family members were permitted to come to his assistance an hour later, it was too late. They arrived at the hospital bearing a limp body. Jade Field was dead.

Though he had almost certainly ordered the public humiliation of Jade Field, Yu Zuomin probably did not want to kill him. When you crossed the line between coercion and crime in China, you invited trouble. Yu now had a delicate problem on his hands. Even if he could command the quiescence of his villagers, he could not ensure silence from the thousands of migrant workers in the village. The Jinghai police were bound to hear of the incident and want to investigate. That in turn might provide the county government with just the pretext it needed to launch another 1982-style "invasion" and "bombing" of the village.

To be sure, the seven thugs had an unshirkable responsibility for the death. But Yu also had a well-founded fear—born of his four decades as a village leader—of seeing his village suffer along with the criminals. By now, he was willing to stop at nothing to prevent that. "We are not afraid of the fact that the legal system is not complete and has loopholes," he would later explain. "But we are afraid that certain powerful people will use their legal powers too flexibly."[3]

Not wanting to be on the defensive, Yu wrote to the Jinghai party committee on 17 April to report the incident. The seven men who had presided over the "criticism meeting" of Jade Field, he wrote, had tried unsuccessfully to prevent angry villagers from inflicting the savage beating that followed. For that, they should be given "lenient and forgiving" treatment. The case was referred to Tianjin leaders immediately.

Not for the last time, the city leadership found itself in an awkward position. Daqiu was a model village, heralded across the nation. While not wanting to overlook flagrant crimes, city leaders were wary of confronting Yu Zuomin directly. The Tianjin mayor was Nie Bichu, a malevolent-looking man with a gap in his upper teeth and narrow squinty eyes. He was in charge of the city because the party secretary, Tan Shaowen, was suffering through the late stages of lung cancer. After dithering for several weeks, Mayor Nie finally authorized the detention of the seven men in late May pending "clarification" of the case. That did not mean much in rural China, though, where cadres accused of crimes regularly got off scot-free.[4]

The death of Jade Field might have passed quietly into history if not for the determination of a forty-three-year-old lawyer from Beijing named Tian Wenchang, a bushy-haired law professor at China Politics and Law University. Late one night in June an agitated peasant came unannounced to Tian's home near Thistle Gate Bridge in western Beijing. Tian ushered him in and closed the metal gate. The visitor was Liu Jinhui, a son of Jade Field who had escaped from detention in Daqiu and made his way to Beijing. Cupping a chipped enamel mug of black tea, he told Tian the story of his father's death and of the subsequent persecution of his family. "You must help me sue Yu Zuomin and redress this injustice," he begged.

It was immediately clear to Tian that this was a case fraught with risk. As he later wrote:

Since this case involved many Daqiu cadres and leaders, there was a political risk that I might be accused of denying the fruits of reform and the contributions of the reformers. It would also be a tricky case to handle because Yu Zuomin was such a crafty person and had a lot of political power. There were limits to what I could do alone as a simple lawyer. I needed to win the shared concerns of senior leaders and the support of the Tianjin political and legal establishment.[5]

Tian opted for a strategy of aiding the prosecution of the accused seven first and worrying about Yu Zuomin later. Liu Jinhui was billeted at a military guesthouse in Beijing to ensure his personal safety. From there, he contacted two brothers back in the village, Liu Jingang and another named Liu Jingong. Within a few days the pair had escaped and fled to Tianjin. There, in late June, they made a successful rendez-vous with Tian, amid the hawkers selling steaming *goubuli* dumplings and fried *mahua* dough twists in front of the Tianjin train station. The lawyer immediately stuffed them into a cab and headed straight for the Tianjin prosecutor's office.

With the evidence provided by the three Liu brothers, Tianjin prosecutors were able to build a strong case against the seven detained men, who were formally placed under arrest in September. Tian, meanwhile, was, in his own words, "running all over the place gathering evidence and at the same time appealing for support from higher authorities."[6] That high-level support remained elusive, however. Yu Zuomin was a prominent national spokesman for the central government's ongoing post-Tiananmen rectification policies. He was also throwing all his resources into a behind-the-scenes effort to have the seven men declared innocent. The accused were tried in secret in late November, but no verdicts were announced. Without Beijing's approval, they were sure to walk free.

Following the trial, Tian took the unusual step of sending his file on the case to the standing committee of the National People's Congress, or national parliament. That at least got the attention of some members of the politburo, including the then-chairman of the parliament, Qiao Shi. Tian's next ploy was to hold a seminar in Beijing in December to discuss the case. There he met a journalist who would figure prominently in the later course of events in Daqiu: Liu Linshan, Tianjin bureau chief of the Ministry of Justice's daily newspaper, the *Legal Daily*.

A veteran reporter, Liu had kept a watchful eye on Daqiu ever since being assigned to the Tianjin bureau in the early 1980s. Like most Chinese journalists, he knew much more than he dared to write. In the case of Daqiu, his own growing suspicions of the autocratic ruling style of Yu Zuomin coincided with the growing fame of the village. The more he learned, the less he could write.

"Yu Zuomin is insufferably arrogant. He thinks he is really great, second only to God himself. Even the Tianjin party committee cannot stand him," he had remarked to Mistress Shi while on a visit to the village in 1985. "Sooner or later something will go wrong here."[7]

Five years later, something had gone wrong, and Liu found himself well positioned to expose it. After meeting lawyer Tian, Liu wrote an "internal reference" report on the Jade Field case to the Ministry of Justice. Such reports are a regular part of any journalist's job in China, providing officials with sensitive information deemed unsuitable for publication. Entitled "A Violent Scandal Occurs in the Model Village for Rural Prosperity," the report had an immediate impact. Besides detailing the direct criminal responsibility of the seven assailants, it also criticized Yu for obstructing justice and fabricating charges against Jade Field. The failure of the Tianjin courts to announce a verdict, Liu wrote, was a bad precedent for a party seeking to restore law and order to rural areas.

Coupled with support from the national parliament, the report spurred the Ministry of Justice to refer the case to "higher levels," presumably meaning the party politburo. The instructions that came down were clear: punish the seven men directly involved in the case, but draw the line there; and forbid any media coverage of the verdict.

On 8 May 1991 the Tianjin Intermediate People's Court declared the seven men guilty in the death of Jade Field. The sentences were substantial: Yu Zuoxiang and Yu Zuoli, cousins of Yu Zuomin who had presided over the street criticism meeting, were given life prison terms for assault with intention to injure. The other five drew jail terms of between nine and fifteen years. Appeals were rejected six weeks later. True to the instructions from Beijing, the case was not reported in the media.

Despite Beijing's attempts to limit the fallout from the verdicts, Yu Zuomin was outraged by the heavy sentences. Already convinced of a growing conspiracy against his village within the Tianjin and Jinghai leaderships, he took the verdicts as a veritable call to arms. Within days of the rejection of the appeals, the Tianjin party committee and the politburo in Beijing were flooded with more than two thousand letters written under the names of Daqiu villagers. The letters complained that the sentences were unjust and an attack on the reforming spirit of the village. The sense of aggrievement was clear from a section of one of the letters later published in a book in China:

> We would like to ask why the chief judge of the court did not come to the village to investigate himself. Just because our pace of reform is quick, it doesn't mean that whenever the crimes of a suspect here are not clear he should simply be convicted. Even more, just because we are an advanced unit of reforms, it does not mean that those who should be punished lightly are punished severely. . . . Not only will this destroy the majesty of the law, but it will also lose the support of the people. . . . Our reforms are already difficult enough. When will these difficulties end?[8]

Throughout the autumn of 1991, journalist Liu Linshan wrote more internal reference reports, this time on the letter-writing campaign. One of them, according to a later report in the *Beijing Youth Daily* newspaper, was read by "the central party leadership and relevant central departments."[9] But Yu and his village were apparently still seen as too important and too powerful to be punished. Beijing leaders refrained from taking action. Lawyer Tian later recalled: "Yu Zuomin's position was in danger a few times. But each time he landed on his feet and consolidated his power by attacking the Tianjin judiciary, saying that they were trying to repudiate Daqiu Village and destroy the economic reform movement."[10]

Eventually, Yu resigned himself to the sentences and called off the campaign. But the experience had a profound transforming effect on Daqiu. In practical terms, it was the first time since 1982 that the village had been forced to defend itself so tenaciously. It also solidified Yu's image within the village as a leader whose causes should command allegiance. Yu had now convinced the people of Daqiu that any attempt by outside authorities to exercise their powers over the village was a disguised plot to undermine its economic success. More important, Yu now believed that China's economic reform movement hinged on his own village's struggle for respect and autonomy. The stage was set for a terrible showdown.

Daqiu's wealth and fame were by the early 1990s crucial ingredients in its ability to challenge the state on a broad range of issues. In 1991 and 1992, those twin resources expanded significantly as a result of an unprecedented wave of further economic reforms that swept the nation.

Daqiu was already investing heavily in new factories when China's economy began to recover from the post-Tiananmen slump in mid-1991. As a result, it was ready and waiting with new capacity as national demand rose, a repeat of its winning bet in the late 1970s. Total output from village enterprises more than doubled in 1991 to Rmb 1.8 billion, while profits rose by a quarter to Rmb 100 million.

But no one predicted the further economic boom that patriarch Deng Xiaoping sparked when he toured southern China in early 1992. Frustrated by the conservative hold on economic policy in Beijing, Deng decamped to the south in January, where he called for faster and bolder reforms. By the time Deng's speeches were made public in

March, every entrepreneur and economic planner in the country was ramping up production. China's economy would grow by an eye-popping 13 percent that year, or even more according to some unofficial estimates.

As a child of Deng's rural reforms, Daqiu responded to the so-called Southern Tour with ebullience. Banners reading "Hello Comrade Xiaoping!" were hung on the village streets, and Yu wrote several articles for Tianjin newspapers praising the renewed reform drive. There were even rumors that Deng had planned to visit Daqiu but the trip was canceled because the road from Jinghai was not entirely paved.[11] Still, the village's close association with Deng was never in doubt. As the official Xinhua news agency said in one dispatch in July 1992: "The village has become a model example of the reform policies."[12]

Caught up in the enthusiasm of the post-Southern Tour boom, Yu set an audacious output goal for the village of Rmb 50 billion by the year 2000. On some arcane calculation, that would make Daqiu the richest village in the world. "We Chinese peasants are no worse than foreign peasants. Indeed, we're much better," he said in announcing the target.[13]

The ambitious goal threw Daqiu into its very own Great Leap Forward. Total village output would more than double that year to Rmb 4.5 billion, accounting for half the entire output of Jinghai county and yielding profits of Rmb 400 million. Each of the Four Hens—now reorganized into four holding companies, Wanquan Group, Yaoshun Group (the former Daqiu Village Industrial Company), Jinhai Group, and Jinmei Group—went through a spasm of expansion that even today boggles the mind. More than twenty new factories were built in a newly created 120-hectare industrial zone on the western edge of the village, involving investment of Rmb 700 million. They included a flashy new motorcycle plant with Japanese partners and several new steel plants. Groundbreaking for the zone was delayed for several months in the late summer so that peasants in the area could harvest their sorghum crop. When the first factories opened on schedule in October, journalists swooned about "Daqiu speed," a flattering reference to the term "Shenzhen speed," used to describe the hectic pace of growth in the special economic zone abutting Hong Kong.

From simply hiring experts, selling products, and running sales offices outside the village in the 1980s, the Four Hens became investors and managers of projects around the country. A new steel pipe factory in distant Zhejiang province was described by the Xinhua news agency as "another shrewd move" by the village, given the central government's plan to revitalize nearby Shanghai.[14] By the end of the year, Daqiu accounted for 3 percent of China's entire steel processing capacity.[15] The Hens also invested in two hot spots for real estate that would later crash spectacularly: Hainan province and Beihai city, both on the southwestern China coast. Closer to home, Yaoshun Group built a sprawling resort named after the eighteenth-century Qianlong emperor. Yu talked about developing raw material sources in inland areas. Indeed, he wondered, why not build little Daqius all over the country, even in Taiwan. "There are riches to be found in even the foulest water," he said.[16] Daqiu was a testament to that fact.

The extension of Daqiu's growing links to the rest of China were its growing links to the rest of the world. Taking up Deng's appeal for more foreign trade and investment, Yu declared that the village's next phase of development would be led by international ventures. Trade delegations were sent to the United States and Europe in 1992, and Yu promised to reward anyone who attracted a foreign investor, even by marrying one. By the end of 1992, the village had thirty-eight joint ventures. Village companies were opened in Russia to source iron and steel, in Thailand for copper, and in Cameroon for yearlings to supply the village's animal husbandry operations. Wanquan Group invested $3 million in a joint venture with a U.S. company to build manufacturing and trading facilities in the Tianjin free trade zone. This would allow the village to handle more of its own trade, which otherwise had to be funneled through state trading companies. Yu even secured the purchase of five decommissioned Russian naval vessels to handle the village's imports and exports, though they were never delivered.

Taking their cue from Deng's endorsement of stock markets during his Southern Tour, the Four Hens also issued shares. Nonvoting "individual shares" had been issued to workers and managers of several companies since late 1991. These entitled them to dividends and bonuses but not control, which remained vested in the groups. Still, many managers got rich by exercising options to buy shares in the companies doing well.[17] Once Deng's endorsement of stock markets was made public, the groups rushed to set up shareholding companies in which they could issue publicly traded stock and bonds as well. Brother Yu was the first off the mark in July with a Rmb 90 million public stock offering, representing 30 percent of a new shareholding company controlled by his Yaoshun Group. This was followed in August by a Rmb 20 million issue in a company under Wanquan Group. The shares were only traded over the counter among Tianjin brokers, as well as on the streets, rather than on an official stock exchange. But that did not worry investors. Few could resist buying a stake in Deng's model village.

The Hens also took on new debt, which totaled Rmb 1.3 billion by the end of the year. The city-owned underwriter of the two share placements, Tianjin Trust and Investment, lent the companies Rmb 100 million from its own funds, such was its confidence in the village. Jinmei Group also placed Rmb 100 million in short-term debentures with an attractive interest rate of 9.2 percent. Tianjin authorities did not approve the issue, but that, again, did not seem to bother anyone. "Isn't it said that we should make use of capitalist tools?" asked company president Zhao Shuzhong, invoking Deng's words, at a press conference in Tianjin to promote the issue.[18]

By the end of 1992, Daqiu was truly the richest village in China. The per capita income of the natives was reported to be Rmb 26,000 that year, more than five times the target for "modest prosperity" (*xiao kang*) in rural areas set by Deng a decade earlier. Hoping to capture some of the savings, the Agricultural Bank of China opened a branch in the village, its first in rural Tianjin.

As in the 1980s, there was little to indicate that Daqiu's 1992 boom was a result of state support.[19] A few suspicious deals came its way, to be sure, such as a Rmb 50 million investment in five steel plants under the Jinhai Group by the central government's Ministry of Materials and Equipment (now defunct). But given that Daqiu was already one of China's biggest steel towns, the deal could hardly be described as unusual. A quarter of the one hundred "key enterprises" designated by the Tianjin municipality were in the village for this same reason. And set against the more than Rmb 1 billion of new investment by the village itself in this year, the amount was quite modest. As Wang Wujing, deputy director of the Tianjin agricultural commission said at the time, "Some central ministries have invested in Daqiu. But they do so because the village is an efficient place to do business, not to support it."[20]

The same sense of the central government following rather than leading Daqiu's development was evident in infrastructure. Yu's big plans included an airport, a railway line spur from Jinghai, and an electrical power station. The latter two, at least, were under active consideration by the Tianjin authorities by late 1992. But this was nothing more than any other booming village or town would expect. "Now that they have grown so much, we are helping them with their infrastructure needs," Hu Chongqing, secretary general of the municipal planning commission, explained.[21]

Daqiu was a model, but it was no sham. Whatever you might say about the way it got rich, one thing was sure: the central government was for the most part an onlooker, not a participant. Its role ended at the village gate.

The burst of economic activity coincided with an intensification of propaganda about Daqiu and its unlikely leader. In mid-1992, the party Central Committee issued a nationwide circular detailing Daqiu's development and calling it a "perfect example" of the merits of the country's rural reforms.[22] That was about as close as any village could get to being declared a model in post-Dazhai China.

Daqiu was not just wealthy and reform-minded: it was audacious too. And audacity is exactly what Deng had called for on his Southern Tour. Daqiu had thumbed its nose at regulators by issuing debentures, circumvented official channels for foreign investment and trade projects, and proudly advertised its money-driven culture. It was almost as if the village's struggle for development was the counterpart to the ideological and political battles Deng had waged in the top echelons of the country's leadership. Giving publicity to the village was like giving publicity to Deng himself.

The most eager participant in this renewed publicity drive was the domestic press. In the ten months after the Southern Tour, China's media was saturated with images and stories of Daqiu and Yu Zuomin. Major newspapers ran multipart series: a four-part series in the high-brow *Guangming Daily* in June; a three-part series in October in the *TVE News;* a seven-part series in the Beijing-run *Ta Kung Pao* in Hong Kong in November; and a seven-part series in the *China Youth Daily* in January 1993. Yu even made it into the who's who of China for the first time.[23] "It is becoming difficult to turn on the television or open a newspaper without seeing Yu Zuomin," the *South China Morning Post*'s Beijing correspondent wrote in exasperation in November. "The gaunt, chain-smoking patriarch of Daqiu is everywhere."[24]

In contrast to the early portrayals of Yu as a simpleton, the village leader was now portrayed as a font of wisdom, a lucid guru of the new rural economy. The *Guangming Daily* compared him to the ancient prince Meng Changjun, who had built his power during the Warring States period (460–220 B.C.) by attracting talented warriors, strategists, and scholars to his camp. China Central Television ran a seven-part series entitled "Yu Zuomin Thought" in late 1992. Yu, meanwhile, began to look and act the part. His suits were better tailored, and his glasses and watch shimmered with gold and silver. For now, at least, he had transcended the image of the lovable rural ignoramus that Uncle Chen had so carefully cultivated.

Following close on the heels of the domestic media came a gaggle of foreign reporters. Unlike the solemn and often hagiographic tone of the domestic media, foreign reporters always had a bemused attitude toward Daqiu. The sight of the upstart farmers plying the dusty village roads in unwieldy sedans provided much wry humor for the postmodern eye. "Outside, Mercedes and Cadillacs cruise the narrow streets, ferrying the new breed of cadrebusinessmen to appointments. Chauffeurs ease their charges past horsedrawn carts that are still used to carry building materials and other goods," noted London's *Daily Telegraph*.[25] Or the *New York Times*, after interviewing Yang Yanru, the wife of a model worker, in her eleven-room house: "Except for her crooked teeth, and a collar that suggested her man-tailored shirt was made in the 1960s, there was little to suggest that Ms. Yang was once a peasant who got her eggs from the chicken coop in the backyard."[26]

This writer's first and only visit to Daqiu took place in July 1992. I was fortunate to bump into five equally curious university students from Tianjin who had come to witness the model village firsthand. Together, we talked to a range of people: Liu Shunmei, an eighteen-year-old Daqiu native working as a secretary in the office of Wanquan Group, who told us how the village had arranged for her job; Zhu Shudong, an earnest former teacher from Shanghai who was now fully engaged as a manager in Yaoshun Group; Li Zhan, a scruffy Hebei native who plied the Shaanxi-Beijing-Tianjin corridor selling electrical welding equipment for the Yaoshun Group; and a host of migrant workers living in cramped dormitories, who complained that there was nothing to do in the village except watch television.

The main impression of Daqiu was of a huge and dusty worksite overrun by migrant workers rather than the tidy and peaceful hamlet portrayed in the domestic press. The luxury villas and spic-and-span school existed, to be sure, but only on the fringes of what was really a sprawling collection of factories and office buildings. Walking along any of the jammed main roads was hazardous as trucks laden with protruding steel bars and building materials (their drivers no doubt working on commission) careened wildly toward their destinations. Dust and noise were everywhere. Still, the village was an impressive sight sitting on the Jinghai plains surrounded by several nearby villages of nothing but mud huts and sorghum fields. What it had lost in rustic charm, Daqiu had more than gained in urban amenity.

Alongside the media came scores of other visitors to "obtain the holy scriptures" of Daqiu's development. Xinhua said that "tens of thousands" of people visited the village in 1992, including "central government leaders" and "senior military officers."[27] Among them were CPPCC chairman Li Ruihuan and the aging Bo Yibo, arguably the village's two most important mentors in Beijing.

Never one to pass up an opportunity to promote his village, or himself, Yu was soon spending the greater part of his time regaling the visitors with tales of the past. "Groups of visitors are swarming to Daqiu to learn from the villagers' experiences, and they all want to meet Yu Zuomin," the *Legal Daily* noted in late 1992. "During the busiest season, the village receives thousands of visitors. Sometimes Yu has to meet eight groups a day, speaking endlessly."[28]

While most came out of respect, some of the day-trippers arrived with ulterior motives, hoping to expose the dark side of this model village. Students, researchers, and cadres whose noses curled at the sight of Daqiu's wealth were eager to gather evidence of corruption, inequality, or undisciplined *guanxi* (personal relationship) politics in the village. As a result, the fortress mentality that had begun to take shape in the village after the 1982 inspection team soon hardened into an almost paranoid fear of ill-intentioned outsiders. A stable of twenty-six sedan cars was put on twenty-four-hour call to meet visitors at the gate and escort them on their excursions. Even foreign dignitaries had to stop and change cars. The *Ta Kung Pao* noted wryly that this rule recalled the imperial edict that everyone except the emperor had to dismount at the gate of the Forbidden City in Beijing, "even foreign advisers and treaty port officials."[29]

The key figure delegated to handle the village's public relations was Mistress Shi. In addition to being his lover, she had always been Yu Zuomin's staunchest defender, warning off *Legal Daily* journalist Liu Linshan several times during the Jade Field incident, for example. Now she took on the role of defending Yu and the village from an influx of outsiders. When journalists and cadres came to town looking for dirt on the model village, Mistress Shi greeted them politely and made sure they left empty-handed.

The mounting fear of visitors intent on scurrying back to Beijing to write scathing internal reference reports about Daqiu came to a head in late 1992. On the morning of 27 November, a busload of twenty-nine students and teachers from the cadre training academy of the Beijing Municipal State Security Department arrived unannounced in the village.[30] Their purpose was to survey its living standards, possibly to criticize its epicurean ways. After lunch, the students fanned out and began peppering shop owners and workers with questions about their incomes and lifestyles. One of the shop owners was Mistress Shi's sister, who immediately reported the intrusion. Before long, village security guards descended on the unauthorized pollsters. Scuffles broke out as students were escorted off the streets. By the time the entire group was brought to the main reception office at about 4 p.m., many were bruised and cut, and several shop windows had been smashed.

Mistress Shi stormed into the room and insisted that the group leader sign a letter of regret for the damages and tumult they had caused. When the leader refused, the group was put under guard in the room and left to think it over. The standoff was only broken when Beijing city leaders got wind of the detention later that evening. Yu spoke with them by phone and it was agreed that the damages would be paid by the city. At 11 p.m., the bruised and tired students climbed aboard their bus, which was escorted all the way back to Beijing, Mistress Shi riding shotgun in the lead vehicle.

The incident was soon forgotten. But it was a telling sign that the debate about Daqiu continued to swirl. For the most part, the tidal wave of publicity the village soaked up throughout 1992 was well intentioned and welcome. It sanctioned the village's approach, protected its flank, and strengthened its struggle. At the same time, some visitors came with preconceived notions that this was yet another sham village waiting to be exposed. For Yu Zuomin, it was a discouraging reminder that a thorough public understanding of the factors that had made Daqiu rich was still a long way off. "All I need now is understanding," Yu told the *Ta Kung Pao.* "Whoever comes to Daqiu and understands us, I will shout: Long live understanding!"[31]

The year 1992 saw the emergence of Yu Zuomin as an avatar of a new kind of peasant rebel in China. Fueled by Daqiu's prosperity and its renown—and backed by a newly galvanized collective spirit in the village in the wake of the Jade Field incident—Yu began to articulate a powerful new discourse of social and economic justice for China's peasants. Until now most of the political battles Yu had fought had been clearly linked to village interests. By 1992, however, his agitation was assuming national significance, and he was taking steps to implant his vision elsewhere in China.

Before we consider this discourse, it is worthwhile to ask why Yu did this, and why his village remained united behind him. After all, both Yu and the village were already flush with success. At least four distinct motivations can be detected driving Yu's dissent. Most obvious was his long-standing determination *to enrich Daqiu.* This factor had explained most of his run-ins with the party and upper-level officials over the preceding fifteen years, and it did not flag despite the village's wealth. Closely related and emerging since 1987 had been *a quest for equality for all of China's peasants.* As he gained stature, Yu used his position to agitate for changes in policies and attitudes that would benefit all rural dwellers. He called himself "the peasant who best understands peasants, their heartbeats, their dreams, their loves, hates, disappointments, and joys. It's just like I understand myself."[32] He said he would "dare to die in order to win honor and credit for peasants."[33] To the extent that he did, he averred, it would be his greatest contribution.[34]

Also emergent since about 1987 had been *a quest for personal recognition*. Yu wanted to be honored for his achievements, indeed honored as highly as Uncle Chen had been. He loved media attention and he loved being surrounded by pilgrims to Daqiu. But personal recognition alone was not enough. In an interview with the *Ta Kung Pao* in October 1992, Yu made this telling remark: "I have enough money, the village is rich, I have plenty of accolades and a lot of face. I could easily retire right now and enjoy all of this. But that would not be the real Yu Zuomin. I would rather be overthrown than just lie down, myself."[35] That suggests a fourth kind of motivation, *a struggle for struggle's sake*. Yu by this time relished a good scrap with those in the party who would have Daqiu revisit its miserable past. He went out of his way to pick a fight with ideologues and petty officials. By engaging in such disputes, Yu vented the accumulated frustrations of years working under misguided party policies.

Given that the latter three of these motivations were not of immediate benefit to Daqiu itself, it is legitimate to ask whether Yu's dissent was really still the voice of Daqiu at all, or just the voice of one man's ego trip. That is, was he still waging true collective action? The best answer seems to be that while the ultimate goals of the two often diverged—Yu seeking personal recognition and the thrill of battle, his villagers direct benefits—their immediate goals remained more or less as one. As a result, more often than not villagers stood behind his actions. To be sure, what masked as collective action could sometimes be the result of silence imposed through fear. But mostly villagers appeared to genuinely support their leader in his campaigns. "Cadre-peasant relations" in Daqiu, to use the party's term, remained excellent, excepting of course some disgruntled families like that of the late Jade

Field. Indeed, this solidarity is what Yu relied on. Had he not been assured of the village's support, he would never have spoken so forcefully. As it was, he won praise and so did the village. Investors came in droves, and villagers prospered.

Gathering together the diverse strands of Yu's dissent is no simple task. Few peasant leaders in China who take a stand against the system ever have their views summarized neatly in books. Indeed, Daqiu villagers themselves were wary of such a coherent manifesto. As the *China Youth Daily* noted, "Daqiu people in general do not like to discuss sensitive theoretical issues for fear of inviting trouble. . . . If you come here to understand these issues, you will leave disappointed."[36] For our purposes, we can group Yu's dissent under three main headings: economic, political, and social.

For more than a decade, Yu Zuomin had explicitly spurned ideological constraints on economic and political policies in Daqiu. Policies that made the peasants rich and more civilized were self-evidently salutary in his view. Leftists who argued about the ideological nature of policies, he believed, were both a threat and a nuisance. "Reforming is not easy," he once said. "There are many difficulties and a lot of risks. You have to constantly fend off attacks by leftists."[37]

There were of course ample antecedents for Yu's pragmatic approach in the sayings of Deng Xiaoping himself. Perhaps the most enduring of these was Deng's "white cat theory," borrowed from the peasants of his native Sichuan province: "It doesn't matter whether a cat is black or white, so long as it catches mice."[38] Yu could also hark back to the memory of Uncle Chen of Dazhai, who had proudly boasted of his ignorance of communist theory.

But Deng's pragmatism and Uncle Chen's ignorance were always conditional on the upholding of certain basic ideological tenets, the party's so-called Four Cardinal Principles. The two most important of these were the incontestable rule of the party and the socialist nature of the Chinese economy. Even for a place like Daqiu, hell-bent on fast growth, both of these tenets had to be seen to be upheld. The problem was that for many on the left, they were not. "There are several areas where we cannot break through," Yu complained to the *TVE News* in 1992. "These include constant questions about our political direction and about our economic direction."[39]

Consider first the economic side. The debate on rural economic policy had shifted dramatically in the fifteen years to 1992. It is almost quaint to recall the *Jiang Han Forum* railing against rural industry in 1981, warning that it might undermine Communist rule in China. It is equally amusing to remember the discomfiture Yu Zuomin brought to senior leaders that same year after he decided to improve incentive pay for his village's reed cutters. Rural industry was now duly sanctioned, while merit pay—the antithesis of the egalitarian iron rice bowl—was widely accepted.

Even in that changed atmosphere, however, those on the left still had plenty of gripes about Daqiu's economy. The market-driven companies and their swaggering executives seemed to differ little from those in capitalist economies, even if the assets were owned collectively. To put it more precisely, collective ownership in the old days meant collective operation as well as ownership. But in modern-day Daqiu, managers took all the decisions and creamed off some of the profits as their reward.

As early as 1987, recall, Yu had argued that a socialist economy should be defined by its ends, not its means, by whether people's stomachs were full and their faces smiling rather than by who or what operated the means of production. By seeking to impose ideological limitations on economic policies, he averred during one trip to the United States in 1991, leftists in Beijing were in effect forcing peasants to work with one arm tied behind their backs. "You guys have always pursued economic development with both hands," he told his hosts. "But we have only one strong hand, and one weak hand."[40]

Fortunately, Daqiu's defense of its economic policies was immeasurably strengthened by events in Beijing in late 1992. Grappling to redefine socialism in a more pragmatic way, Deng formulated a "new cat theory."

This held that it did not matter whether the cat was market driven or planning driven as long as it pursued the general good and was largely owned by the state.[41] With this new notion of a "socialist market economy" incorporated into the country's constitution, rural industrial leaders like Yu breathed a collective sigh of relief. Since TVEs were owned by collectives, they easily fit this new definition of socialism. In effect, operation and profit distribution were no longer an issue, since Deng's theory said socialism could be market driven. "Some people say that we are going capitalist. But we are just following the road to riches laid down by the party center," Yu said. "The issue of what is socialist and what is capitalist is a matter for the party center to decide, not the peasants. And we know that the party center would not go capitalist."[42]

In stark contrast to the waning debate on Daqiu's economic policies, the debate over its political system went from bad to worse. Daqiu's political system had long been dominated by Yu, of course; but the structure through which he ruled became a source of controversy. Three related issues were at stake: the weakening of the party structure in Daqiu; the concomitant strengthening of the role of the village conglomerate; and the domination of the village conglomerate by Yu and a few families. Together, these issues added up to a striking challenge to Communist rule in peasant China, a new vision in which the party was confined to the sidelines and a new rural moneyed class took its place.

As far back as the 1980s, recall, Yu's willingness to hire people with problematic class, ideological, historical, or family backgrounds had won him praise. Paeans about "Yu Zuomin's employment doctrine" (*Yu Zuomin yong ren zhi dao*) filled official publications. "Yu Zuomin's standards for judging people are very pragmatic," one typical Ministry of Agriculture–sponsored handbook had explained in 1988. "Is the enterprise developing? Are profits high?"[43] Or as the *TVE News* noted in 1987: "Yu Zuomin has broken through the leftist constraints of the past and boldly employed people of all sorts."[44]

By the 1990s, however, Yu wanted to extend this ideology-blind system from the factories to the political system. Good cadres, like good

managers, he believed, should be judged by their economic performance, not their political rectitude. The *China Youth Daily* explained
gingerly: "It's not that there are no political, moral, or ideological issues
here. It's just that they are simplified. When the village chooses its outstanding workers *and party members,* they simply decide according to
who has the highest salaries. So it's all very simple."[45]

As early as 1987, the *TVE News* had been wary enough of Yu's non-
doctrinaire hiring code to note: "This does not mean management is
lax, of course. Yu insists that cadres remain unanimous with the party
center in matters of politics and ideology."[46] But by 1992 Yu was even
dissenting from this central tenet, asserting that leaders should think
and act for themselves. "Reforms cannot wait for unanimity," he said.
"If we wait for unanimity, there would be no reforms. And in any case,
there would never be any unanimity in a hundred years."[47]

The obvious result of this was that the role of the party, specifically
the village party branch of which Yu was secretary, withered. Daqiu
had paid lip service to Beijing's appeal to strengthen rural party
branches in the wake of the Tiananmen Square protests by quadrupling
its party membership to 813 by 1991. In that year, Yu was even honored
at a lunar new year reception in Beijing as a representative of a "national
advanced ideological and political work unit." But in reality, the party
in Daqiu disappeared from view. "In all reports produced by the village
and its holding company since 1984," sociologist Lin Nan noted, "party
functions and activities at the local level are completely absent . . . all
local economic, political and social functions proceed without any need
for the party apparatus."[48] Or as the *China Youth Daily* put it: "Pretty
much everything in Daqiu is aimed at promoting business. Even politics
is adopted here to promote business, not to be an obstacle to it."[49]

Indeed, more than just allowing party structures to die from neglect,
Yu began to advocate the formal abolition of some. In particular, he
took aim at the organization department, the key part of every rural
party branch which controls cadre appointments. Yu's subversive idea,
like so many others that came off his lips, was couched in a catchy slo-

gan that rhymed in Chinese. Even now, it jolts with its baldness: "If you want to get rich," it went, "abolish the party organization department" (*yao zhi fu, quxiao zuzhibu*).[50]

The corollary of the shrinking role of the party in Daqiu was the growing role of the village conglomerate. Since its formation in 1983, the village conglomerate had been steadily expanding its reach into all aspects of village life and governance. By 1992, Yu was ready to formalize that role. The conglomerate, now renamed Daqiu Village Enterprise Group Corporation, was reorganized into two divisions, one handling business and one government. Yu became the chairman of a newly constituted twenty-six-member board of directors. The village party branch and the villagers committee—the two would-be organs of administration in such a village—were nowhere to be found.

Beijing never explicitly criticized Yu for his attempt to weaken the hold of the party in Daqiu. But at least one exchange has been recorded in which its disapproving attitude was clear. In mid-1992, an unnamed "senior cadre" from the Organization Department of the party's Central Committee—the same department whose rural tentacles would be hacked off if Yu had his way—came to inspect Daqiu. Yu was not much for listening to lectures from Beijing officials. Instead, he turned the tables and delivered this lecture to the visitor on the failings of his department:

Whether China can become rich or not all depends on your department. For a long time, many local cadres have considered poverty to be glorious and idiocy to be admirable. Without exception, they would pass on documents from the Central Committee without changing a single character, pasting them up on walls and turning them into slogans. They would not come up with a single concrete idea themselves. They wouldn't say a single incorrect word, but neither would they do a single useful thing. These kinds of people were considered good cadres. But could they make the economy develop?

The Organization Department leader was clearly affronted. His cryptic reply was, "I'll try to have a positive understanding of your point of view." Yu never heard from him again, but he guessed aloud that the silence indicated disapproval. "How could he have a negative understanding?" he asked.[51]

It is important to note that Yu's reworking of the political structures of Daqiu did not give rise to anything like a pure meritocracy, much less a democracy. Rather, it gave rise to a highly authoritarian ruling structure in which family ties often appeared to count for more than merit. As the head of the village conglomerate, Yu himself increasingly took on the trappings of an emperor, moving around with a large cortege and rarely being interrupted by anyone, much less questioned. As Hong Kong's *South China Morning Post* noted of an interview with the famed peasant hero: "Mr Yu was accompanied by a small army of secretaries and assorted hangerson, who noted down his every word and leapt to attention every time he spoke to them. As soon as Mr Yu finished a cigarette, one of his assistants brought him a fresh pack, which was opened and another cigarette lit for him."[52]

There was no better example of how nepotism rather than *nengli* (ability) was guiding cadre appointments than Yu's plan to hand over his power to the younger of his two sons, a plump and awkward twenty-six-year-old named Yu Shaozheng. Under the revamp of the village conglomerate, Little Yu, as he was called, was named president, second in command to his father as chairman. Little Yu was also the head of the village's Communist Youth League, which suggested that he would take over as village party secretary as well. Boss Yu justified the nepotistic succession saying, "It's important that the successor is someone the people trust."[53] A Chinese reporter also claimed that the installation of Little Yu would bolster investor confidence.[54] But unlike his gaunt, workaholic father, Little Yu was more a sultry playboy than a charismatic leader. His house was stuffed with luxuries like a grand piano, a big-screen TV, and a gym, and an even more splendid manor was under construction for him in Jinghai.[55] His wedding in 1991 reportedly cost more than Rmb 1 million.[56] If Boss Yu was not corrupt, the odor of improbity hung heavily over his corpulent son.

Similarly nepotistic appointments colored the entire top leadership of the village. Liu Wanquan, Mr. Do-It-All, made his son, Liu Yonghua—known by his given name, Eternal China—president of Wanquan Group in 1992, retaining only the company chairmanship. Boss Yu's eldest son, Yu Shaowei, meanwhile, was put in charge of enterprise management in the village conglomerate. Mistress Shi, who was now the head of village administration, also doled out plum jobs to the eleven members of her family she had brought from Tianjin. One brother ran the local power station, another a village trade company, and another a village electronics factory; her father ran the village guesthouse; and a sister headed the village office in the Tianjin free trade zone.[57] The entire interlocking family system can be seen in table 3.

This, then, was the entrenched family-based system that Yu Zuomin constructed as an alternative to party rule in Daqiu. It was not unique; similar conglomerates had been formed in other places grown rich on TVEs. But the leaders of those places at least made gestures to uphold the role of the party. Not Yu Zuomin. He explicitly spurned the role of the party, even proposed to disembowel rural party branches.

Left-wing critics claimed that Daqiu's ruling system was indistinguishable from feudalism.[58] That may be too strong a criticism. As mentioned earlier, family networks had proved remarkably effective in running the village companies in the early years of China's reforms. Most important, all indications are that the ruling structure in Daqiu enjoyed broad support in the village. In any case, the issue was not whether Daqiu was run according to democratic principles or feudal ones. Rather, it was a question of whether the village had the right to rule itself as it pleased, whether through consensus-based family networks or some other agreed-upon method. To be sure, the Daqiu

TABLE 3   DAQIU VILLAGE LEADERSHIP IN 1992

Top Leaders

Yu Zuomin: Chairman of village holding company. Village party secretary.
Yu Shaozheng*: Son of Yu. President of village holding company.

Administration

Shi Jiaming*†: Mistress of Yu. Head of village administration.
Li Fengzhuang: Nephew of Yu. Head of village personnel.
Yu Zuozhang†: Cousin of Yu. Head of village finances.
Yu Shaoguo†: Son of Yu Zuozhang.
Zhang Yupu: Village patriarch. Head of village ethics committee.

Enterprises

Yu Shaowei†: Eldest son of Yu. Head of village enterprise management.
Zhao Shuzhong*†: Son-in-law of Yu. Jinmei Group president and chairman.
Yu Zuoyao*†: Brother of Yu. Yaoshun Group president and chairman.
Li Fengzheng*†: Nephew of Yu. Huada Group president.
Yu Shaodong†: Son of Yu Zuozhang. Deputy head of village enterprise management.
Zhang Yanjun*†: Son of Zhang Yupu. Jinhai Group president and chairman.
Zhang Yuyin†: Cousin of Zhang Yupu. Wanquan Group executive vice president.
Shi Jiafu: Brother of Shi Jiaming. Manager of a village trading company.
Shi Jiashi: Brother of Shi Jiaming. Manager of a village electronics company.
Liu Wanquan*†: Former brigade leader. Wanquan Group chairman.
Liu Yonghua: Eldest son of Liu Wanquan. Wanquan Group president.
Liu Yunzhang: Son of Liu Wanquan. Wanquan Group personnel head and secretary.
Liu Shaosheng: Cousin of Liu Wanquan. Wanquan Group vice president.
Liu Wanmin: Brother of Liu Wanquan. Wanquan Group vice president.

*Vice chairman of village conglomerate.
†Vice president of village conglomerate.

model had problems. Dissent from families outside the ruling elite—such as that of the late Jade Field—was stifled, and it was not clear that a single economic entity could efficiently coordinate such vast and diversified business interests forever. But one thing was sure: together they symbolized a kind of quiet revolution in the countryside in which the role of the party was being diminished. That, more than anything, accounted for Beijing's concerns about exactly what kind of monster this model village was becoming.

The social policies of Daqiu—in particular its culture of conspicuous consumption—were the other aspect of Yu Zuomin's new vision of peasant China. As early as the 1982 inspection team, recall, county officials had fussed about the village's visible wealth. Ten years later, as village companies put on another burst of speed and per capita income rose to about Rmb 26,000 for every Daqiu native, that disquiet finally broke onto the national stage.

There were really two overlapping issues. One was the bureaucratic issue of whether cadres in Daqiu, in particular Yu Zuomin, were living beyond their means, surrounding themselves with trappings that violated prescribed living standards for party cadres. The second was more the heart of the matter: Was it good or bad for peasants to flaunt their success?

By 1992, it was hard to overlook the fact that Yu Zuomin was living quite well. His salary in that year was Rmb 1 million. His 700-square-meter house was a palatial three-story structure inside a walled compound that also contained the houses of thirteen other company presidents and vice presidents. The main floor featured a marble and granite-faced reception room complete with a bar, as well as separate quarters for Yu's bodyguards. Upstairs was a sauna and a karaoke lounge near the bedroom. Yu's car was a golden Mercedes 600, and a backup Lincoln limousine was parked in the garage. He smoked Chung Hwa brand cigarettes, China's most expensive. He wore finely tailored ersatz Pierre Cardin suits. His watch and glasses glittered as he gesticulated before guests.

"For a peasant leader to dare to be rich really means undertaking political risks on behalf of capable people in the enterprises," Yu said, defending the appurtenances. "Of course I'm not the only rich man here, but I am the one whose wealth sparkles the most. So, anyone who wants to kill the rich, please just criticize me alone!"[59]

The issue of Yu's lifestyle first came into the open in late 1991 after a churlish vice minister from the Ministry of Agriculture named Ma Zhongchen came to dinner. Yu was fond of entertaining guests at home. But the sight of his dwelling could incite resentment from visiting central government officials, many of whom worked for a pittance despite their grand titles and lived in shabby dormitories with shared kitchens and bathrooms. Ma returned to Beijing after dinner and wrote a scathing internal report that accused Yu of living beyond his means, a veiled charge of corruption. The report contended that Yu's house was as big as a minister's house. Soon, that allegation got twisted into a rumor in which Yu boasted that his house was bigger than a minister's. "I've never even been to a minister's house. How could I know how big that is?" Yu protested when the issue became public.[60]

The prescribed living standards for party cadres may not have applied in a place like Daqiu, where virtually every cadre was concurrently an executive of the village conglomerate. That meant cadres could draw salaries and own houses beyond those allowed by their "levels" (*dengji*). Indeed, the whole point of the conglomerate was that it had leveled the playing field among workers and cadres in Daqiu, wiping out the artificial "distinctions" (*bie*) based on cadre rank and introducing differences based on merit alone. As Yu told the *TVE News:*

> One of the hardest things is dealing with appearances. . . . Certain people, including certain leaders, accuse us of being privileged and exceeding the levels of leaders themselves; but we peasants have no distinctions [*bie*], so why are we always compared to those official distinctions?[61]

Merely proving that cadres in Daqiu were technically *allowed* to live the high life was not enough, however. Yu's main concern was to prove that deserving cadres *should* lead the high life. For Yu, wealthy cadres were a sign of success—providing, of course, that the wealth was a result of hard work, not corruption. To the extent that local cadres in places like Daqiu played a critical role as entrepreneurs in the industrialization sweeping China's countryside, there was no reason why they should not be remunerated accordingly. As he put it: "We have no restrictions on the wealth of cadres. The house and the car you have depends on your abilities. The only thing to be afraid of here is of being incapable."[62]

Besides fairness—to each according to his work—Yu also believed that the initial income disparities caused when some cadres got rich would encourage changes that led to common prosperity.

> Someone once wrote a report to senior levels saying that I smoked Chung Hwa cigarettes. But what's so privileged about that? If every peasant smoked them, wouldn't that mean that we were developed? From this point of view, special privileges are really just a kind of reform. First they are special privileges, and then they become widespread, so we are constantly reforming and advancing. When the whole country's peasants are like Daqiu, we will no longer be special.[63]

The debate about Yu's ostentation soon coalesced around one issue: his car, the Mercedes 600. "People often ask Yu why he dares to ride in a car that exceeds his administrative level," the *China Youth Daily* wrote. "In that sense, the car is seen as a challenge to bureaucratic interests."[64] Yu defended his flashy vehicle on all the grounds mentioned above. For one, he was theoretically exempt from cadre regulations governing cars. In addition, he had earned the car. When one "senior retired cadre" from Jinghai groused that, having "fought tooth and nail in the revolutionary war," he was now riding only in a common sedan, Yu retorted with characteristic flair: "Sure, but just remember: You led the poor to overthrow the rich. I led the poor to become the rich!"[65]

Most important, Yu believed that his car, like that of every other made-good cadre and manager in Daqiu, could be a force for change. Luxury vehicles were exactly the kind of respectable transport that peasants needed in order to reverse their image as bumpkins and achieve true social and economic equality in China. "If we were still riding around in donkey carts, wearing grass belts and white *yangduzi* on our heads," he asked with barely concealed reference to Uncle Chen of Dazhai, "would any foreign investors want to cooperate with us?"[66]

The criticism of Yu's car was really a proxy for the criticism of the village's ostentation itself. For that reason, the car soon gained a sort of iconic value in the village. As long as the golden chariot was parked in front of the village office each day, the minds of the villagers were set at ease. If it was missing, panic would ensue. On at least one occasion, the car's sudden absence sparked a run on the local bank. Yu was away on business, but rumors swirled that he had been summoned to Beijing for criticism. Informed of the clamor, Yu sped back and parked the vehicle in its accustomed place. After that, he made a point of leaving it there any time political tensions were high. The car, the *China Youth Daily* concluded, had become a sort of "political stability sedative" for the villagers as Daqiu's struggle against the state intensified.

The debate about Yu's lifestyle, and that of other Daqiu cadres, led naturally to a more general debate about the wealth of Daqiu as a whole. The 1992 boom had brought several flashy symbols of the village's wealth to public attention. These included an imposing traditional Chinese gate at the village entrance and a cable television system that allowed villagers to watch foreign stations for free. A huge dance hall was built as well, complete with karaoke and disco systems imported from Japan. Perhaps most symbolic of the material aspirations of the village was the hundred-shop commercial strip built with Rmb 50 million of village money in mid-1992. After the last flagstone was laid, a sign was unveiled in glitzy chrome and neon naming the strip after the capitalist paradise that most Chinese could only dream of—Hong Kong Street.

Rewards for model workers also continued their upward spiral. Top workers were now handed the keys to three-story villas—of which there were 120—and swank Japanese or American sedans—of which there were 260. Money culture in Daqiu also went beyond mere remuneration for work. Children were paid for good marks in school, pensioners were paid to stay well dressed and take daily baths, parents were paid to have only one child, in line with national policy. Even wives who treated their parents-in-law with respect were rewarded in coin.[67] This did not mean that Daqiu was ignoring the ethical and spiritual needs of its people, Yu insisted; but cold cash was a better incentive than party slogans to induce change, he believed. As he put it: "When we earn money, we learn about material culture, and when we spend it, we learn about spiritual culture."[68]

Daqiu's money culture was in many ways the realization of Yu's now-famous money slogan. But seeing the slogan incarnate in the village resurrected criticisms from the left. The influential leftist magazine *Search for Truth,* for example, renewed its attack on the slogan in 1991, calling it a "vulgarization" of Deng Xiaoping's theories. "Such sayings reflect this vulgar outlook," it warned. "They cause people to become confused about the meaning of socialism, making them think that socialism is merely the pursuit of material benefits."[69]

In defending the village's extravagance and money culture, Yu and his lieutenants used largely the same arguments they made in defending their own wealth: that it was allowed; that it was deserved; and that it was beneficial.

The most fundamental justification for Daqiu's wealthy lifestyle was that it accorded with party policies. Communist China, after all, was built on the premise of making peasants better off. "How can it be that the same people who liberated the peasants are now afraid of the peasants getting rich?" Yu asked.[70] Especially since 1978, economic reforms had been introduced explicitly to improve living standards in the countryside. "Is it better for peasants to be rich or poor?" Yu asked. "Several leaders can't seem to get this point straight. [Deng] Xiaoping said we should let some people grow rich first. How are we supposed to interpret this?"[71]

Deng was also the one who had famously noted that "socialism does not mean being poor." This, more than anything, provided the high-level sanction for Daqiu's wealth. As Yu explained:

> Poverty is not socialism, and nor is being poor together or becoming rich together socialism. . . . Collective wealth under socialism is not the same thing as moving together to achieve collective wealth, otherwise that's just egalitarianism and we might as well go back to the iron rice bowl and all be poor together.[72]

Those leaders who, despite policies aimed at enriching peasants, became inexplicably perturbed when confronted with the spectacle of rich peasants, Yu charged, were like the famous Lord Ye of Chinese legend. Lord Ye was a lover of dragons who had adorned his home with paintings and carvings of the mythical beast. But when a dragon came to visit one day, he gasped in horror and fled. "Many people are like Lord Ye," Yu said. "When they see Daqiu, they're scared to death."[73]

Policies aside, the Daqiu people deserved their prosperity, Yu averred. "Our wealth was not stolen or robbed from others. It is the result of our hard work using the opening and reform policies."[74] There was also a moral claim that perhaps was greater than this economic one. A party that had turned its collective back on the starving peasantry during the Great Leap Famine and its aftermath had little right to sanction rural wealth now. When an unnamed senior leader warned Yu of the "negative effects" of his village's wealth, he snapped back: "Why didn't you come here when we were poor and consider the negative effects of our poverty?"[75]

Most of all, wealthy enclaves like Daqiu had a salutary effect on the country at large. They provided jobs for outsiders, sprinkled their wealth around through aid programs, and supplied a model for others to follow. "If we have nice houses and nice cars, it reduces the urban-rural income gap, improves the investment environment, and shows

the fruits of reforms," Yu explained.[76] Without these material improvements, China's peasants might have risen up in protest, as their
urban counterparts did twice in the 1980s. "The ten years of reforms
have been very turbulent. But the countryside has remained stable.
Why?" Yu asked. "Because the policies have made the peasants better
off."[77]

As with its economic and political system, Daqiu's social compact
was not unique in rural China by the early 1990s. But unlike the heads
of other rich villages, Yu Zuomin and his lieutenants staunchly defended this inchoate new vision of the future, rather than paying lip
service to party criticisms and hoping to avoid attention. London's
Daily Telegraph described how "one village official defended Daqiu's
striking inequalities with almost as much vigour as officials at Dazhai
once championed egalitarianism."[78] And when a large delegation of
city mayors, central government ministers, and State Council (cabinet)
officials came to Daqiu on an inspection in mid-1992, Yu openly chided
them for their feigned frugality:

> You are all senior cadres. But does that mean you really don't like
> money? You all know that once inflation begins, you never have
> enough money to spend. So do you really not want higher salaries?
> Aren't your salaries already higher than most cadres' anyway? So
> doesn't this show that you want to have wealthy lifestyles too? . . .
> Everything I say is what each of you would like to say but dare not.
> So what's wrong with that?[79]

To be sure, Deng Xiaoping's Southern Tour in 1992 did much to al-
leviate criticism of the openly materialistic social policies pursued in
Daqiu. Of all the periods in post-1978 China, this may have been one of
the most liberal in terms of an acceptance of material aspirations. The
campaigns against "bourgeois liberalization" of the 1980s seemed to
have abated, while new party chief Jiang Zemin's focus on "spiritual
culture" was still a few years off.[80]

Yet even under such accommodating conditions, Daqiu found itself the target of attacks. That was a sign that neither side was likely to concede defeat in this epic struggle for the future of the Chinese countryside. Certainly the white flag would never be raised by Yu Zuomin, whose plucky attitude had added to the outrage some felt about the village's social reality. "If we can't live as we please," he said, "then what's there to fear in death?"[81]

On a sunny autumn morning in October 1991, a battered minibus from Jinghai swung into the Daqiu terminus and disgorged its rumpled passengers. Among the arrivals were two men wearing black cloth shoes and carrying synthetic-leather handbags. After asking directions, the pair walked directly to the village administration office and introduced themselves to Mistress Shi: Wang Zuoshan, head of the villager committee of Xiaojin Village, and Wang Jian, the party secretary (no relation).[82]

Xiaojin, it will be recalled, was the village in the northern reaches of Tianjin whose revolutionary song and dance troupe was praised by the Gang of Four during the Cultural Revolution. Yu visited the village three times in the 1960s and watched Daqiu's grain output plummet after trying to emulate its melodic example. In the aftermath of the arrest of the Gang of Four in 1976, Wang Zuoshan was stripped of his positions as Xiaojin party secretary and vice chairman of the National People's Congress and sent to toil in the fields in rural Tianjin. But villagers called him back to lead them through the hurly-burly of reform China. In 1985, he returned and was elected head of the villager committee.

Mistress Shi was well aware of the symbolic importance of the visit by the two Xiaojin leaders: a Maoist model village had come calling on a Dengist model village. Leaping from her desk as they walked into her office, she turned them right around and led them up a flight of stairs into the office of Boss Yu. An initially ill-disposed Yu soon warmed to his guests, seeing the opportunity for publicity.

The two Wangs explained how their seven-hundred-person village remained mired in poverty. Its only factory, a metals processing plant, had fallen into disuse. After an hour of talk, Yu handed them a check for Rmb 60,000 to finance renovations and repay back wages at the idled factory. He also promised large orders from Daqiu companies to restart production at the plant. Following a lavish banquet at the village hotel, Yu ushered the pair into a waiting limousine that bore them back to Xiaojin.

For several years, Yu Zuomin had thought of his political agitation as a struggle waged on behalf of all of China's peasants. He was "the peasant who best understands peasants," and he believed that the battles he fought were as much for his rural brethren as for his fellow villagers.[83] His articulation of economic, political, and social policies that he believed would bring true equality and justice to rural China had application across the country. What better place to implant that vision than one of the greatest model villages of the Maoist past?

Relationships between villages in rural China had always caused disquiet within the party when they were not sanctioned. Such relationships could weave the strands of a web of political power that would be impervious to state control. Since the late 1980s, Daqiu had forged several "twinning relationships" to provide material and technical assistance to poor areas such as Wuwei prefecture in northwestern Gansu province and the poor villages in its purlieu, like Guankeng, Xiaoqiu, and Wanghu. But these had all been sanctioned by the central and county governments. The creation of relationships outside the sanctioned system was different. It was bound to alarm upper-level officials, especially at a time when Yu's influence was expanding quickly. Through business deals, Daqiu already had several close relationships with other villages in coastal provinces like Jiangsu and Zhejiang. Now it seemed to be making friends for political reasons too.

When Wang Zuoshan returned to Xiaojin, one of the first things he did was to drive to the county seat of Baodi, in which his village lay and where he had served as party secretary during the Cultural Revolution, to report the good news. The moment he did, however, the face of the Baodi party secretary, Zheng Shousen, clouded over. "I don't want to hear about your sixty thousand yuan from Yu Zuomin," Zheng sniffed. "It's not such a big deal. I could have given you the same amount from my own pocket." Zheng ordered Wang to return the money and sever all relations with Daqiu. If he did not, the party chief warned, the county would "no longer concern itself with the affairs of Xiaojin"—a menacing threat that could mean everything from canceled grain orders to electricity cuts.

The injunction was odd, and the Xiaojin leaders voiced their surprise to the media. "I cannot understand the instructions of the county," Wang Jian said. "They have been exhorting us to build village enterprises in recent years. But the moment we find a way to do so they try to stop it." Wang Zuoshan was more trenchant: "How can it be that we are allowed to have joint ventures with the Americans and the Japanese, the people who used to exploit us, but not with our own people?"[84]

The flimsy official excuse offered by Zheng was that Xiaojin had lost face by going cap in hand to Daqiu. Few doubted the real reason, though: Zheng was obviously alarmed at the prospect of having Boss Yu operating inside Baodi county lines, encouraging Xiaojin to be as much a maverick as Daqiu. As the pro-Beijing *Mirror* magazine in Hong Kong commented: "The Baodi party committee was afraid of the power of Yu Zuomin, because under the pretense of helping others, he was in fact looking for allies and trying to expand his influence. . . . If they allowed him to set up an enterprise in Baodi, there would never be any peace in the county."[85]

Wang Zuoshan consulted Yu Zuomin on the issue. Not surprisingly, Yu exhorted him to stay the course. Daqiu's own experience was proof positive that success often meant rubbing county officials the wrong way, he said. No matter what their self-interest in the taxes generated by successful TVEs, county-level officials never liked uppity village leaders who threatened their power. "You can't eat rice without knocking your chopsticks against the bowl," a Chinese saying goes. Yu's advice to Wang was to keep eating.

> There are hundreds and thousands of difficulties when you're involved in economic development. If you are determined, you can overcome all these difficulties. . . . We gave you help in order to stir your spirits to fight against the difficulties. But only if you have a will that does not yield and a spirit that does not flag will you be able to accept this help from us without any complaints. . . . You have to walk on your own and take your own road. . . . No matter how much friction you encounter, it will be worth it.[86]

Wang was convinced. The two villages signed an unsanctioned cooperation agreement in late 1991, and the Xiaojin metals factory came back to life. In May 1992 Wang made a second trip to Daqiu. This time he came away with promises of Rmb 400,000 to be invested in a new steel pipes factory and further technical assistance. As before, Baodi leaders assailed the ties. But Wang's resistance was stouter now:

> Since Daqiu is a national rural reform model, why are we wrong to learn from it? The Xiaojin people are frightfully poor, so why can't we aspire to riches? If the county wanted to help us, they should have done so long ago. . . . I admit that in the past I made mistakes. But this time I'm not wrong, that's for sure.[87]

Throughout the conflict over Xiaojin, Yu skillfully used the domestic media, in particular the *TVE News,* to portray the issue as a showdown between reformers and leftists. As the newspaper wrote, "Deng Xiaoping has warned us to beware of leftism and there's nothing like a lively story to make us understand what leftism really means." The same theme was taken up by the *People's Daily* and other national newspapers.

Frightened by the onslaught, Baodi leaders even declined offers of stories that would support their case.[88] Wang Zuoshan, meanwhile, felt his in-itially fragile confidence rise. "From now on," he said, "if we can't get a straight answer from the county, we will take our case directly to the Tianjin municipality or even to the party Central Committee.[89]

The Xiaojin incident had barely died down when a far higher pro-file pilgrim came seeking the holy scriptures in Daqiu: Guo Fenglian, the party secretary of the greatest model village of them all, Dazhai.[90]

Guo had been the head of the celebrated "Iron Girls" work team in Dazhai in the 1960s, a sickle-wielding unit of militant women who built terraced fields and harvested grain with rifles strapped to their backs. When the Cultural Revolution erupted, she formed the village's Red Guard brigade and trucked in several senior provincial officials for "struggle sessions" of verbal and physical abuse. When Chen Yong-gui—Uncle Chen—joined the politburo in 1973, Guo took over as Dazhai's party secretary and joined the party Central Committee.

Like Uncle Chen, Guo was stripped of her positions when the Cul-tural Revolution ended and sent into political oblivion, first at a fruit research institute and then at the provincial highways bureau. But she also followed the path of thousands of other former village leaders in reclaiming her leadership as the uncertain new reform era dawned. In late 1991, she was fully recycled as Dazhai's party secretary.

The moment Deng Xiaoping's Southern Tour speeches were made public in early 1992, Guo began planning a trip to Daqiu. Thoroughly disabused of her leftist ways, she was determined to learn from this lat-est paragon of rural development. Yu Zuomin, fresh from his success-ful tussle over Xiaojin, welcomed the opportunity to plant his flag on another Maoist model village. After months of careful preparations, during which a raft of reporters was assembled to cover the event, Guo was welcomed at a lavish ceremony at the brand-new Kowloon Hotel on 25 October.

In what was becoming a habit, Yu spoke first with his wallet, hand-ing Guo a check for Rmb 500,000 to help refurbish an old chemicals factory in Dazhai. He also promised assistance to develop stone quarries near the village and to find joint-venture partners for other projects. "If *you* get rich," he told her, recalling Dazhai's leftist past, "it will really make a splash."[91]

Just as the Xiaojin leaders had done, Guo felt emboldened to speak her mind in the presence of this iconoclastic colleague as they sat down to lunch: "We peasants have to stand up together," she said. "In the past, everyone in China looked down on peasants. Cadres were sent down to the countryside, students were sent down to the countryside, anyone who had made a mistake was sent down to the countryside. . . . Secretary Yu, you have forged a new road for the countryside. I'm a newcomer here, but I know it has not been easy to achieve all this."[92]

Guo also complained openly about the obstacles to Dazhai's development thrown up by county and provincial officials. Predictably, Yu urged her to ignore their complaints and beat her own path:

YU: The important thing is to change our thinking, because it was the leftism of the past that caused poverty.

GUO: Sure, but the problem is that people nowadays tell us to change our thinking, but they don't change their own.

YU: Then don't wait for them to change. Even if they never change, you should change. Sure there will be risks and obstacles. But trust in yourself and don't be afraid. If you agree with me, then let's march forward together!

GUO: Right! We peasants have to stick together! In future, whenever I have a problem, I'll come to Daqiu for help.

YU: Good! From now on we'll walk down the same road. You follow our lead. Eventually we'll be marching together. This is far better than just studying a lot of party documents![93]

The spectacle of the former Maoist village stooping to learn from the reformist village made for great copy. Reuters News Agency picked up Xinhua's report on the meeting and retitled it "Capitalist Tips for Mao Model." But behind the cheap irony was a more profound message. By urging Dazhai to follow in his path, Yu was seeking to legitimize his own vision of rural development. That vision in its many facets could only be realized, he believed, through quite blatant confrontations with higher authorities, usually those at the county and provincial level. It also demanded stiff repudiations of ideological complaints about capitalist-style development and ostentatious wealth.

Through both the Dazhai and Xiaojin incidents, Yu made clear his belief that combating leftism required a very real and open struggle against political interference. Never did he mention the importance of following central dictates or of coordinating with central policies. His creed was go it alone and the critics be damned. If his vision could germinate in the two reddest villages of China's past, it could grow anywhere.

In that sense, the incidents represented a very tangible spread of the Daqiu approach to other parts of the country. It was one thing for Yu to sound off about this and that from the confines of his remote village. But now he was taking his struggle on the road. The official *China Peasant* magazine would later refer to Yu's forging of a new kind of "peasant identity" (*nongmin yishi*) in which TVE leaders like himself felt emboldened by their wealth to ignore outside criticism. Add to that "a web of relationships at all levels and an impervious ruling system in their own localities," the magazine would write, and you had the makings of a dangerous new trend.[94] Peasant leaders were banding together for the common cause of autonomy and enrichment. And leading the march was Yu Zuomin, who had now become a very real threat—both in word and in deed—to the party's rule in rural China.

It is probably safe to say that by the end of 1992 Yu Zuomin was quite firmly stuck in the craw of official China. The range of bad feelings toward this outspoken and subversive peasant leader ran the gamut: from the austere disapproval of some party leaders and ideologues in

Beijing, to a more charged hostility among many local leaders in Tianjin and its rural counties.

As early as 1985, recall, journalist Liu Linshan had warned that "even the Tianjin party committee cannot stand" Yu. Yu's stepped-up struggle of dissent and resistance throughout 1992 only intensified these antipathies. At the local level, the *Mirror* commented, Tianjin and Jinghai leaders had "serious reservations" about Yu by late 1992. "They felt he was acting like a great local official of the Qing dynasty, overstepping his authority as a mere delegate to the national CPPCC and interfering in all sorts of local affairs."[95] A later article in the Beijing magazine *Law and News* asserted that the Tianjin authorities were "disgusted" with Yu and as a result had denied him the opportunity to represent the municipality as a delegate to the National People's Congress.[96] "Everyone says you are not obedient," the *TVE News* told Yu frankly in an interview, to which he responded: "Sometimes it is best to obey in public but resist in private."[97]

Some senior leaders in Beijing obviously shared this antipathy. The cold reply of the Central Committee Organization Department official to Yu's lecture on bad cadres was one sign. On another occasion, a delegation of officials from the powerful State Economic Reform Commission left the village grumbling that Yu was nothing but a "mountain rebel" (*shanda wang*) after he lectured them for an hour on how to improve their work.[98] Perhaps most indicative was Yu's inability to rise above his modest status as a CPPCC delegate, as Uncle Chen had done. After predicting that he would be elected a vice chairman of the CPPCC, or even a state premier, Yu got nothing better than renomination as an ordinary delegate at the annual CPPCC meeting in Beijing in March 1992.[99] An even bigger snub came a few months later when he failed to win a place as a delegate to the party's fourteenth national congress, to be held in October. Every party secretary of even minor repute was usually invited to the congress, and Yu complained openly about the indignity: "The fact that I am not a delegate to the party congress despite heading China's richest village shows how difficult it is for us to be accepted."[100]

During the frictions over the death of Jade Field in 1991, recall, one unnamed senior leader had scribbled, "Why is this lawless ruffian Yu Zuomin still at large?" in the margins of one of journalist Liu Lin-shan's reports.[101] It is a question we might well ask too. For if Yu was so despised, why wasn't he simply sacked as party secretary of Daqiu? After all, Yu—aged sixty-three in 1992—was well past the guideline retirement age of fifty-five for party cadres at or below the county level.

Several reasons can be advanced for why Yu remained in place. First and foremost was Daqiu's wealth and fame, which we have traced throughout this narrative. By 1992, Yu had a formidable armory of political resources at his disposal; a powerhouse economy that employed thousands and propped up most of Jinghai county; lateral ties to other villages and companies; a profile in the media as a pioneer of the party's successful rural reforms; and even the makings of a reputation outside China. If you shook Daqiu's tree, a lot more than just one village would come tumbling down.

Yu also appeared to enjoy the support of a few key leaders in Beijing, in particular Bo Yibo and Li Ruihuan. One can only imagine the internal debates of the politburo over this irascible leader and his village. For now, in any event, Daqiu continued to reflect the greater glory of the party. "Even though Yu Zuomin's many problems were already well known by the end of 1992," the *Mirror* observed, "at the central level he was still seen as a roaring success."[102]

Moreover, despite the personal rancor between Yu and his detractors, it was difficult to accuse him of any clear wrongdoing. While many worried about the "direction" of Daqiu's policies and habits, no one could find any egregious violations of laws or directives in the village. Yu had been careful to couch his dissent in the rhetoric of official policies where possible, to make his resistance "righteous," as political scientists say. When he stepped out of that safe shelter, he usually did so in a nuanced way, one that could be explained away by his supporters as the naughty mutterings of an uneducated peasant. As the *China*

Youth Daily said of Yu's many outrageous sayings, "They are Deng Xiaoping Theory translated into peasant slang."[103]

That studied ambiguity had manifested itself in an equally ambivalent approach to the village by many leaders. Afraid of being called leftists, they would troop to the village for photo-ops in order to display their reformist credentials. While there, they could listen politely to descriptions of the village's development without voicing open approval. If worse came to worst and the political winds shifted, they could always wash their hands of the place and claim to have been "concerned" (*guanxin*) about its policies from the start. But in the absence of a top-level move against the village, there was nothing to be gained from attacking Daqiu. Just ask the leaders of Baodi.

Another intriguing reason for Yu's resilience may relate to the changed nature of peasant politics in China by this time. In sharp contrast to the uncompromising official attitudes of the Mao era, the Deng years ushered in a more tolerant period, in which peasants in particular could complain about policies within wider limits.[104] China's economic reforms depended crucially on a bustling rural economy. The entrepreneurial initiative shown by Daqiu needed to be emulated elsewhere if the whole enterprise were to succeed. Crushing every sign of peasant defiance would be a disaster. And so Yu Zuomin lived on.

For all these reasons, Yu found himself embattled but still firmly entrenched in late 1992. He had "successfully brought Daqiu through many political storms," the *China Youth Daily* commented, and showed no signs of buckling under pressure.[105] Yu, of course, was resolved to fight on, no matter what the costs. His statement about preferring to be "overthrown" rather than just "lie down" like an obedient dog continued to inform his behavior. Or as he said on another occasion: "I have always believed that the smartest way to proceed is just to shoot the rapids valiantly. I have absolutely no doubts on this point."[106]

It was well that he was prepared. For he was about to shoot the most turbulent rapids of his career.

FIGURES

Figure 1.   Yu Zuomin, the leader of Daqiu Village, while attending the annual meeting of the Chinese People's Political Consultative Conference in 1992. (Source: *South China Morning Post*)

Figure 2.   Daqiu in the mid-1970s. The village was long known for its mud
huts and poverty. (Source: Xinhua News Agency)

Figure 3.   By the 1990s, Daqiu had been transformed by industrial development. Its wealth allowed the village to turn its public spaces and private homes into potent symbols of comfort and plenty. (Source: Xinhua News Agency)

Figure 4.   Inside one of Daqiu's steel factories in the 1990s. Steel products were the mainstay of the village companies, despite attempts to diversify. (Source: Xinhua News Agency)

Figure 5.   Daqiu was famous for its stable of luxury sedans and limousines, which ferried officials and visitors around the village. (Source: Adrian Bradshaw)

Figure 6. The economic development of Daqiu helped finance several new projects, including this village gate. Curbside bicycle repairmen catered to a growing number of factory workers. (Source: Adrian Bradshaw)

Figure 7. (*Left*) Liu Wanquan, known as Mr. Do-It-All, founded Daqiu's first factory. He went on to become the village's most famous entrepreneur as the head of the Wanquan Group. (Source: Wanquan Group)

Figure 8. (*Right*) Yu Zuoyao criticized his brother, Yu Zuomin, for failing to develop the local economy when a crucial village meeting was held in 1977. Yu Zuoyao founded the village's second industrial group, the Yaoshun Group. (Source: Yaoshun Group)

Figure 9. (*Left*) A former head of the Communist Youth League in Daqiu, Zhao Shuzhong founded the village's third industrial group, the Jinmei Group. (Source: Jinmei Group)

Figure 10. (*Right*) A former scientist from the village's pig feedlot, Zhang Yanjun founded the Jinhai Group, Daqiu's fourth industrial group. (Source: Jinhai Group)

Figure 11.   In the 1984 allegorical short story "Yanzhao Elegy," Yu Zuomin was portrayed as a savvy local cadre who had enriched his village with an unorthodox factory-building program. (Source: "Yanzhao beige" [Yanzhao elegy], *Renmin wenxue* [People's literature] 7, no. 298 [1984]: 42)

Figure 12.   Dazhai, the greatest model village of China's past, was promoted in propaganda posters like this one for its abundant harvests and industrious spirit. (Source: Chinese Poster Collection, University of Westminster)

Figure 13. Chen Yonggui, the leader of Dazhai, shown here terracing fields, reached the highest levels of power as a state vice premier before being removed from office in 1980. (Source: Xinhua News Agency)

Figure 14. Yu Zuomin, photographed here by the official Xinhua News Agency after having been named a national model worker, won acclaim for leading Daqiu to prosperity. But like Chen Yonggui, he fell from power when his political support collapsed. (Photo: Xinhua News Agency)

FOUR

Outlaws of the Marsh

There are more than a thousand armed police surrounding our village, waiting to force their way in to search us using dogs, tear gas, and artillery. We cannot accept this! . . . They are trying to attack the achievements of Daqiu's reforms!

Yu Zuomin, February 1993

It was the last day of November 1992 and a chill wind blew through the steel factories and worker dormitories of Daqiu Village. On this day, Yu Zuomin found himself standing in the small mortuary attached to the village hospital. Before him lay the body of his nephew, Li Fengzheng, the late president of the village's agricultural holding company, Huada Group.

Fengzheng, or Righteous Wind, had been one of the village's most trusted and capable managers. Under his leadership, the Huada Group had assumed a key role alongside the Four Hens as a major incubator of the Daqiu economy. But like many Daqiu executives, he was badly overworked. That morning, he had tumbled from his desk in the throes of a massive stroke. Resuscitation efforts had failed and now he lay dead, aged just forty-five. Yu felt like he had lost a son.

"Fengzheng!" he cried, finally pulling the white sheet over the pallid face. "You've worked yourself to death!"

The next day, Yu ordered a full appraisal of the Huada Group's business. It was supposed to be a routine matter. But rather than neat columns of cash flow statements trickling through the space-age feed lots and miracle grain yields, village accountants found complex money transfers and confusing sleights of hand. It soon became apparent that Righteous Wind had been anything but righteous. When the accountants toted it all up, they found debts in excess of Rmb 300 million and tens of thousands in missing funds. A four-person investigation team was immediately constituted to look into the affairs of the Huada Group, which was put under the temporary administration of the Wanquan Group. The team was composed of Little Yu, Mistress Shi, Eternal China (the son and designated successor of Liu Wanquan), and Zhou Kewen, the head of the village's public security committee.

In the course of a week, more than a dozen senior employees of the Huada Group were questioned in the third-floor conference room of the village office over possible corruption. There are no independent eyewitness accounts of what went on inside that room, but it appears to have been a ruthless inquisition. At least three senior Huada Group employees were physically abused and detained in the course of the questioning. Some reports speak of the use of electric cattle prods and whips to exact confessions. While most of the abuses seem to have been carried out by toughs from the Wanquan Group, it was clearly done with the complicity of the investigating quartet, and of Yu Zuomin himself.

Ever since his return from Japan in the mid-1980s, Yu Zuomin's authoritarian streak had grown deeper and wider. By the early 1990s, this had developed into an almost paranoid fear of dissent and a cavalier disregard for the law. Yu's absolute power had strengthened his hand in the spirited tussle he had waged against the state on issues of ideology, politics, and economics. For that, he continued to enjoy wide support in the village. But it had also retarded his sense of fairness and the law. Those who found themselves on the wrong side of Boss Yu were bound to suffer. Justice in Daqiu was at his discretion alone.

Among the holes in the Huada Group accounts was a sum of Rmb 29,000 missing from an experimental animal husbandry farm that had been set up with top-level support from Beijing earlier in the year.[1] After two weeks of chasing the paper trail, investigators zeroed in on an unassuming twenty-seven-year-old accountant attached to the farm named Wei Fuhe, an "outside expert" from neighboring Hebei province who had worked in the village since 1990. On the afternoon of 13 December, Wei was summoned to the third-floor conference room for questioning. As with the others, the purpose was to force him to explain where the missing money had gone. He had little choice but to explain what he knew. When he refused, he was left to think it over in the company of four thugs from the Wanquan Group.

What followed can only be described as a brutal murder. Wei was strapped to a chair and stripped of his shirt and shoes. When he refused to talk, he was assailed with a leather whip. As the ordeal continued, heavier instruments like bamboo canes and wooden planks were used. By around 10 P.M., the stout young man had been beaten unconscious. Most of his body was bruised and bleeding. There was little point asking him questions now. The thugs decided to send him to the hospital for treatment, but it was too late. Wei Fuhe was dead on arrival, having succumbed to a traumatic coma induced by external injuries.[2]

Where was Yu Zuomin, and why didn't he stop the beating? We know that he was in the village. And clearly he must have known that one of the key figures in the alleged corruption at Huada Group was being interrogated, and roughly. Perhaps because dozens of others had already been "successfully" questioned without serious injuries, he expected this one to proceed smoothly as well. One thing is clear: if only for his personal sake, a murder is the last thing he wanted. The death of Jade Field had proved that violent crimes could provide the county and the city governments with just the reason they needed to bring the village into line. Especially by late 1992, when Yu's outspoken struggle with the state had brought tensions to a crescendo, any criminal wrongdoing would be costly. If Yu had known that Wei was being tortured to death, he probably would have stopped it. But by this time, Yu was too used to acting with impunity. Now he would pay.

At about 10:30 P.M., Little Yu and Eternal China sheepishly knocked on Yu's door to report the death. When he heard the news, Yu was furious. "Goddamnit!" he swore at the pair. "You've let this one get out of control. And there are too many people involved!"[3]

Yu lit up a cigarette and began to think what to do. If the death of Jade Field had taught him one lesson, it was that honesty was the worst policy. In that case, he had forthrightly handed over the seven assailants to the Tianjin police in hopes of lenient treatment. The Tianjin court had then thrown the book at them. This time, Yu would not be so naive.

The first thing he did was order the bloodstains in the conference room scrubbed clean and the blunt instruments of torture disposed of. A confession of "serious economic crimes" was then hastily drafted and the fingerprints from Wei Fuhe's dead corpse impressed on each page. At midnight, when all was ready, Yu called the Jinghai public security bureau to report the murder. Dozens of unidentified people had rushed into a conference room during a normal questioning session and beaten Wei to death, he explained. Attempts by village officials to stop the beating had been thwarted and the man had died. Just another raucous night in China's richest village. No big deal. But he thought they should know.

Early next morning, 14 December, two Jinghai police officers arrived in the village to investigate. The story of the sudden swarm of uninvited assailants was repeated. But when the police examined the conference room they became suspicious. The cleanup of the room had been hasty. A large carpet that had been pulled over the floor to conceal stubborn bloodstains also showed the muddy footprints of the four Wanquan Group thugs. Clearly, they had been the only ones in the room when Wei died.

Their names and positions were duly noted down: Liu Yunzhang, twenty-nine, the younger son of Liu Wanquan, brother of Eternal China, who handled personnel matters and was company secretary of the Wanquan Group; Liu Shaosheng, forty-four, a company vice president and cousin of Liu Wanquan, uncle of Eternal China; Li Zhenbiao, twenty-nine, a staffer in Eternal China's office; and Chen Xiangqi, fifty-eight, a company security guard. They were now the prime suspects.

The following day a police van bearing the markings "Tianjin City Public Security Bureau" came bouncing across the bleak landscape as evening fell on Daqiu. Inside was a six-member team led by the second in command of the Tianjin police department's criminal investigation bureau. He and his Jinghai counterpart wore their uniforms, even though forensic work was usually done in plainclothes.

The arrival of the high-level team was a blow to Yu Zuomin's plan to pass off the murder as the accidental result of a melee. Things were also happening fast, as if the Jinghai and Tianjin authorities were determined that this time the case should be cracked speedily, before politics intervened to slow the process. Yu allowed the team to go over the murder scene again. But as they did, he began faxing angry letters to the Tianjin city government. The death had been reported to the county police, so why were the city police involved? Such an investigation required the prior approval of the village. Even worse, the team had crept into town under cover of darkness, like villains. "This has affected our economic life and hurt our people's feelings," he wrote in one fax.[4]

At 10 P.M. the conference room in which the investigators were working was suddenly cleared of all village officials and barred from the outside. Yu Zuomin had rashly decided to detain the team until the city authorities explained its presence. When the team did not return to its van parked near the village gate, the quick-witted driver sped away to report the detention.

If Yu's attitude toward the 1982 county inspection team had been one of cautious protest, and toward the 1990 Jade Field investigation one of spirited defiance, this time he seemed to be verging on outright rebellion. His bold actions suggested that he was girding for a bruising confrontation with those who would destroy Daqiu. Perhaps he sensed that this was the battle he had long expected. The moment may have come when he would be overthrown. If so, he would live up to his promise and go down with a fight.

The next morning Tianjin mayor Nie Bichu stormed into the colonial mansion that served as his office and brushed aside his usual mug of black tea. "Who does Yu Zuomin think he is?" he hollered to no one in particular. "It's like dealing with a kidnapper!"

News of the detention of the police team had reached Tianjin overnight. Yu was demanding direct talks with the mayor, who had long ago lost patience with this renegade peasant. Still, when he eventually patched through to Daqiu, Nie's tone was conciliatory. After listening politely to Yu's complaints, he promised that the investigation would proceed only with the consent of the village. It was a stiff ransom to pay, but Nie appeared to have little choice. The hapless police team was finally released at 11 A.M.

In the classic Chinese novel *Shui hu zhuan* (Outlaws of the marsh), written in the fourteenth century, a renowned soldier in a border garrison town named Lu Da murders the local butcher in a petty dispute.[5] Despite the evidence of several eyewitnesses, the local garrison commander hesitates to arrest the skilled warrior because of his great reputation, and the fact that Lu Da is a good friend and former soldier of his father, the regional commander. "Since he has committed a capital offense," the local commander tells the court prefect, "you may interrogate him according to law. But if you get a confession and the crime is proved, you must inform my father before passing sentence. Otherwise it might be very embarrassing if, at some future date, my father should ask for him back."

As in the novel, there was little doubt that a serious murder had been committed in Daqiu. But Yu Zuomin had a great reputation and good connections at the top. Though they had long despised Yu, the Jinghai and Tianjin authorities had to act carefully. After all, you never knew when the Beijing leadership would "ask for him back"—to build a top-level national experimental zone for animal husbandry, for example.

In the weeks after the release of the police team, Tianjin police made little headway in the murder investigation. As Yu traveled back and forth to Tianjin for talks with city leaders, the four suspects were sent into hiding, family members stopped talking, and Wei Fuhe's body was returned to his hometown and cremated. Unless they could win the support of Beijing, Tianjin and Jinghai leaders knew they would never be able to "pass sentence."

Fortunately, Tianjin police had taken *Legal Daily* journalist Liu Linshan to Jinghai to interview the members of the detained police team the morning they were released. Liu's internal reference reports had been critical to winning Beijing's support in the Jade Field case. Maybe he could do it again.

Liu's first internal report on this incident was titled "Violence without End: Another Murder Case in Daqiu, Investigators Are Illegally Detained." It wended its way up the hierarchy, reaching the party politburo by the end of December. There, an unnamed senior leader scribbled in the margins the Chinese expression *wu fa wu tian,* meaning roughly "neither God-fearing nor law-abiding."[6] That note was just the supportive high-level *pishi,* or "written instruction," that Tianjin authorities needed. On 7 January, the Tianjin procuracy issued arrest warrants for the four suspects.

Beijing's attitude was crucial, but perhaps not surprising. Yu Zuomin's welcome in Beijing had always been more resilient than his reception in Tianjin or Jinghai. But there were limits. By decrying the lawless state of affairs in Daqiu, Beijing was indicating that its patience with this model peasant leader was wearing thin. Still, Yu had survived such run-ins with the law before. If he played his cards right, he could ensure that the damage ended with the four accused men.

For more than a month, the Tianjin and Jinghai police made fruitless efforts to locate the four suspects outside the village. Mayor Nie, meanwhile, was distracted by the long-awaited death on 3 February of the city's party secretary, Tan Shaowen, after a long battle with lung cancer. Tan's death gave the embattled mayor a chance to discuss the Daqiu situation with politburo standing committee member Hu Jintao, who was dispatched to attend the funeral ten days later.[7] Official attitudes in Tianjin hardened perceptibly following the meeting.

On 16 February, Tianjin authorities informed Yu that a police team would be coming to search for the four suspects in the village and to post warrants for their arrest. Yu immediately fired back a faxed letter. The letter deferred to the authority of the police, but it warned that if they tried to storm the village, they would meet resistance. It also included this forbidding passage:

> I don't understand much about the law, and my people understand even less. So please tell the investigating team that they must proceed according to the law. They must absolutely be aware of the effect of their actions on reforms, economic activity, and people's feelings. . . . They should ensure that no unfortunate incident occurs, because if it does I will plead ignorance and not accept responsibility.[8]

Those terms might have been acceptable to a police force merely trying to stamp its authority on the village. But there were several practical considerations that may have warranted a more assertive approach. The fate of the first police team was ample warning that some show of strength was needed for the police to execute their duties in the village. It was possible (and indeed true) that the four suspects remained under Yu's protection, and unless the police could operate freely, the four would never be apprehended. In addition, it was known that Daqiu's public security committee under Zhou Kewen had equipped itself with a small armory of weapons in recent years. Merely for purposes of self-defense, the incoming police team would need to be prepared for violent contingencies. "There were still many weapons in the village, and it was hard to predict what would happen," Liu Linshan would write.[9]

With these considerations in mind—and possibly emboldened by verbal support from Hu Jintao—Mayor Nie sought and received approval from Beijing to mobilize a small contingent of paramilitary soldiers for the operation. The soldiers would be called out from the Number 8630 Unit based in Tianjin of the People's Armed Police, or PAP, the internal security corps formed in 1983. PAP headquarters in Beijing insisted that the troops should remain on standby outside the village. If the operation proceeded smoothly, they would return to Tianjin with as little commotion as possible.

When the sun rose over Daqiu on 17 February, lookouts had already been posted to await the police team. Around midmorning, they spotted the now-familiar markings of three Tianjin police vehicles trundling toward the village. The team was composed of just seven police and procuracy officers as well as the county head and party secretary of Jinghai. Their duties that day, they informed Yu and his aides, included searching for the four suspects, serving subpoenas on the family members for questioning, and posting the arrest warrants. The team was led to the village reception room for talks on how this would be done.

As the talks dragged on into the early afternoon, the PAP soldiers were taking up their positions. It was a sinister sight as the camouflaged troops moved into surrounding villages and hid inside sheds and huts. The biggest concentration was assembled in a steel factory in nearby Pang hamlet, just up the road from Daqiu toward Jinghai town. The exact number of paramilitaries called out is unclear. The official report on the incident would say it was four hundred.[10] Other estimates in the mainland press put it at over a thousand.[11] Whatever the figure, it was a formidable muster.

It did not take long before word of the siegelike placement of the paramilitaries reached Daqiu. Within minutes, the village was abuzz with rumors of a veritable army massed on its doorstep. Yu, informed of the troop movements, brought the police team immediately into a separate meeting room attached to his office and demanded an explanation.

"We were afraid that the four suspects might flee. We had to have enough men to watch all sides," one team leader explained.

Mistress Shi, who had been at Yu's side throughout the day, shot out: "We have been living well for only a few years. And now you guys come here to ruin our way of life!"[12]

"That's not our intention. We are here to investigate the murder," came the reply.

"Well, it's a clear breach of faith," Yu interjected. "Since you have dispensed with all niceties, so will we."[13]

With that, Yu Zuomin ordered the team detained. He then walked into his adjoining office and commanded a mobilization of the village against a potential attack. It was now 5 P.M.

Within minutes the village was a flurry of activity. Flatbed trucks and an assortment of tractors were placed at every road portal to act as barricades, their gas tanks filled to cause explosions if they were rammed. Zhou Kewen assigned several teams to guard the periphery and search anyone entering or leaving.

"Daqiu was suddenly on a war footing," the official report on the incident would say. "The situation was rapidly deteriorating."[14]

If the paramilitary troops came within half a mile of the village, a peasant militia would be there to confront them. Besides wooden clubs and steel bars, the villagers would be equipped with sundry firearms. The village public security office had a cache of fifteen handguns and about two thousand bullets. Another eighty-four smoothbore guns with about twenty thousand cartridges were collected from a village factory that exported hunting guns to the United States. A few company executives also contributed their personal handguns and rifles. Within hours, this motley but earnest peasant army—a faint image of the revolutionary People's Liberation Army that had seized power with wide popular support across China in 1948 and 1949—was staring down the CCP itself. The two sides remained entrenched, often within sight of each other, as night fell.

At daybreak on 18 February, Yu Zuomin summoned every person in the village to a mass rally in the village square. The square was soon thronging with thousands of people, natives and migrants alike. Many of the migrant workers had even donned their orange hard hats in case of a battle.

Yu had lost none of his energy and spunk from a long night keeping watch along the village ramparts. Indeed, he seemed to be rising to the occasion.

"Fellow villagers," he called through a bullhorn. "There are more than a thousand armed police surrounding our village waiting to force their way in to search us using dogs, tear gas, and artillery. We cannot accept this!"

A hum of assent ran through the crowd.

"I doubt very much that they have come here about the case. They are not trying to solve the case. They are trying to attack the achievements of Daqiu's reforms!"

Everyone knew about "the case," and no one doubted that Yu was right.

"We must defend our village!" Yu cried out.

Cheers went up as the villagers answered the call to arms. Yu's ability to rally his people had not diminished. Now he was their commander.

"Let the Jinghai and Tianjin party committees come here themselves to hold negotiations!" clamored one man.

"I'm with Boss Yu. He cares about us more than the party does!" shouted another.

Wave after wave of cheers enveloped the scene. Daqiu was united behind Yu Zuomin, prepared to take its long struggle against perceived injustice to the limit.

The shift to a more aggressive stance by Daqiu had the desired effect. After a tense day of staring down the paramilitary troops on his doorstep, Yu induced Mayor Nie to compromise. A truce was made. The PAP troops would be withdrawn in return for Yu's agreement to release the detained police team and allow another team to carry out the posting of arrest warrants and a formal search for the four suspects. Mayor Nie—the local garrison commander who feared the famed warrior as much for his connections to the top as for his skills—had backed down.

Official reports on the incident would assert that all but thirty of the paramilitary PAP troops had been pulled back to Jinghai the previous night "to prevent clashes with the people who were being deceived by Yu Zuomin."[15] But at least two other domestic reports say that the troops had merely fallen back to critical road junctions to seal off the village from a greater distance.[16] Whatever the truth, by 10 P.M. on 18 February, village scouts confirmed that the PAP had fully withdrawn.

Daqiu, however, was ready for a protracted campaign. Yu announced a one-month work stoppage with full pay to allow villagers to defend their home against further incursions. Schools would also be closed. Anyone unwilling to fight was free to leave, but those who remained would be rewarded—with money, of course. Notices were posted in the village to explain the siegelike conditions to unwitting outsiders who might come on business:

> As a result of a decision by the Tianjin leadership to send a contingent of over one thousand police and armed police officers to our village for reasons unknown to us, all production has stopped here. We ask you to refrain from visiting our village at this time and to please pardon the inconvenience. We also ask for the understanding of the media.[17]

True to his word, Mayor Nie sent an unarmed police team, this one composed of twenty officers, to the village on 19 February to discharge the agreed-upon tasks. As they moved deliberately around the village posting the arrest warrants on light poles, the officers were followed by hundreds of eyes. Village officials, workers, even the elderly and children, stalked them, a repeat of the harassment meted out to the 1982 inspection team. After posting the warrants, the team was led to the homes of Liu Shaosheng and Liu Yunzhang, the two suspects who were native Daqiu villagers. To no one's surprise, the homes were silent and the doors locked. The simple wooden beam placed in brackets across the front doors was the traditional sign that the tenants were away and that the house was not to be disturbed. The dormitory beds of the two suspects who were migrants, Li Zhenbiao and Chen Xiangqi, were also vacant.

The police team probably knew, and the checks confirmed, that the four had by this time been bundled out of the village. In fact, all four were now on the run in various parts of the country, with orders from Yu to lie low until the investigation ran out of steam. When the team finally left the village in the late afternoon, Yu's confidence began to rise. The withdrawal of the paramilitary troops seemed to be an admission of guilt by the Tianjin authorities; now, it appeared, the investigation was proceeding on his terms.

Emboldened by this apparent turn of the tide in his favor, Yu launched a prolific media campaign the next day to gain the sympathy of the country's newspapers. Articles were sent to several major newspapers which asserted that Tianjin authorities had overreacted to the murder of a worker in the village by unknown assailants. The Tianjin police investigation, one article said, "is aimed at the reform undertaking and at the village itself."[18]

Already on the defensive, Mayor Nie was furious at being publicly ridiculed as a leftist conspirator. On 22 February, he phoned Yu and accused him of violating party "organization principles" with the attempt to sway public opinion in his favor. A good cadre would sort out differences behind closed doors and then display a facade of unanimity to the people, Nie noted. Yu had done neither.

Nie's appeal, though, flew in the face of everything Yu Zuomin stood for. The party's organization principles were to him a byword for the docile acceptance by the peasantry of policies that hurt their interests. How many Chinese peasants had been starved, exploited, excluded, and misrepresented by such "principles" in the forty-odd years since the Communists came to power in China?

"I don't understand what you mean about violating organization principles," Yu told the mayor. "The best thing would be for you to reply to our articles point by point rather than to argue about such principles."[19]

Mayor Nie never responded. He didn't need to. For unbeknownst to Yu Zuomin, the village's cause had taken a turn for the worse in Beijing.

After approving the use of the armed police for the 17 February operation, the party's highest organ of power, the politburo standing committee under General Secretary Jiang Zemin, had met to consider the Daqiu issue more fully. Among the documents informing their discussion were two of the latest internal reference reports by journalist Liu Linshan. One of them described the authoritarian nature of Yu's rule in the village and how it had contributed to the senseless murder of Wei Fuhe. The other gave an in-depth account of the melee involving the students from the Beijing Municipal State Security Department college. The two reports were later described as a "turning point" in Beijing's hitherto accommodating attitude toward Daqiu and its defiant leader.[20]

Like the authorities in Tianjin and Jinghai, Beijing had every reason to treat a reform model like Daqiu with kid gloves. Reprimanding Daqiu could be seen as a sign of leftism, especially in this period of reformist zeal following Deng Xiaoping's Southern Tour. What's more, the names of several senior leaders—among them party elder Bo Yibo, former Tianjin mayor and now politburo standing committee member Li Ruihuan, and scientist Qian Xuesen—were closely associated with the village. The *New York Times,* calling the Daqiu case "the hottest mystery in China," speculated that Li Ruihuan was shielding the village from retribution.[21]

Still, things seemed to be getting a little out of hand in Daqiu. The conviction of those involved in the death of Jade Field was supposed to have chastened Yu Zuomin. Instead, it had emboldened him. Standing on his fame, he had begun to articulate opposition to a range of party policies and principles. If he was allowed to continue, one committee member averred, other peasants might follow suit, marching in step behind the banner of Boss Yu and his irascible village. In addition, the murder of Wei Fuhe and the Beijing students incident suggested that Yu's authoritarian rule was turning Daqiu into a violent tyranny, heedless of all laws.

After some debate, the committee issued an order to Mayor Nie in Tianjin to personally take over the murder investigation and to "handle matters according to law." That unremarkable expression was imbued with deep meaning in Communist China. It meant, forget personal relationships and political ties and throw the book at them. A brief handwritten *pishi* was delivered to Mayor Nie on 22 February, which stated:

We would ask that the Tianjin party committee and government pay attention to this case and earnestly investigate it. As far as we know, this is not the first time such a case has happened there. Daqiu Village has become too arrogant and their methods are completely lawless. Yesterday, the politburo standing committee was unanimous in agreeing that this case should be handled according to law.[22]

Yu Zuomin had misjudged his position. It was a puzzling mistake because certainly he knew by this time that the power provided by his village's wealth and fame were increasingly hemmed in by a range of bad feelings at all levels of government. Whatever his sense of self-righteousness, this alone should have dictated prudence. The fact that a blatant murder had taken place under his nose only reinforced the need to be careful. The pendulum swing in Beijing indicated that Yu was not being careful enough.

Within a few days of the edict reaching Tianjin, Yu was aware of its contents. His source was a thirty-six-year-old staffer in the general offices of both the State Council and the party Central Committee named Gao Chao. Gao had visited Daqiu for the first time in July 1992 and become one of Yu's best informants about developments in Beijing. In the coming months, Gao would provide a constant stream of reports about high-level views on the Daqiu issue. In return, he would be given Rmb 25,000 in bribes and another Rmb 10,000 worth of stock in village companies.[23] Yu was "like a spy buying state secrets," according to one official report, "playing for high stakes," according to another.[24]

The reports of Beijing's ebbing patience with Daqiu seemed to chasten Yu Zuomin. As February turned to March he adopted a lower profile, and an eerie silence crept over the village. "The richest of Chinese villages now broods under a cloud of suspicion far murkier than the pall of pollution from its primitive smokestack industries," the *Far Eastern Economic Review* reported.[25] On at least one occasion, Yu was reported to have traveled to Beijing to explain his side of the story to the politburo.[26] But those efforts were far too little too late. In Beijing, leaders continued to read a stream of unflattering internal reference reports on the village by Liu Linshan:

> Protecting murderers: Daqiu stops production to mobilize its people, and a clash is avoided, but legal officials who enter the village are surrounded and viciously beaten.

> Daqiu deceives national public opinion through the telephone while the four suspects are sheltered and the police come up empty-handed.

> Tianjin public opinion feels that Yu Zuomin's behavior is a crime.

In one report, Liu even suggested that several national media organs had hesitated to submit similar internal reports to Beijing because their editors owned shares in Daqiu companies. The *Beijing Youth Daily,* for example, would later prominently quote an official from Tianjin Trust and Investment, the underwriter of the village stocks, appealing to investors to "join hands and help the village companies get past this rough period, since this will be in the interests of everybody."[27]

Yu Zuomin's defiance of party authority and discipline was already well known. But Liu's avalanche of reports revealed the frontierlike lawlessness of the village in all its colors. "If not for your reports," a senior official of the Tianjin procuracy would later tell Liu, "there's no way we could have moved Yu Zuomin. You gave us the backing we needed."[28]

In early March, Beijing finally decided to lower the boom. Daqiu was to be occupied, by force if necessary. The endgame had begun.

On the night of 9 March, Mayor Nie phoned Yu to inform him that a work group (*gongzuo zu*) directly under the Tianjin party committee would enter Daqiu the next day. The group would oversee the murder investigation and "rectify" the village's baleful public order situation. Yu already knew that the tide of opinion was turning rapidly against him. He had little choice but to agree. It was exactly a decade since the first occupation of Daqiu by a county inspection team.

The work group sped into the village the next morning in a cloud of dust and commandeered the Kowloon Hotel for its headquarters. Every key Tianjin organ was represented: the police, the procuracy, the government, and the party committee. Its first act was to dissolve the village public security office under Zhou Kewen and confiscate its tiny stash of weapons. Then it issued a back-to-work order to get the factories producing again. That done, signs were posted to explain the group's presence. These read in part:

> The work group has come here to investigate the murder case. It
> is our hope that villagers will continue their normal life and work
> during this time, as well as safeguard the legitimate duties of the
> work group and enthusiastically provide leads on the crime.[29]

This was not a full-scale crackdown by any means. Daqiu was still a valuable economic asset for the county and the city, and neither government wanted to be known as the home of the model village that went wrong. "Taking into consideration the fact that Daqiu was a model for the country's rural reforms and that it had a great reputation in China and abroad," one local newspaper explained, "the Tianjin party committee made sure that it strictly abided by the law in handling this case in order to protect the fruits of Daqiu's reforms."[30]

Yu made a point of attending the annual gathering of the CPPCC in Beijing when it opened on 14 March. There, he was duly reelected to another five-year term. Although the media were under a gag order from the party Propaganda Department,[31] reporters still peppered Yu with questions about the parlous situation. For the first time, Yu was reticent and cautious. "Everything is normal," he commented as he strode out of one meeting. "Other than that, I have no comment."[32]

Returning to the village, though, Yu found that his control was slipping. The work group had seized the village broadcast system and begun relaying a message claiming that the Daqiu party committee had welcomed the group's presence as "correct and timely." The broadcast system was also used to offer an amnesty for all those who turned in their guns and other weapons to the Kowloon Hotel headquarters by 30 March.[33] "The entry of the work group frightened Yu to death because it challenged his longtime iron grip on the village," the *Legal Daily* would later say.[34]

In Yu's absence, the work group had managed to get most factories restarted, putting losses for the monthlong halt at Rmb 400 million. In a last-ditch effort to rescue his position, Yu sought to reimpose the work stoppage. But this time, his appeals fell on deaf ears. Indeed, it led to a hitherto unthinkable breaking of ranks by the leaders of two of the Four Hens, Yu's brother Yu Zuoyao of Yaoshun Group and Zhao Shuzhong of Jinmei Group.[35] Both men accused Yu of mishandling the delicate situation with his defiant attitude. When Yu dismissed their criticisms, they fled the village, fearing his wrath. For the first time since he was bombarded with criticisms at the 1977 village meeting, Yu found his position deteriorating from within.

Now a cascade of events engulfed Yu Zuomin. On 19 March, Wanquan Group vice president Liu Shaosheng, one of the four murder suspects, was arrested in adjoining Hebei province. Six days later, police detained company security guard Chen Xiangqi, also in Hebei. The country's minister of public security, Tao Siju, triumphantly revealed the two arrests to reporters at the end of the annual meeting of the National People's Congress on 8 April, the first public statement on the case by a senior Beijing official.[36] Tao admitted that there had been "initial difficulties" in the case caused by people who "opposed the investigation"; but he rejected charges that he had deployed more than one thousand PAP officers in the February standoff. "I would not have sent so many officers to deal with an incident in a small village," was his haughty remark. Now, he was confident in bringing the hitherto untouchable village to heel. "I believe that Daqiu will learn from this incident and become a more ethical and civilized place as a result," he said.

The final breach in Yu Zuomin's defenses came in early April, when informant Gao Chao was unmasked after an internal Central Committee investigation into leaks about the case. When the politburo standing committee met again to consider the case on 12 April, the unanimous feeling was that Yu had finally gone too far. Complicity in murder was one thing, but subverting the party at the highest levels was quite another. In any case, pressure within the party for Yu to be purged was growing, and he was losing support in Daqiu itself. With the party preparing to launch one of its perennial anticorruption campaigns, Yu would make a fitting example.[37] A vote was taken in the politburo standing committee and the signatures of each of the seven members were affixed to an urgent directive to the Tianjin party committee.[38] Yu Zuomin, it said, was to be detained immediately on criminal charges.

Yu Zuomin was not a difficult prey to capture. The rapid deterioration in his position had made him nervous and careless. Once Tianjin police had the authority to detain him, they stalked him at close range looking for a chance to leap. It came within days. Yu went to Beijing on 14 April in a final effort to save himself. He failed to make any headway. As his motorcade of four sedans sped back along the Beijing-Tianjin highway the next day, Tianjin police cars surrounded the procession and brought it to a halt.[39] Yu was pulled out of his golden Mercedes and informed that he was being detained for questioning on charges of obstruction of justice and harboring criminals.

"Aiya!" he is said to have exclaimed. "It's over! It's over! I never thought it would happen so quickly!"[40]

Late the next day, 16 April, the official Xinhua news agency issued a brief report on the detention, which was broadcast on the evening news of China Central Television and carried on the inside pages of the

People's Daily the following day. "We have learned from the Ministry of Public Security that Yu Zuomin, chairman of the Daqiu Village Enterprise Group Corporation, was detained on criminal charges by the Tianjin Public Security Bureau on April 15," it said. "On December 13 last year, an illegal detention and beating took place in Daqiu Village which led to the death of worker Wei Fuhe. In the course of the investigation, it was discovered that Yu Zuomin had exhibited criminal behavior like protecting and harboring criminals and using illegal methods to obstruct the course of justice. Judicial officials have thus begun to interrogate him in accordance with the law."[41]

Yu was not referred to as the party secretary of Daqiu, a post he had symbolically abandoned in February to protest the use of the PAP to surround the village. But no one was in any doubt that he was still the boss of the village, the Lord of the East of northern Hebei. Shares in Wanquan Group, already plumbing all-time lows, fell further to just Rmb 0.4 the day of the announcement, after a high of Rmb 5.2 in late 1992. "One investor on the streets of Tianjin said he received a sharp smack in the face by this news when he returned from a business trip to the south," the *Beijing Youth Daily* reported.[42]

Back in Daqiu, the disappearance of Boss Yu's car from its accustomed place stirred the usual disquiet. News of the detention confirmed that the game was up. Police attached to the work group led a parade of senior village officials into the Kowloon Hotel, where each was detained in turn. First came Little Yu, accused, along with his father, of having bribed Gao Chao for information. Then came the other members of the probe into the Huada Group: Mistress Shi, Eternal China, and Zhou Kewen. More came in their wake. Daqiu had surrendered.

On 21 April, with the clamps firmly placed on Daqiu, Yu was formally placed under arrest in Tianjin. All media organs were again instructed in a message from the central Propaganda Department that "it is inappropriate to conduct interviews or write reports on the situation in Daqiu Village."[43] But speculation in the foreign press rose to a new crescendo. The *South China Morning Post* predicted that Yu would be "let off with a strict warning," while United Press International reported that Yu had been set free on direct instructions from Deng Xiaoping.[44] But Beijing was not budging. Xinhua issued a special report to refute the UPI story, saying that Yu "is still under arrest and prosecution proceedings against him are continuing."[45]

No one familiar with the legal system in China was in any doubt that this fallen peasant hero and his fellow conspirators were headed for jail. One of the few reports on the case that managed to escape censors made it plain enough: "Yu Zuomin has protected and harbored criminals and obstructed justice in a way that amounts to a crime," the *Southern Weekend* newspaper declared. "He is sure to be punished according to law."[46] Throughout May and June, Yu remained at the police detention center in Tianjin. During that time he was denied his customary foods and kept in mostly solitary confinement. Some reports speak of attempted suicide.[47] With this majestic lion finally in captivity, just about everyone took turns poking sticks through the bars. Police, state security, procuracy, and court officials, not to mention several Jinghai and Tianjin politicians, all played chief inquisitor with Yu. There were thirty-eight formal interrogation sessions and dozens of informal ones, filling up eighty-six bound volumes of testimony.

On 23 July, journalist Liu Linshan—the man whose reports had been so instrumental to Yu's arrest—and three other reporters were allowed into the detention center to observe the trophy at close range. The four reporters had been asked to submit questions in advance. As with the report in the *Southern Weekend,* the arrangement clearly prejudiced the case. But Yu's conviction was already a foregone conclusion. Switching his cigarette nervously from one hand to the other, he "looked more like a caged wolf than the famous person we were used to seeing on television, always talking without end," Liu wrote.[48] Asked about his hopes for the resolution of the case, Yu replied:

If they're going to jail me, I wish they'd do it faster. If they're going to free me, I wish they'd do it faster. If they sentence me to jail, I'll obey, but I will be bitter. I worked hard as a cadre for forty-one years and my merits exceed my faults. If the government forgives me this time and sentences me to serve my punishment outside jail, then I'll go back to Daqiu and work for several more years.

That hope appeared forlorn. By the time of the interview, the two remaining fugitives, Liu Yunzhang and Li Zhenbiao, had turned themselves in to Tianjin police. Preparations were under way for a mass trial of the Daqiu incident, involving twenty-six people in all. The sixty-four-year-old Yu's dream of building a village that would radically alter the precepts about wealth, politics, and society in rural China was now hopelessly fallen about his oversized ears. He was on the verge of being overthrown, and he knew it.

On 31 July 1992, more than eight months after Yu Zuomin had pulled the white sheet over his dead cousin and set in motion the train of events that would bring his village into disrepute, the Daqiu trial opened in Tianjin. The first batch of eighteen people led into the dock included the four murder suspects and fourteen other workers who had taken part in the subsequent cover-up. It is not known if they pleaded guilty or not, but the defense arguments were brief. A hand-picked audience sat silently as a battery of television cameras captured the proceedings for later broadcast. By 11 August, the entire group had been tried and sent back into detention centers to await the verdicts.

The trial of the second batch, consisting of eight top village leaders, lasted for two weeks from 14 August. The five key defendants—Yu Zuomin and the four who had overseen the probe into the Huada Group, Little Yu, Mistress Shi, Eternal China, and Zhou Kewen— were charged with crimes ranging from bribery to obstruction of justice, collusion, and harboring criminals. All but Mistress Shi pleaded not guilty.

Court officials hurried through the prosecution of the first seven defendants as onlookers fanned themselves in the packed courtroom. Again, defense arguments were brief. Most stated that they merely had followed the orders of Boss Yu. Mistress Shi, though, remained loyal to her lover to the end, asking only for lenient punishment in return for her guilty plea. Little Yu, defending himself against a charge of bribing Gao Chao, said the money was for consultancy services rendered, not for information on the murder case. The proceedings went quickly. Everyone was waiting for the main draw: the trial of Yu Zuomin.

Yu was led into the hushed courtroom on the morning of 24 August wearing a simple white dress shirt, blue trousers, and—most unusually—traditional Chinese cloth shoes. The cloth shoes, or *bu xie,* had not been seen on Yu since the early 1980s, when he had begun issuing sartorial edicts in Daqiu including the wearing of leather shoes. Like Uncle Chen's white headcloth, or *yang duzi,* the cloth shoes were a sign of Yu's roots. Perhaps they were his way of showing that on this day he was representing all of China's peasants.

The importance Beijing attached to a sound prosecution was evident from its choice of a defense lawyer for Yu. Rather than leave the task in the hands of a court-appointed lawyer from Tianjin, Beijing entrusted the job to one of its most loyal attorneys, Wang Yaoting, from the Ministry of Justice's Beijing Municipal Number Two Law Office. Yu was a wily player who might steal the stage and confuse proceedings if a less reliable lawyer were overseeing things. Wang's job was to ensure that his "client" went to jail quietly.

The first two charges against Yu, harboring criminals and obstruction of justice, referred to the murder of Wei Fuhe. But the prosecution did not end there. Three more charges were read aloud that created a stir in the courtroom: bribery to obtain "important and top secret state information" (*guojia zhongyao jimi*), a charge relating to Gao Chao that went back to August 1992; unlawful detention, this involving the teachers and students from the cadre training academy of the Beijing Municipal State Security Department in November 1992; and unlawful detention and restraint of the relatives of the deceased Jade Field since 1990. It was a laundry list of Yu's misdeeds. Evidence for the Jade Field charge was presented by lawyer Tian Wenchang, who had continued to represent the family. "That day was the culmination of my three-year tussle with Yu Zuomin," Tian later recalled.[49]

While the charges were carefully phrased around the alleged criminal acts, the prosecution left little doubt that Yu Zuomin was on trial for more than just legal misdemeanors. Rather, his whole vision of a new kind of rural China was on trial as well. Yu was brought to court for breaking the law, but his true crime was being an ideological enemy of the Communist state.

"Being rich does not mean you can use your money and power to violate the law *and shirk political discipline,*" the *Southern Weekend* newspaper later explained.[50]

In their statements, prosecutors went out of their way to detail Yu's immoderate lifestyle and his autocratic rule. "He smoked cigarettes like a fat-cat Westerner smokes cigars," charged one prosecutor.[51] Added another official from Jinghai: "In the last two to three years, he began to accumulate wealth and indulged more and more in luxury and extravagance. His residence became more and more luxurious. He went from his home to his office by car, although the distance was only 200 meters. He spent money like water. He had six telephones in his home, and his leather belt cost more than Rmb 10,000."[52]

As for his rule, prosecutors called Yu "the greatest despot of the 1990s" and decried his attempts to reform Daqiu's political system.[53] "It was said that Daqiu Village had no laws but only the instructions of Yu Zuomin, which were like the imperial edicts of feudal emperors," said one prosecutor.[54] And another prosecutor: "Yu Zuomin became insufferably arrogant in the face of his achievements and honors. As his wealth grew, his governance became more brutal, and he failed to pay heed to state laws. He only cared about money and did not give a whit for spiritual culture or legal development."[55] And finally, there came this simple and powerful statement by one prosecutor, which summed up the political revulsion: "There is not even the shadow of a Chinese Communist Party member left in him now."[56]

It did not seem to matter that such arguments about Yu's life and his rule had only a passing relevance to the charges under consideration. Yu Zuomin was on trial as much for what he was as for what he had done.

In the lengthy *Legal Daily* report on the Daqiu trial—given the burlesque title "Crazy Village Boss" (*fengkuang zhuangzhu*) and running to twenty-four thousand characters—journalist Liu and a colleague described how Yu defended himself.[57] Like a wounded bird, he spun helplessly on the ground as others watched him exhaust his last stores of energy. The Jade Field incident was a closed case, he argued, while the melee involving the Beijing students resulted from their unapproved visit to the village. The detention of certain members of the Huada Group, meanwhile, had been justified by the gaping holes in the company accounts uncovered by a village investigation. And the village had been put onto a war footing because of inaccurate reports of an impending attack by rogue paramilitary troops.[58] Whatever mistakes he had made in handling these incidents, Yu argued, his merits far exceeded those faults, and he should be sent back to the village on probation. In any normal trial, good deeds are no defense against one's crimes. But Yu and everyone else in the courtroom knew that the trial was about much more than crimes.

On 27 August, the court reconvened to announce the verdicts of all twenty-six defendants. The unseemly dispatch of the proceedings— few courts could fairly hear cases against twenty-six people in less than a month—was no surprise. Guilty verdicts were clearly waiting in the dossiers of each. One after another, accompanied by the whir of television cameras, they were led into the courtroom to learn of their fate.

The jail terms announced for the first batch of eighteen directly involved in the murder varied widely. The stiffest sanctions went to the four Wanquan Group thugs accused of the murder itself. The young secretary of the president's office, Liu Yunzhang, was handed a suspended death sentence, while the other three—president's office staffer Li Zhenbiao, company vice president Liu Shaosheng, and security guard Chen Xiangqi—all drew life in prison. The other fourteen were all jailed for between five and fifteen years.

Then came the eight village leaders, including Yu. Three lesser lights—Ma Deshui (a brother of model farmer Ma Deliang), Huang Naiqi, and Chen Guanghong—received two to three years each for harboring criminals. The sentences handed down to the four leaders who oversaw the probe into the Huada Group were also varied. Mistress Shi, the only female defendant, got off with only one year in jail for collusion. Eternal China drew four years for unlawful restraint and harboring criminals, while Zhou Kewen took five years for unlawful restraint and obstructing justice. A heavier term was given to Little Yu, who was jailed for ten years for bribing Gao Chao and for unlawful restraint. This young man, for whom the world was opening like an oyster just a year earlier, was now destined to spend his prime years behind bars.

Yu Zuomin came last. Like the others, he was forced to remain standing while his fate was announced. The presiding judge also stood, and then read the verdict: guilty on all counts, with stiff jail terms for each. Six years for harboring criminals in the murder. Three years for obstructing justice in the subsequent investigation. Ten years for the bribery of Gao Chao. Three years for the unlawful restraint of the Beijing students. And three years for the unlawful restraint of the Jade Field family. A total of twenty-five years, reduced to twenty by concurrent terms. Yu would be in prison until the year 2013—when he would be eighty-four.

The stunned village leader stared in disbelief and slumped into the dock. The day had finally come. He was overthrown. Back in 1977, he had promised to go to jail if he failed to enrich the village. Now, he was going anyway, leaving behind the richest village in China. Not for a long time, perhaps never, would he walk again through the village where he had spent his entire life. Whatever defiance remained, that prospect alone sent a chill through his bones.

Lawyer Wang hastened to the dock to hand Yu a statement of regret to be read aloud. It was the last act of the courtroom play. Yu straightened up and read: "There are ideological as well as historical reasons for my crimes. As the village grew, my head swelled and I forgot about the law and about spiritual things. I was muddle-headed and unaware of the serious crimes I had committed."[59]

That was the last image anyone in China would ever see of Yu Zuomin. He was helped from the dock by court guards and led out into a waiting van.

It remained only for the national press—long accustomed to heaping praise on Yu Zuomin and his village—to make the 180-degree turn and heap scorn on them as if it were the most natural thing. With the former model now in official disgrace, reporters were free to "mercilessly beat the dog who has fallen into the ditch," as the Chinese saying went.

Much of the reporting was simply a gleeful rehashing of the sensational details of the murder incident, spiced with as much salacious rumor of village life as could be credibly mustered. Even the foreign press joined in the orgy: "The nationally renowned boss of a model village was unmasked yesterday as a corrupt feudal lord," the Associated Press reported on 27 August in one of several articles that appeared in world newspapers the following day.[60]

As with all cases of political wind shifts, official media went to great lengths to explain how a model formerly praised by the party was suddenly an antiparty enemy. Yu, Xinhua wrote in the most authoritative commentary on the case, "played an active role when he accepted and implemented the party line, principles, and policies" but played a destructive role when he "violated state law and policies and did bad things."[61] No matter what the merits of any person, "they must still learn to properly handle relations with their organization and with the state." Most important, it asserted, was the need to strengthen party rule in villages like Daqiu. "We must not allow 'fortified villages' and 'local tyrants' that do not subject themselves to any authority to emerge again inside the party." The political, rather than legal, revulsion of Yu was never so clear.

Several days later the *Legal Daily* weighed in with an editorial. "Yu Zuomin's selfishness reached shocking proportions and a miniature independent kingdom was created," it said. "Now, this epic struggle between socialist China's legal system and a little prince wearing the robes of an emperor has finally been resolved. And victory has gone to the former."[62]

Several months later, the CPPCC standing committee would strip Yu of his status as a delegate to the national body.[63] The case also earned the dubious distinction of mention by China's chief prosecutor in his report to the National People's Congress in April 1994.[64] The last piece of business was concluded in December of that year: Gao Chao, in detention since April 1993, was jailed for thirteen years for taking bribes in return for state secrets.[65]

Yu Zuomin had been Daqiu's party secretary since 1964. His effective reign as village chief had been more than thirty years. Perhaps he had known that this day would come. Indeed, he may have relished the day when he would be "overthrown" for his impertinence toward the party's leadership and its ideology. Anything else, as he had said, would not be "the real Yu Zuomin." Now "the real Yu Zuomin" was beginning a long spell in jail along with a host of his ex-comrades in rebellion. Daqiu Village faced an uncertain future, deprived of its leader and of its fame. And an important chapter in China's rural development was at an end.

FIVE

Conclusions

The rise and fall of Daqiu Village is a portentous tale of rebellion in rural China. Through a combination of luck, leadership, and hard work, a small and unassuming village rose from the alkaline soil of the northern China plains to become an industrial powerhouse. The arresting development of the village and the charisma of its leader, Yu Zuomin, made it a perfect model for the rural reforms of the 1980s and early 1990s. But power and fame also allowed the village to flex its political muscles in ways that caused increasing disquiet in the national leadership. When those tensions finally came to a head in an astonishing armed confrontation, it caught the attention of the world.

The Daqiu story finds its historical context in the shifting tectonic plates of reform China. Its rise reflected all the elements of the decade after 1978 in which villages gained autonomy, economics replaced ideology as the highest guiding policy, and a more malleable relationship developed between peasants and the state. There was also at this time an endorsement of private rural wealth related to the deprivations of the 1950s and 1960s and the emergence of a visible "rural lobby" in the media and leadership. Following the 1989 Tiananmen Square protests, however, other shifts began: a renewed drive to prop up party rule in the countryside, a higher-profile campaign against official corruption, and an attempt to moderate the materialism of the 1980s. Daqiu's rise and fall reflected both these periods.

Daqiu's story has obvious historical affinities to the rise and fall of Dazhai. Both villages boasted genuine economic achievements and a charismatic leader prior to their "discovery" as models. They were then born as models because they fit perfectly into the party's propaganda needs at the time. Yet model status exerted a corrosive effect on both village leaders, Boss Yu and Uncle Chen. The adulation bestowed on them became like an opiate, encouraging them to pursue any means to keep the positive publicity flowing. The result was that Yu became a tyrant and Chen a fraud.

Author Jiang Zilong, the man whose short story, "Yanzhao Elegy," brought Daqiu its early fame, has wondered aloud whether it was a historic inevitability that Daqiu should fall from grace. "Peasants in China cannot help but notice that every era of rural reform since 1949 had its model village and that the life span of these villages was never long," he wrote. "The models were different, but their basic qualities and the stories of their rises and falls were essentially the same."[1]

Yet it is important to distinguish the paths that took both villages from humble beginnings to ignominious ends. Most important, Daqiu's economic "miracle" was for real, while Dazhai's was for the most part a sham. Daqiu's political power also depended less on high-level state patronage and more on a mesh of allies and grassroots organization. For these reasons and others relating to personal factors, Boss Yu waged a political struggle against the Communist state that would have been unthinkable for Uncle Chen.

In many ways, these differences reflect the fact that Dazhai's story unfolded under the strong Maoist state, while Daqiu's took place during its collapse. Economic activity in the Maoist period was inextricably linked to the strong central state, which meant that Dazhai's economic fortunes depended on favorable treatment from that state. By the time

Daqiu came along, however, a village's wealth depended far more on its own initiative. Likewise, patronage from the strong central state was critical to Dazhai's political fortunes, while Daqiu exploited the collapse of that structure to accumulate its own political resources. The economic and political dimensions of the Daqiu story tell us much about how post-Mao China has empowered the peasantry. Let us consider each in turn.

Daqiu's experience in industrialization remains an important case study for students of China's rural economy. The founding of its four factories between 1977 and 1981 reflected several currents at work in the countryside, among them the breakup of the communes and the delegation of authority and fiscal incentives to the village level; the growth of demand for simple industrial goods and the resulting higher returns for industry than agriculture; and the psychological impetus provided by memories of poverty and famine. Daqiu was also blessed with entrepreneurial talents in the form of Yu Zuomin and the leaders of the Four Hens. They sketched out and initiated the village's industrialization and took the political risks necessary to succeed.

The period from 1984 to 1992 was the golden age of Daqiu. The scattered village factories were brought under a village conglomerate that also gradually took over the functions of governance. Facing hard budget constraints, the factories expanded into immediately profitable lines, especially steel products. Large numbers of migrant workers were hired alongside skilled technicians and managers from outside; they supplemented the local family-based networks that sat atop the companies. The companies also created networks of sales agents and offices throughout the country. There is evidence of some involvement in the illegal trading of materials—*zhanwu* and *daomai*—for the benefit of village companies, but this appears to have been a small and shrinking part of the village's economic success.

The economic boom set off by Deng Xiaoping in early 1992 came at a time when the village was already investing heavily in new factories. Coupled with greater publicity, the village economy grew mightily. It also diversified, producing services as well as goods, entering into more complex arrangements to finance its growth, and expanding its activities abroad. All evidence points to an authentic economic boom in which state support was minimal and came as an adjunct rather than as an inducement to the village's growth.

The importance of TVEs in China's national economy continues to grow apace. By the end of 1998 there were twenty million TVEs in China, employing 130 million people or 20 percent of the entire national labor force. They accounted for two-thirds of rural GDP, a third of national GDP, and half of national exports. In coastal provinces like Jiangsu, Shandong, and Zhejiang, TVEs have eclipsed state industry in terms of output and exports. All indicators point to an acceleration of this trend since then.

TVE expansion differs across China in several respects, such as the extent of foreign capital used, the amount of production that is exported, and the mix of private and collective ownership. At the same time, several factors are common to all, including an amenable macroeconomic environment and fiscal incentives for county and township officials to encourage TVE growth. The role of local cadres as entrepreneurs also appears critical; having served under the strong local state in the Maoist era of the 1950s, 1960s, and 1970s, these officials have become their own natural successors in the post-Mao era, since they have both the power and the incentives to work for TVEs.[2]

The Daqiu case brings out one additional factor that seems to be increasingly common: the role of the village conglomerate (*cun zong-gongsi*), or VC. In Daqiu, the company that eventually became the Daqiu Village Enterprise Group Corporation was created in 1983 to draw together the village's TVEs into one unit. Other examples of VCs in China are now legion. The village that succeeded Daqiu as the richest village in China, Huaxi in Jiangsu province, operates its TVEs under the Huaxi Group, which listed shares on the Shenzhen stock exchange in 1999. Another famed village, Beijiao in the Pearl River Delta, turned itself into an industrial powerhouse in the 1980s and early 1990s with most of its enterprises under the Meidi Group (whose air conditioners are advertised by Chinese actress Gong Li).[3] Even Dazhai has followed the VC model. After her 1992 visit to Daqiu, Guo Fenglian established the Dazhai Economic Development Company to run the village's five new companies. The conglomerate registered turnover of Rmb 57 million in 1998, and Guo earned five times as much from her corporate position atop the Dazhai VC as from her post as party secretary of the village.[4] One scholar found that VCs accounted for half of all TVE output in Shandong province and more than a quarter of the province's entire GDP.[5]

The emergence of VCs is clearly linked to an enduring communal spirit that survived the breakup of communes in small, tightly knit villages. Villagers in such places prefer the VC structure because it retains the egalitarian virtues of the communes while discarding their economic shortcomings. VCs then prove their economic worth in several ways: by providing loose coordination among a village's TVEs so that they can share resources in areas like materials procurement and sales; by allowing some TVEs to ride out short-term slumps through cross-subsidization; and by their ability to collectively represent the companies in political struggles with the state. One major distinction between a VC and a commune is that VC leaders have to deliver the economic goods to stay in power. If they do not, their tenures are sure to be short lived.

The foundations that gave rise to Daqiu-style wealth are unlikely to change anytime soon. Seemingly endless supplies of surplus labor from agriculture coupled with strong industrial demand will prompt more and more villages, especially in inland areas, to establish TVEs. Access to new sources of capital from overseas and from a reformed banking sector will make these start-ups easier. At the same time, the lack of an open and predictable legal and political structure will mean that wily local cadres will continue to play a critical role in the success of TVEs—this despite the fact that a growing number of TVEs, and indeed even VCs, are being privatized. In addition, enduring communal sentiments and the facility of using family and clan structures in management will continue to induce the creation of VCs. In short, Daqiu-style villages will sprout for many years to come across the Chinese countryside. This will further the long process in which China's peasants have gained increasing economic autonomy vis-à-vis the state, a process which more than anything else has furthered the goals of equality that Yu Zuomin espoused. As the best-known pioneer of this style of development, Daqiu will always be "China's First Village."

One of the central purposes of this narrative has been to exhume the political nature of the Daqiu story. Many terms have been used to describe the politics of Daqiu here: resistance, dissent, struggle, subversion, rebellion. These are imperfect terms to cover a variety of conflictual interactions with the state in pursuit of political, economic, or social goals—what scholars generally call "collective actions."

Of course, this assumes that the actions of Daqiu were indeed "collective." As mentioned, there was some divergence between Yu and his villagers in later years. Yu Zuomin relished a good scrap with the party, sought personal accolades, and believed in his mission to fight for all of China's peasants. The villagers generally had more immediate concerns. Still, the villagers stood to benefit from Yu's campaign because of the fame and influence it won for Daqiu. That is why they largely supported him as the storm grew, writing down and repeating his every word and rallying to defend him against outsiders. There were signs of dissent to be sure, but by and large Yu was usually leading genuine collective actions.

How and why did Daqiu rebel? A full sociological analysis is far beyond the scope of this work. But the question can be answered briefly with respect to the four dimensions of any instance of collective action: the issue, the goal, the means, and the methods.[6]

The *issue* of collective action refers to the matter at stake, ranging from a simple issue, such as the conversion of a piece of agricultural land into a factory site, to a complex one, such as a matter of national policy or ideology. The range here is from petty quotidian issues to more enduring and nationally significant ones. The *goal* of collective action, meanwhile, can range from an immediate and quantifiable goal, such as monetary returns, to a more protracted and diffuse goal, such as some sort of psychological benefit. In rural China, the struggle by a group to be recognized as *junzi* ("gentlemen") rather than *tubaozi* ("country hicks") is an example of the latter.

The issue and goal are sometimes called the "demand-pull" factors because they are concerned with the motivations behind collective action.[7] But an equally important aspect is the ability to mount collective action, sometimes called the "supply-push" factors.[8] This leads us to the means and methods.

The *means* may be divided into material and nonmaterial resources.[9] Material resources include things like money to pay for the action and the provision of benefits to those who take part. Nonmaterial resources are a more varied category. Critical ingredients include the skills of the "entrepreneurs" who lead and organize the action, the solidarity of the participants in the action, and the passions of those involved. In addition, nonmaterial resources include those aspects of the institutional environment that lend themselves to the action, often referred to as the "political opportunity structure."[10] Examples would be the tolerance for collective action, the availability of allies within the political system, and the responsiveness of the system in the face of collective action.

In many respects, the means will determine the *methods* chosen. Here we have a kaleidoscope of possibilities: passive resistance, open protest, verbal dissent, covert subversion, or even violent rebellion. One way to categorize the methods when studying an authoritarian state like China is to ask whether they use the rhetoric and political mechanisms of the state—what is often called "righteous resistance"—or whether they use unsanctioned rhetoric and actions, or "unrighteous resistance." The latter is the best known and studied, since it is usually more conflictual. It can range from "everyday forms of resistance" like lying and stealing to the rare and spectacular forms like armed uprising. Righteous resistance, meanwhile, presents a more fascinating aspect, and one that scholars believe is growing rapidly in rural China.[11] This is the appeal to sanctioned, authoritative statements or policies as the method of resistance, even if the people using them do not believe what they are saying. In a country like China, where overlapping and often conflicting values emanate from a wide array of authoritative sources—party leaders, government officials, the media—and in a variety of forms—laws, regulations, editorials, "important speeches" (*zhongyao jianghua*), appeals (*haozhao*), etc.—there are always many options for righteous resistance. This leaves us with a simple road map with four points of the compass—the issue, the goal, the means, and the method—to use in recapping the story of Daqiu's collective actions.

Daqiu's poverty and its sense of historical grievance were major factors affecting the nature of its collective actions in the early years. The actions tended to be over simple issues and aimed at immediate, material goals. While in every other respect it was deprived of the necessary resources for action, Daqiu did enjoy the leadership of Yu Zuomin, whose charisma could mobilize the village in ways that the cadres of other villages could not. Still, Yu himself was but the leader of a small, poor village, so the actions were largely righteous in method. Unrighteous actions, such as the diversion of money from county irrigation funds to build its first factory, were over minor issues only.

The formal ending of the Cultural Revolution and the onset of economic reforms in the late 1970s allowed Yu to make righteous appeals to central government policies (*fangzhen*) in order to introduce merit pay for oil well diggers and reed cutters, for example, and to hire people with "dubious" backgrounds. Likewise, as Maoist agricultural policies came under fire in Beijing and "brigade enterprises" were encouraged,

Daqiu leaders forged ahead with plans to make steel for the cities despite the opposition of county cadres still wedded to the notion of "three locals" production.

In the early 1980s, more complex issues naturally arose between Daqiu and upper-level officials who worried about the rapid expansion of the village's factories. While county and township officials had a vested fiscal interest in promoting village industry, they retained an ambivalent attitude toward Daqiu—enjoying the fruits of its economic success but unable to overcome lingering feelings of jealousy and insecurity. Yu's jousting with the county leadership, which culminated in the 1982 inspection team, and his indifference to hostile ideologues in Beijing involved more complex issues of national policy direction. Still, Daqiu's actions were largely righteous, that is, based on appeals to national policies and ideological shifts. The reasons for this should be clear: at this early stage, the village did not have the ability to mount collective actions over such important issues in any unrighteous form; it had to accept the entry of a county inspection team into the village, and it had to accept ideological criticisms from Beijing with a stony silence rather than open rebuttal.

The publication of "Yanzhao Elegy" in 1984 won for Daqiu national fame. Coupled with the flowering of the village economy, this provided a bounty of new resources beyond the leadership of Yu with which to mount collective actions. Indeed, these resources were complementary, since Yu was now able to build a more impregnable political structure on the back of the expanding village corporate structure. As a result, we see a sudden decline in attacks on the village by the county leadership, a kind of induced collective action.

The golden age of Daqiu from 1984 to 1992 saw the emergence of collective action, driven by the ability of the village to mobilize resources as well as by its simple desire to develop. That is, the supply-push factors began to have greater explanatory power than the demand-pull factors. The village continued to develop rapidly; it was seen as a model of rural reforms. The internal sense of solidarity was bolstered by Yu's disciplinarian rule. And Yu's many new accolades—top peasant entrepreneur, national model worker, TVE association vice chairman, national CPPCC delegate—allowed him to forge allies both in Beijing and across the country. With those resources, Daqiu went on the attack.

The wrangle over the money slogan was a complex national issue that seemed to hinge ultimately on whether peasants could openly exhort the moneymaking ethos that patriarch Deng Xiaoping's policies had sanctioned. Few village leaders could have taken the heat for this issue that Yu did. But by now the village's resources were up to the task. While at first assuming an unrighteous stance by refusing to rephrase the slogan in terms of party rhetoric, Yu later met state leader Bo Yibo halfway, agreeing that the slogan was consonant with party policies. Given that Daqiu gained little in the way of direct benefits from the dustup over the money slogan, this episode also suggested that Yu's goals were changing. He seemed to relish butting heads with leftists in the party, enjoying the national attention it brought him. Clearly, he was being motivated by less immediate goals than in the past, having now to do with the state's attitude toward peasant wealth and the recognition of his own fight against perceived injustice.

The years 1991–93 saw a sudden surge and then noisy confluence of the two subterranean rivers driving the history of Daqiu: its resources and its collective action, its power and its purpose. The wealth and fame that came to Daqiu in these years provided it with the means to mount new forms of collective action on several fronts. The village continued to act on many simple issues that brought immediate benefits, like issuing stocks and bonds without authorization and fending off an in-depth inquiry over the death of Jade Field.

Complex issues, however, stole the show. In these years, Yu articulated a new vision of rural China. Its aim was nothing less than an end to a perceived political, economic, and social discrimination against peasants in China that he believed had continued through the post-1949 period. Yu's vision often struck at the heart of Communist rule in

China by challenging ideological approaches to economic policy, political leadership, and social behavior. While ideology often disappears from the local agenda in rapidly growing villages, Daqiu was different. Ideological issues were the cornerstone of its collective actions in these years. The reason: they provided a much richer potential payoff than more pedestrian issues, not only for Yu Zuomin's ego but also for Daqiu's livelihood. Yu could achieve only so much by haggling with the county over taxes; but if he took on leftist ideologues and senior cadres on behalf of all of China's peasants and won, he and his village stood to reap rich rewards. If he lost, the village would suffer greatly.

On economic issues, Yu outlined a pragmatic approach to the definition of socialism that was centered on social welfare, while on social issues he advocated a new ideology of conspicuous consumption for China's peasants. In both these cases, Yu made largely righteous appeals by drawing attention to the party's stated goals of raising rural living standards and to Deng's sanction of some inequality in the initial period of economic reforms. In this way, he sought to highlight what he believed was the hypocritical reaction of many party leaders to peasant wealth in China.

On the issue of political leadership, however, Yu's actions were largely unrighteous, a bald threat to Communist rule. His appeal to discard ideological qualifications for political leaders uprooted the entire justification for rural party branches. His slogan "If you want to get rich, then abolish the party organization department" was as subversive in a one-party state as it was catchy. While they may have shared Yu's resentment toward the party, few leaders of other villages had the resources to mount such outlandish challenges to its power.

Yu's desire for recognition—to be "overthrown rather than lie down," in his words—changed the nature of Daqiu's resistance. Virtually the entire hopes of the village, the reasons for standing behind Yu, rested on the belief that through his struggles he would garner still greater long-term benefits. Nor were these hopes forlorn: Yu's audacity brought untold fame to Daqiu. It also brought county and city leaders with plans for new infrastructure investments, and national leaders with plans for new model pig farms and experimental grain projects.

Daqiu's collective actions were also notable at this latter stage because they showed signs of expanding to include other members of China's rural constituency. That is, they appeared to be verging on a genuine "social movement," defined as a series of collective actions mounted by an informal network of participants who share a common goal and a sense of solidarity.[12] By the late 1980s, for example, Yu was not only addressing nationally significant issues, but he was doing so with explicit reference to all of China's peasants. The money slogan incident of 1987 was one case. Then as he sat surrounded by a hundred of his fellow peasant entrepreneurs to receive his national award later that year, Yu declaimed on the need to treat rural enterprises as more than just a "supplement" to the state-owned economy and argued for the need to redefine socialism in terms of the welfare of the peasants. By making these assertions surrounded by others like him, Yu was showing signs that he might be trying to create an informal network of peasant industrialists and their allies, including possibly the then–party general secretary, Zhao Ziyang.

In the early 1990s, the inklings of such an informal network grew stronger. Yu's forging of close and open political ties with the two model villages of China's revolutionary past, Xiaojin and Dazhai, showed an emerging solidarity that is the very stuff of a social movement. While the leaders of these supplicant villages couched their ties to Daqiu in righteous terms—appealing to the party's sanction of various economic reforms—Yu himself made largely unrighteous appeals to them in turn, exhorting them to fight upper-level interference in their governance whatever the case. Other potential members of this would-be social movement appeared in the media (especially the *TVE News*), the senior party leadership (Li Ruihuan and Bo Yibo), and the government (the Ministry of Agriculture).

But Daqiu's would-be social movement was cut short. Indeed, fear of just such a movement may have been one of the biggest factors in its downfall. When the Tianjin and Jinghai leaders worried that Yu was "acting like a great local official of the Qing dynasty, overstepping his authority as a mere delegate to the national CPPCC," they seemed to be expressing a recognition that this local emperor's constituency was expanding by the day.

The result of Yu's more active resistance throughout 1992 was a sharp intensification of frictions between the village and the state. While Yu and his village remained firmly entrenched with their formidable political resources, disgust for the village on the part of party authorities at all levels was apparently growing. Under those charged circumstances, a man was murdered in the village with at least the complicity, if not the active encouragement, of an investigation team appointed by Yu. Although both sides acted cautiously over the murder, the deep pool of suspicion and resentment between Yu and higher-level party authorities made it seemingly impossible that the case could be handled dispassionately. Each side overreacted to the actions of the other. The result was a dramatic armed standoff between perhaps one thousand paramilitary officers and ten thousand village residents. After that, convinced of a conspiracy to chasten his village, Yu blocked the investigation and bribed officials for inside information. For a Beijing leadership becoming tired of this maverick village leader, it was all the evidence required to arrest, try, and jail him along with several other Daqiu leaders.

Looked at in these terms, the Daqiu story is a case study in the possibilities and the evolution of collective action in rural China. It shows not only the changes in the *issues* and *goals* of collective action as development proceeds, but also in the *means* and *methods* used. The Xinhua news agency asserted after the Daqiu trial that "the criminal activities of Yu Zuomin were not caused by the party's reform policies." But if anything, the opposite was true. The reforms did not sanction crime, of course. But they did facilitate the collective actions of Daqiu. As one Chinese official commented after the incident, "We had people like Yu Zuomin in the past too, but under the planned economy they lacked any economic base or power. They could fight for power, but they could deploy only so many resources. Yu Zuomin, on the other hand, had huge economic power."[13] More important, the same facilitating process is at work across rural China today. According to one party commentator, "The fall of Yu Zuomin is a rarity among peasant entrepreneurs; but the 'Yu Zuomin phenomenon' [*Yu Zuomin xianxiang*] is not at all unusual."[14] Let us conclude with a brief look at the Yu Zuomin phenomenon elsewhere.

For a Chinese Communist Party still reeling from the effects of mass student protests in cities across China in 1989, the insurrection at Daqiu seemed to presage the rise of a dangerous new trend in the countryside. It suggested that in villages, as in the cities, the country's economic reform program was fatally weakening the party's grip on power. "We must not allow 'fortified villages' and 'local tyrants' that do not subject themselves to any authority to emerge again inside the party," the *People's Daily* declared the day after the Daqiu trial.[15]

The party has made several attempts since the Daqiu incident to reinforce its presence at the village level, where it admitted that half of its 750,000 branches were essentially dormant by the mid-1990s. The entire annual party plenum of 1994 was devoted to this issue, and a wide-ranging "rectification" campaign for rural party branches was carried out in the following three years. The party also lighted upon a new model town called Zhangjiagang, in Jiangsu province, which boasted both an upright party branch and a booming economy—the perfect antidote to Daqiu syndrome.[16]

Still, most evidence suggests that the party is waging a losing battle. The development of TVEs and other economic and political changes continue to give peasants more autonomy vis-à-vis the state, pushing the party further and further to the margins of peasant life. Even more, those changes are providing peasants with new means to mount ever more diverse and effective collective actions, which further tip the balance of power in their favor.

The *issues* and *goals* of rural collective action are bound to become more complex as rural China's market economy and China's legal system develop in tandem. Already there are signs that new issues of rural protest are arising, such as environmental degradation and business dealings with state entities.[17] At the same time, the old-hat issues like taxes, land, and cadre misbehavior will continue to expand in scale.

More than anything, however, it is the new *means* and *methods* of collective action—the supply-push factors—that are unsettling the countryside. Among these, economic development may be the most important. Growing incomes furnish the means for groups of peasants to assert their interests with the state. Examples of wealthy villages rising up to defend their interests are now legion.[18] This overflow of economic power into political protest is well known in Beijing. The *People's Daily* in April 1997 named Yu Zuomin as "the best example" of a worrying phenomenon in which "some people are using economic means to build political capital."[19] "Since the 1980s, a class of people has been born which is not directly controlled by the government or the state," it said in another editorial. "The party and the government must make them understand the correct relationship between the individual and the state. We must do everything we can to prevent the recurrence of tragedies like the Yu Zuomin incident."[20] The incident showed Beijing that, far from remaining or becoming docile, peasants who grew rich could instead become more politically assertive. "If peasants are allowed to develop their private interests without control, they will want to become like emperors," one scholar told an official magazine after the incident.[21]

Besides economic resources, rural actions are also being spurred by the emergence of charismatic leaders in villages. Such leaders are gaining power because of their ability to develop the local economy rather than toeing the line from Beijing. And they are a crucial resource for the mounting of collective actions. The doyen of party sociologists in China,

Dang Guoyin, warned in an internal report in 1998 of "a new power class" that was forming in rural areas, which was forming "independent interest groups" that openly challenged central policies.[22] Similarly, the *Southern Rural Daily* said in 1998 that the countryside was "hanging by a thread" as a result of the proliferation of "village chieftains" (*zhuangzhu*), naming Yu Zuomin as one of the best examples.[23]

Examples of *zhuangzhu* are now everywhere. One of the best known was Pei Anjun, "the cement-eating cadre with an iron heart," as he was known during his time as party secretary of Shanxi province's Qiancun village. Pei led the 630-household village to modest wealth by developing factories and making deals in the early 1990s. But he began to anger local officials by ignoring state policies on land transfers and grain procurement and by developing allies among other villages. In early 1996, Pei was finally ousted by the provincial government along with seven of the village's fifteen-member party committee. "Although he had just the minor position of a village cadre, he threw his weight around beyond his status," the provincial party newspaper, *Shanxi Daily,* said in a charge reminiscent of those made against Yu Zuomin.[24]

Another example was Chen Yiner, the party secretary of Qiuer village in Zhejiang province, often referred to as the southern counterpart of Daqiu because of its enormous wealth.[25] Chen was a mirror image of Yu Zuomin: a former commune cadre who had taken the lead in the early 1980s by opening up a metals factory in the village that by the mid-1990s had expanded into a forty-four-factory village conglomerate called the Yinfa Group. Indeed, in many ways Chen was even more of a model rebel than Yu. In addition to being a national model worker, he was named a delegate to the party's fourteenth national congress in 1992, an honor that Yu had tried but failed to achieve. Like Yu, Chen alarmed Beijing by throwing his weight around as his village's wealth and fame grew. His favored way of building political capital was to hand out shares in village companies to local officials. He even built a resort in the United States where he sent political allies on vacations in return for their support. Ironically, Chen happened to be visiting

Daqiu when he got wind of Beijing's decision to purge him in late 1996. After fleeing first to the United States and then to the Philippines, he was arrested and sent back to China in early 1997, where he was jailed for six years on bribery charges.

New forms of collective organization are another resource for the mounting of resistance. Both the village conglomerate and the villager committee—one authoritarian and the other democratic—have proved to be valuable instruments in this regard. Village conglomerates can be a powerful means of action both because they concentrate wealth and power internally and because as corporations they are perfectly suited to developing the kinds of external supports that can further empower action. As one scholar has noted, many village conglomerates "are establishing dominant positions in their localities and regions," even becoming "local empires."[26]

Villager committees, meanwhile, are also providing the kind of rallying point that helps collective action.[27] This is ironic because the committees are far more subject to upper-level control than village conglomerates. But like the conglomerates, they increasingly are led by charismatic leaders with local interests firmly in mind. In a village named Datong in Guangdong province, for example, a local brickmaker named Tan Fuhua defeated a party cadre from the district government in a 1998 election after villagers accused the latter of being arrogant. Tan, who won the election with a 68 percent mandate, promised a government "every bit of which will closely accord with the interests of the people."[28]

Scholars have also pointed to factors like decollectivization, increased migration, weaker rural party structures, and new legal and political rights for peasants as providing new means for action.[29] These multiple factors were brought into startling focus in August 1999, when the leaders of a highly organized peasant group called the Southwestern Yangtze Column of the Anti-Corruption Army of the People's Workers and Peasants were arrested in Sichuan province for subversion.[30] Members of the group, which agitated over the typical issue of cadre corruption, carried identity cards, produced documents with special seals, and worked within a complex hierarchy.

The political opportunity structure for collective action also continues to change in favor of peasants.[31] The media have become more open and willing to report the point of view of protesting peasants. And the legal system has become more amenable to lawsuits against state and party organizations.

Last but not least is the revolutionary, although still unclear, effect of the Internet in providing peasants in China with a new means for collective action. In surveys conducted by the official China Internet Information Center in 1999, just two-tenths of 1 percent of all Internet users in the country—or about 180,000 people that year—described themselves as "peasants." That modest figure, however, did not include rural cadres and rural businessmen, key agents of collective action in the countryside. The vast number of Web sites belonging to village and township governments and to TVEs—including the Four Hens of Daqiu—that have appeared in recent years suggests that these two groups are increasingly making use of the Internet. One can speculate that by facilitating faster communications and information flows, creating constituencies through participatory Internet sites, and widening the knowledge of government regulations, the Internet will have a profound transforming effect on collective action in rural China.

All of this flows naturally into a much wider array of methods, both righteous and unrighteous, for collective action. The Daqiu story and others suggest that peasants increasingly use a mixture of righteous and unrighteous methods to launch their collective actions. One of the best other examples was the campaign by ten thousand peasants in Hunan province's Daolin township in 1998 and 1999 over excessive taxation and official corruption.[32] The very righteous-sounding name of the Daolin protest group was Volunteers for the Publicity of Policies and Regulations. It was aimed at drawing attention to local contraventions of provincial and central government edicts. But that was backed up with open protests, which eventually led to an armed clash with paramilitaries on 8 January 1999. In short, peasants are finding that righteous resistance can offer both support and cover for unrighteous rebellion, that it can be a strategy as well as a reflection of beliefs.

One implication of the wider range of methods available for collective action is that, more and more, it will be concealed from view. The Daolin case, for example, came to light only because of the armed clash. But how many more actions succeed without such an outward display? If a village strongman can march right into the office of the county party secretary and list his demands, we are less likely to see villagers storming that same office bearing placards. The same "action eclipse," if we can call it that, occurs when a village simply refuses to implement unpopular state policies and the state has little choice but to accept the situation. A less resolute Beijing might have simply accepted Yu Zuomin's rebuff of the Tianjin police's search for the four murderers. Instead, it dispatched a PAP team, and the same "invisible" act of resistance became "visible."

Where will all this lead rural China? Toward a broadly more democratic future, or toward warlordism and disorder? Certainly, Beijing prefers to emphasize the latter possibility in order to strengthen the grounds for cracking down on growing political power in the countryside. As the *People's Public Security News* charged in a 1997 article:

> Village tyrants and local ruffians often form gangs, claiming unilateral supremacy, stirring trouble, taking things by force or deceit, bullying men and terrorizing women, endangering the common people, and resisting the government. Some rely on clan forces, enlisting henchmen to control local grassroots political power, controlling township enterprises, and monopolizing market transactions. Such rogues have the most direct and widespread impact on agricultural production and peasant life. . . . Until new management and control forces to suit the market economy have been effectively established, rural disorder will remain quite prominent.[33]

Such fears of warlordism and crime are not entirely misplaced, of course. The Daqiu story itself shows how growing political power in the countryside led to a new kind of village-level authoritarianism and to the sanctioning of crime. However, important democratic principles also emerge, ones that distinguish powerful village leaders like Yu Zuomin from the rural warlords of old, or the criminal gangs of today. Yu and others like him are populists who act in the interests of their villages. That is, they represent them, an important democratic principle and a key departure from the hated warlords and gang bosses. Moreover, the politics of a place like Daqiu was mostly the politics of livelihood and economics, not the politics of power. As in nineteenth-century Japan and medieval Europe, what came to hold sway was an organization and articulation of common demands from a growing class of merchants whose aim was to push back and control the predatory state, not overthrow it.[34] This also is an important foundation of democracy, and a stark difference from warlordism, if not criminality. That is why one can remain cautiously optimistic that the "Yu Zuomin phenomenon" will bring benefits to the country's rural population, and possibly to the country as a whole. As National People's Congress chairman and former state premier Li Peng said unwittingly while inspecting village elections in Fujian province in early 1999: "The work you are doing here is tantamount to laying the cornerstone for China's democracy."[35]

If so, it suggests a renewed agenda of research and reporting on rural China to uncover the changing nature of collective action there. For those exploring this important issue, there will be no better reference point than Daqiu, the onetime richest village in China.

Afterword

Three-story tiled houses, their sloping roof ridges adorned with ceramic figures of mythological animals ... White marble bridges engraved with cranes and clouds ... Children with rosy cheeks ... Fathers and mothers astride moto-scooters ... Happy ... Healthy ... Rich.

Those were the images of Daqiu Village broadcast to the nation by a team of reporters and photographers from the official Xinhua news agency in December 1998 as part of media coverage to mark the twentieth anniversary of China's economic reforms.[1] Daqiu was again prospering as the storm clouds dispersed, the news agency said. Though it had latterly challenged the role of the party and raised a small army against the state, "the most legendary village of the reform period," as the news agency called it, was apparently not so easily airbrushed from the official memory.

Life in Daqiu after the storm of 1993 is a complex tale of continuity and change, a tale of largely undisturbed social and economic endeavors alongside a wrenching political transformation. Simple curiosity is reason enough to recall these events. But there is also a didactic reason—for in many ways the story after the fall reveals the true significance of what had gone before.

In the wake of the trial and jailing of villagers involved in the incident, the Tianjin party committee work group remained in Daqiu for several months. A thorough audit of the village's finances was conducted and remaining legal issues tied up. After the work group withdrew, the village was put under the direct governance of the Jinghai party committee.[2] The county's main task was to remake the village's political system in order to prevent a resurgence of its rebellious ways—to prevent a "flip of the pancake" (*fan laobing*), as the Chinese saying goes.

The single most important change was the elevation of Daqiu from the status of a village (*cun*) to a town (*zhen*) in November 1993.[3] As an administrative village, Daqiu had enjoyed a significant degree of autonomy under China's political system. In party matters, it had borne only a "guiding relationship" (*zhidao guanxi*) from the county. In government affairs, the village had been empowered to elect the head of its own villager committee through direct, popular elections. It had also been autonomous in matters like public security, education, and family planning. All that changed when it became a town. In party matters, the county now exercised a "leading relationship" (*lingdao guanxi*) over Daqiu. The leaders of the new Daqiu town government, meanwhile, were chosen by a people's congress that was appointed by the county. The county government also gained a supervisory role over the town's administration. In short, Daqiu became a ward of the county.

To no one's surprise, the post-1993 Daqiu leadership was stacked with Jinghai county loyalists. Four of the nine members of the first party committee chosen in 1994 were from the Jinghai party committee itself, including the new party secretary, Tao Runli.[4] The first town head, meanwhile, "elected" by the town congress in July 1994, was Wang Qingwu, concurrently a deputy county governor. Twenty-four officials were seconded from the county, the city, and the central government to staff the ruling apparatus.[5] Mistress Shi's position as head of general affairs was assumed by a retired Jinghai official. As Xinhua put it at the time, "Daqiu people are marching forward with a new posture in the direction pointed by the party."[6]

The new town government set up a raft of new departments to answer to their counterparts in the county. In law enforcement, these included a court, a prosecutor's office, and a five-hundred-officer police station. If another murder occurred in the village, a Tianjin newspaper noted, "the police can organize quickly and no criminals will escape."[7]

Alongside the establishment of new structures was the dissolution of the village conglomerate, Daqiu Village Enterprise Group Corporation. This of course was expected: the conglomerate had been the instrument of Yu Zuomin's rule and the edifice of Daqiu's rebellion. From now on, there would be only one power center in Daqiu: the party committee and its affiliated town government. Beijing had clearly noted the impact of village conglomerates on political resistance. "Empty public ownership easily turned into village boss ownership," the *People's Daily* commented in 1997.[8]

On the ground, a rigorous indoctrination campaign was launched to disabuse the village of its maverick mentality. For more than a year after the purge, staff of the Four Hens attended daily lectures focusing on "party policies and ideological education." These were supplemented by legal seminars, "so that the masses know the law, understand the law, obey the law, and handle matters according to law."[9] Daqiu, of all places, was suddenly known for "enthusiastically subscribing to the *People's Daily*."[10] The Four Hens also established party branches for the first time and accepted party secretaries appointed by the county. As Jinhai Group chairman Zhang Yanjun told the *People's Daily*, "We have to learn from this bloody lesson, haul in our tails, and act more like humans."[11]

Another fascinating, if little-reported, aspect of the political clampdown was the blurring of the former rigid distinction between natives and migrants in Daqiu. After the purge, migrants were for the first time registered as temporary residents, and many more than before were allowed to become permanent residents, gaining access to education and health care. As in troublesome ethnic areas like Tibet and Xinjiang, Beijing's policy in Daqiu was apparently to encourage an inflow of migrants in order to dilute its indigenous sense of identity. The *People's Daily* pointedly noted in 1995 that per capita income "for the town's 30,000 residents, just 5,000 of whom are locals," was between Rmb 2,000 and Rmb 3,000, just a tenth of the previously reported figures.[12] By including migrants as residents, Daqiu was no longer ten or twenty times richer than its rural cousins. Even if it had remained a village, this change would have cost it its title as the richest village in China.[13] In the event, Daqiu was now nothing more than a modestly prosperous town marching in lockstep with the party.

With the county in firm control, "state socialism seemed to have returned in full force" to Daqiu.[14] Certainly, Daqiu's political direction would never again be in doubt. But in other respects, what the village lost in political freedom after 1993 it more than gained in administrative and economic freedom. For a start, the family-based networks that had long formed the basis of the village's leadership actually seemed to strengthen. Virtually all of the village's top executives not implicated in the murder were left in place. Most remarkable was the survival of the founders of the Four Hens: Liu Wanquan, Yu Zuoyao, Zhao Shuzhong, and Zhang Yanjun. Their role in guiding the village's economic affairs was apparently just too important to revoke. Other members of the core families—in particular those of Yu Zuomin, Mr. Do-It-All Liu Wanquan, and patriarch Zhang Yupu—also continued to percolate up into senior positions in the companies.[15] As one newspaper assured its readers, "The sky has not fallen without village boss Yu Zuomin. The people of Daqiu are not suffering."[16]

The powers of the Four Hens were also enhanced. For one, they exacted from the town government the right to continue operating autonomously in return for assuming the Rmb 300 million debt left over by the defunct Huada Group, the nova of the village's rebellion.[17] For all its political power, the new town government had few economic resources and was forced to accept the terms. In addition, since the village conglomerate had run schools, hospitals, elderly homes, and other welfare services, its abolition left a welfare lacuna; these responsibilities were now taken over by the Four Hens, leaving the town government with responsibility for only utilities, public security, and public finances. The village's residential areas were carved up into four "street administrative districts" (*jiedao guanli qu*), one for each of the Four Hens to supervise and keep safe.[18] Houses built and owned by the village were sold off to their tenants, while new ones were individually financed and owned. Wanquan Group built a four-story primary school that was bigger than most offices in the village.[19]

In short, the Four Hens largely took over the functions of government from the town after 1993. While Daqiu's political fealty was no longer in question, the party's role in the day-to-day life and administration of the village continued to recede. Yu Zuomin's vision lived on.

Despite the ignominy of the 1993 purge, Beijing continued to uphold Daqiu as an "advanced model" for economic reforms, warning on one occasion that "discriminating against and attacking" the village because of its political indiscretion "will not be tolerated."[20] There was of course an overriding political reason for retaining Daqiu as a model: it was important to show that the village's wealth had been mainly the result of sagacious party policies rather than the rule of one man. Indeed, the party wanted to demonstrate that Daqiu's wealth was burgeoning now that it was a star pupil of party policies. There was also the unavoidable fact that Daqiu continued to be an economic powerhouse, paying Rmb 530 million in state taxes between 1993 and 1999. Too many jobs were at stake to allow its good name to suffer for long.

The renewed official promotion of Daqiu echoed from the top down. Party general secretary Jiang Zemin detoured to Daqiu when he made an inspection tour of Tianjin in 1998, exactly ten years after his disgraced predecessor, Zhao Ziyang.[21] Authorities in Tianjin also continued to publicize Daqiu, including it as one of four stops on the city's standard tour of rural areas for visiting cadres as of 1998.[22] The Tianjin Tobacco Company even launched a "Daqiu Village" brand cigarette that year, a tribute to the village's enduring place in peasant minds as a symbol of rural wealth.[23] When a Tianjin company tried to register and sell the name "Daqiu Village" as a trademark in early 2000, the opening price was set at Rmb 10 million.[24] As the *People's Daily* chirped: "The wheels of Daqiu's reform continue to roll forward. Following the storm, the spirit of the people of Daqiu is even more excited, no less mighty than in the past."[25]

The maintenance of Daqiu's model status led to some tangible economic benefits to be sure. These included funding for infrastructure as part of a model town program launched by the Tianjin municipality and the central government, and research grants for several steel factories.[26] The benefits were ironic because they were exactly the kind of state support that Daqiu had long spurned, an attitude that had set it apart from sham model villages like Dazhai. Still, the combined impact of the positive propaganda and the tangible rewards appeared to be limited. Rather, Daqiu's strong economic performance after 1993 appears to owe to many of the same factors that drove it to prosperity in the first place. "Daqiu's recovery," London's *Guardian* newspaper wrote when the village held an investment fair in Hong Kong in 1995, "is the latest twist of a saga that illustrates the momentum of policies based on money-making rather than ideology. . . . Maoist models sprang from ideology. They crumbled as soon as the political wind shifted. Money, as Daqiu knows, provides far sturdier foundations."[27]

By the end of 1993 several business deals that had been suspended during the uprising and subsequent trial were recommenced.[28] In an effort to wean the village off steel products (which still accounted for 80 percent of output), Brother Yu launched a plan called the "second pioneering effort" (*dierci chuangye*), a sort of paradigm shift in which the emphasis would be placed on a more diverse and technologically ad-

TABLE 4   RANKINGS OF DAQIU COMPANIES
AMONG CHINA'S TVES, 1996

	Output	Gross Profits
Yaoshun Group	2	11
Jinmei Group	7	5
Jinhai Group	15	9
Wanquan Group	28	33

SOURCE: *Zhongguo xiangzhen qiye nianjian 1997* (China TVE yearbook 1997) (Beijing: Nongye chubanshe [Agricultural Press], 1997), 512, 520.

vanced industrial base.[29] To emphasize quality over quantity, Boss Yu's initial target of Rmb 50 billion in total output by 2000 was scaled back to Rmb 40 billion. Although the target was not reached, the Four Hens continued to hold their own as some of the biggest TVEs in China (table 4).

Daqiu's continued prosperity despite its fall from grace probably reflects three main factors. One, as mentioned, is the continuation of the policies that allowed it to get rich in the first place. Indeed, official attitudes toward TVEs actually became more favorable in 1997 when they were put on par with state-owned industry as part of a newly defined "publicly owned" (*gongyou*) sector.[30] The second potential reason relates to the entrepreneurial diversity that the abolition of the village conglomerate facilitated. Boss Yu had played a crucial role in the village's early development, but by the time he and his fellow leaders were purged, the village economy may have outgrown the one-man cadre-entrepreneur model. The Four Hens were now virtual village conglomerates unto themselves and required more diverse talents in order to flourish. "For many years, Daqiu was run like a family," Xinhua commented plausibly in 1998. "While this system of rule by one man's diktat helped unite people's strength and attitudes at the beginning, . . . it increasingly constrained the village's advance as the scale of enterprises grew and markets became more complex."[31]

The third important reason for the ongoing prosperity of Daqiu relates to the changing ownership of rural industry in China by the late

1990s. About the time that Daqiu's leaders were being thrown in jail, a major transformation was sweeping rural China, in which TVEs were privatized in all but name.[32] The introduction of the shareholding system (*gufen zhidu*) went in different directions in different parts of rural China. Indeed, within individual villages like Daqiu it could have several meanings. But whatever the details of each scheme, they generally had the effect of putting ownership into private hands, while at the same time improving the efficiency of TVEs.

As we saw, Daqiu companies had begun using the shareholding system in the early 1990s. The abolition of the village conglomerate after 1993 and the disappearance of the strict collectivist spirit that had been so carefully nurtured by Boss Yu provided an added impetus for experiments with shareholding. Dozens of new companies were created, expanding the Four Hens into a complex web of over one hundred limited-liability companies and close to four hundred factories.[33] Wanquan Group was considerably downsized when the Daqiu Steel Rolling Mill, its key enterprise and the cradle of the village's industrial development, was spun off entirely into a separate company in 1996.[34] All of these new companies then became the fodder for shareholding experiments, with the long-term target being for individual shares (*geren gufen*) to represent 70 percent of the village's entire corporate assets. Scholars Lin Nan and Chen Chih-Jou call the ownership changes "no less dramatic than the initial rise" of Daqiu.[35]

The official excuse for the shareholding experiments in Daqiu were both political and economic. Politically, it was seen as part of the wider attempt to dilute ownership to prevent the rise of another village conglomerate. In economic terms, the efficiency gains from shareholding were believed to hold the key to the "second pioneering effort" that would vault Daqiu from primitive smokestacks to advanced processing. Still, evidence gathered by Lin Nan and colleagues suggests another motivation behind the changes: greed. For not only did this process turn into a de facto privatization of the village's assets, but the bulk of the control over those assets ended up in the hands of the top company executives. Managers of enterprises, who usually remained village party cadres, transferred ownership of both the collective shares (*jiti gufen*) and many of the individual shares (*geren gufen*) into their own hands. At Yaoshun Group, for example, shareholding had turned the group into the virtual fiefdom of the two Yu cousins by the late 1990s. They not only controlled the 70 percent of shares owned by the collective (which might normally have been controlled by the town or county) but also a large part of the remainder, which had been distributed as "occupation shares" (*gangwei gu*) to top managers. At Jinmei Group, this quiet privatization and elite asset grab went even further. A total of fifteen separate companies were set up, and managers and executives in the group claimed between a half and three-quarters of the shares in each. While Yaoshun elites at least maintained the fig leaf of socialism by continuing to call most shares "collective," those in Jinmei argued that the more shares held by individuals, the better. The result was that by the end of 1997 collective shares represented just 27 percent of the ownership in the group.[36] As Lin and Chen comment, "The shareholding system has become one means by which actors, the local elites, have wrested the control of collective assets from the public sector."[37]

Whatever the economic implications, the impression gained from the ownership changes was that individual greed had finally supplanted the collective spirit that Yu Zuomin had nurtured. To be sure, Yu had enriched himself as head of the former village conglomerate; but in many respects his all-powerful presence also kept greed in check in the absence of any properly regulated asset ownership system. With his departure, the character of Daqiu changed fundamentally. Its collective sense of identity and purpose was now virtually gone. In its place was a hollow town government concerned mainly with political correctness and four rapacious hens pecking their way through the village's wealth. As Lin and Chen wrote:

When Yu was in charge, he was a ruthless entrepreneur but also a powerful cadre. . . . Yu's system was to allow some enterprises and individuals to become rich fast, and yet maintain and enhance the collective level of well-being. The village retained ultimate control of the assets of the enterprises. After becoming a town, the local government for all intents and purposes has become a powerless resourceless entity. It does not control the enterprises, it does not manage the residents and neighbourhoods, and it does not even control any land. . . . As a result, the real economic, political and administrative resources were clearly shifted from the town to the Big Four Groups.[38]

With the demise of Daqiu's collective identity, it follows that the village's political resistance has evaporated. While its economic resources remain plentiful, Daqiu now lacks a charismatic figure like Yu Zuomin to use those resources for political struggle. Only in the sense that the Four Hens have wrested economic and administrative power from the state can we say that Daqiu has continued to be a rebellious model village. But in stark contrast to the ideological and social battles which Yu fought, the battles now are decidedly mundane and pecuniary. The cadre-executives who run the Four Hens retain their party roles now almost exclusively for the purpose of minimizing political interference in their operations. Most would no doubt be happy to shuffle off those roles if the threat of such interference dissipated.

Still, there may be a bright side to all this. Sooner or later, the last shreds of collectivism were bound to fall from rural China. That process may be proceeding in a distasteful fashion in places like Daqiu. But the transition itself may be salutary insofar as it enhances individual freedoms by further attenuating the state's role in economic affairs. Daqiu may be leading this next great transformation as rural China marches into the post-Communist era. The story of this remarkable village is far from over.

For years after he began serving his twenty-year prison term in 1993, Yu Zuomin labored through the daily rituals of life behind bars. But the confines of a Tianjin prison were hard on this free-ranging peasant used to rural life and the privileges of power. All the more so because, unlike jailed political dissidents in China, who often commanded the grudging respect of their captors and with it some measure of compassion, Yu was viewed as a despicable criminal who should suffer his condign punishment. His customary foods were denied him and visitors were kept to a minimum. All that took a heavy toll. Yu's health deteriorated rapidly as he was beset by bronchial conditions caused by chain-smoking and by stomach ulcers that prevented him from eating for days at a time.[39]

By early 1999, Yu had also developed a heart condition that could not be treated from prison. At the request of his erstwhile defense lawyer, Wang Yaoting, he was moved to the Tianhe Hospital in southern Tianjin for treatment.[40] Although official media commentators had argued in 1993 that Yu should never be granted parole given the odious nature of his crimes, time had moderated that vengeance, and the ravaged old man was put in the best wing of the Tianhe Hospital, reserved for high-level cadres, as part of a medical parole deal.

Life was slipping away from Yu Zuomin, and he seemed to know it. By day, he would sit in a trance watching events unfold on the streets below his hospital window. By night, he would lie naked on his bed in typical peasant fashion, as if recalling the comfortable flue-heated *kang* brick platforms of village life. The train of events that had brought him to this point must have passed repeatedly through his mind. Perhaps he remained defiant at heart, but his demeanor suggested that he now viewed that long-ago day in 1977 when he had promised to make his restless village rich as the opening act of a long folly.

Yu's health did not improve one bit in the Tianhe Hospital. Friends and family visited more often, sensing that the end was nigh. In the small hours of Sunday, 3 October 1999, hospital staff detected abnormal signals coming from his bedside monitors. When they reached his room, he lay limp in bed, dead at age seventy. The official word was that Yu had succumbed to a heart attack. But other reports spoke of a suicide by drug overdose—a possibility that cannot be discounted. Yu was known to be deeply depressed, and he had made an earlier attempt on his life after being arrested. Whatever the truth, the six-year incarceration had certainly sped his demise. Like Uncle Chen before him, Yu Zuomin died a sad and broken man.

News of the death spread quickly to Daqiu. But there, the reaction was muted. The memory of Boss Yu and his cronies was by now long out of official favor in the village, and county officials banned all memorial activities to ensure that it was not revived. Yu's ashes were returned to the village and placed on a makeshift shrine in a simple brick house. Villagers could only sigh in dismay. "We'll miss the old guy. He did a lot for our village," said one company official.[41]

As of this writing, many of those jailed in 1993 have returned to the village and been reintegrated into daily life with little fuss. Eternal China was reinstated as a vice president of Wanquan Group in 1997, shortly before his father, Mr. Do-it-all, Liu Wanquan, retired. Ma Deshui, a brother of model farmer Ma Deliang, now heads the Wanquan Group's copper subsidiary. Only those closest to Yu, like Mistress Shi and security chief Zhou Kewen, have disappeared from sight. The same fate is no doubt in store for Little Yu, Yu's eldest son, when he regains his freedom in 2003.

Yu Zuomin was ultimately a flawed character. His achievement was to have created a model for rural industrial wealth in the most unlikely place. As an individual, he was hardworking and principled. His undoing, however, was that as a leader, he retained a strong sense of authoritarianism and little tolerance for dissent even as he fought against the party's own tyranny and intolerance.

The story of Yu Zuomin and Daqiu Village is now indelibly marked on the mind of the Chinese Communist Party as the embodiment of rural economic power leading to political incorrectness and re-bellion. No other place has brought so clearly into focus the political implications of the forces unleashed in the Chinese countryside by the country's economic reform program. Daqiu is no longer China's rich-est village. But its memory lives on.

APPENDIX

The tables contained in this appendix were compiled from a variety of sources. The main ones include Jinghai annals; TVE Yearbook; Tianjin annals; company reports; CYD series; TKP series and Lin Nan. In many cases multiple figures have been published for the same variable. This may be due to rounding, revisions or even the provision of different figures by different departments. The ones given here represent the author's best guess about which is the most reliable.

TABLE A-1   VILLAGE OUTPUT, PROFITS,
AND TAXES (IN MILLIONS OF RMB)

Year	Output	Net Profits	Taxes Paid
1978	1.4	0.7	0.2
1979	2.3	0.9	0.1
1980	4.1	1.7	0.2
1981	8.8	1.2	0.4
1982	12	3.4	0.8
1983	30	6.0	1.0
1984	46	8.7	1.6
1985	79	17.4	2.8
1986	110	25.0	7.4
1987	203	42	10
1988	403	75*	NA
1989	603	100*	NA
1990	662	82	21
1991	1,800	100	35
1992	4,500	510	100
1993	5,600	420	70
1994	7,100	560*	NA
1995	9,200	650*	NA
1996	10,500	750*	NA
1997	13,130	880*	NA

* Figure includes taxes.

TABLE A-2   NATIVE POPULATION
AND MIGRANT LABOR FORCE

Year	Native Population	Migrant Labor Force
1933	1,156	0
1949	1,650	0
1963	1,929	0
1979	2,828	0
1989	3,886	5,000
1990	4,035	7,000
1991	4,400	15,000
1994	4,500	22,000
1996	5,000	25,000
1997	6,000	20,000

TABLE A-3   INCOME PER CAPITA (IN RMB)

Year	Income
1977	121
1978	167
1983	1,266
1984	4,100
1986	10,000
1989	21,800
1990	19,754
1991	26,700
1992	23,240

TABLE A-4   GROWTH OF ENTERPRISES

Year	Number of Enterprises	Foreign Joint Ventures
1977	1	0
1979	5	0
1987	107	NA
1989	117	NA
1990	195	21
1991	226	33
1992	262	33
1993	280	59
1994	258	34
1995	335	40
1997	360	NA

TABLE A-5   COMPANY DEVELOPMENT

1978   Daqiu Village Cold-Rolled Steel Strip Factory (1)

1979   Daqiu Village Pipes Factory (2)

1980   Daqiu Village General Printing Plant (3)

1982   Jinhai Electrical Equipment Factory (4)

1983   Daqiu Village Agriculture, Industry, and Commerce United Co.
       Daqiu Village Cold-Rolled Steel Strip General Factory (1)
       Daqiu Village Pipes General Factory (2)
       Daqiu Village General Printing Plant (3)
       Daqiu Village Electrical Equipment Factory (4)

1986   Daqiu Village Agriculture, Industry, and Commerce United Co.
       Daqiu Village Number One General Factory (1)
       Daqiu Village Industrial Company (2)
       Daqiu Village Number Three General Factory (3)
       Jinhai Electrical Equipment General Factory (4)

1988   Daqiu Village Agriculture, Industry, and Commerce United Co.
       Wanquan Industrial Group (1)
       Daqiu Village Industrial Co. (2)
       Jinmei Industrial Co. (3)
       Jinhai Industrial Co. (4)

1992   Daqiu Village Enterprise Group Corp.
       Wanquan Group (1)
       Yaoshun Group (2)
       Jinmei Group (3)
       Jinhai Group (4)
       Huada Group (5)

Daiqiu's four original companies, and its village holding company, went through several name changes to reflect their evolving business. The companies are numbered to help readers track their changing names.

NOTES

PROLOGUE

1. The name of the village in Chinese is *Daqiuzhuang,* or Daqiu Village. Although *zhuang,* meaning village, is part of the name, like town in Jamestown, for convenience I use simply Daqiu in this narrative. In the administrative terms of China's political system, Daqiu was a *cun,* also meaning village, so the complete formal name was *Daqiuzhuang cun,* or Daqiu Village village.

2. Xu Rujin and Zhang Sutang, "Guofa bu rong: Yu Zuomin fanzui jishi" (A case that the national law will not tolerate: an account of the crimes of Yu Zuomin), *Renmin ribao haiwai ban* (People's Daily overseas edition), 28 Aug. 1993.

3. I prefer this term to the more neutral "farmer" as the best translation of the Chinese word *nongmin,* since, as others have noted, despite its perjorative sense it best captures the realities of social and political discrimination faced by rural residents in both imperial and Communist China.

4. Little has been written about the village in scholarly publications or books. The one exception is the works by Lin Nan of Duke University (see references). Several general books on China have included brief accounts of the village, including: James Miles, *China in Disarray: The Legacy of Tiananmen*

(Ann Arbor: University of Michigan Press, 1996), 304–6; Nicholas Kristof and Sheryl WuDunn, *China Wakes: The Struggle for the Soul of a Rising Power* (New York: Vintage Books, 1995), 110–13; and Bruce Gilley, *Tiger on the Brink: Jiang Zemin and China's New Elite* (Berkeley: University of California Press, 1998), 205–8, 272–73.

5. Han Yi, "Fengjian sixiang yingxiang shi xiangzhen qiye fazhande jiban" (The effects of feudal thinking are a yoke on the development of township and village enterprises), *Dongfang luntan* (Eastern forum) (Qingdao shiwei [Qingdao party committee]), no. 3 (1993): 56–58.

ONE. YANZHAO ELEGY

1. Details on village history are from Jinghai xianzhi bianxiu weiyuanhui (Jinghai county annals editorial committee), *Jinghai xianzhi* (Jinghai county annals) (Tianjin: Tianjin shehui kexue yuan [Tianjian Academy of Social Sciences], 1995) [hereafter cited as Jinghai annals], "Daqiuzhuang," chap. 24, 813–38; and from Jiang Zilong, "Yanzhao beige" (Yanzhao elegy), *Renmin wenxue* (People's literature) 7, no. 298 (1984): 5–55 [hereafter cited as "Yanzhao Elegy"].

2. Jinghai annals, 125.

3. Fang Ling. "'Zhongguo diyi cun' Daqiuzhuang jianwen" (Sights and sounds of "China's richest village" Daqiuzhuang) (7-part series), *Dagong bao* (*Ta kung pao*), 11–17 Nov. 1992, pt. 1 [hereafter cited as *TKP* series].

4. *TKP* series, pt. 5.

5. Various dates, raging from 1958 to 1974, are given for Yu's promotion to party secretary. I believe 1964 is correct.

6. Sun Qitai and Xiong Zhiyong, *Dazhai hongqide shengqi yu zhuiluo* (The rise and fall of the red flag of Dazhai) (Zhengzhou: Henan renmin chubanshe [Henan People's Publishing House], 1994), 138.

7. *TKP* series, pt. 6.

8. Sun and Xiong, *Dazhai hongqi*. See also Wu Si, *Chen Yonggui fuchen lu* (The Rise and Fall of Chen Yonggui) (Hong Kong: Tiandi tushu [Cosmos Books], 1993); Tan Chengjian, *Dazhai: Zhongguo mingcun jishi* (Dazhai: The true story of China's famous village) (Zhengzhou: Zhongyuan nongmin chubanshe [Zhongyuan Peasant Press], 1998).

9. In Chinese, it is called Xiaojinzhuang or Xiaojin Village.

10. Yu Zuomin, "Shinian gaige, shinian ju bian" (Ten years of reform, ten years of great change), *Renmin ribao* (People's daily), 13 Jan. 1989, 5 [hereafter cited as *PD*]; *TKP* series, pt. 6.

11. On peasant versus official memories of rural China, see Ralph Thaxton, *Salt of the Earth: The Political Origins of Peasant Protest and Communist Revolution in China* (Berkeley: University of California Press, 1997), xiii–xv.

12. Yu Hongfeng, *Huihuangzhongde yinying: Zhongguo "shou fu cun" Daqiuzhuang jiemi* (The shadow amid splendor: Revealing the secret of China's "first rich village" Daqiuzhuang) (Beijing: Jingguan jiaoyu chubanshe [Police Officer Education Press], 1993), 170.

13. *TKP* series, pt. 1.

14. "Yanzhao Elegy," 11.

15. In Chinese, *qiong ze si bian*.

16. See, for example, William Hinton, *Shenfan: The Continuing Revolution in a Chinese Village* (New York: Vintage Books, 1984), 697–99.

17. David Zweig, *Freeing China's Farmers: Rural Restructuring in the Reform Era* (Armonk, N.Y.: M.E. Sharpe, 1997), 254–59.

18. Cited in Dali L. Yang, *Calamity and Reform in China: State, Rural Society, and Institutional Change since the Great Leap Famine* (Stanford: Stanford University Press, 1996), table 35, 214.

19. Ibid.

20. *TKP* series, pt. 7.

21. "Yu Zuomin xiao da 15 wen" (Yu Zuomin happily answers 15 questions), *Zhongguo xiangzhen qiye bao* (China township and village enterprise news) [hereafter cited as *TVE News*], 14 Oct. 1992 (pt. 2) [hereafter cited as "15 Questions"].

22. "Yanzhao Elegy," 7, 15–16. Other details about the 1977 meeting from "Daqiu," Jinghai annals, 821–22.

23. *TKP* series, pts. 1 and 5.

24. Details from "15 Questions," 12 Oct. 1992 (pt. 1); Wu Wei and Wang Ke, "Daqiuzhuang de laoshao 'zhuangzhu'" (The old and young leaders of Daqiuzhuang), *Zhonghua ernu* (Sons and daughters of China) 1 (1993): 45–47; *TKP* series, pt. 1; and "Yanzhao Elegy," 11–16.

25. See Jean C. Oi, *State and Peasant in Contemporary China: The Political Economy of Village Government* (Berkeley: University of California Press, 1989), chap. 9.

26. *TVE News*, 9 Sept. 1987, 1.

27. Yu Hongfeng, *Huihuangzhongde yinying,* 107.

28. Yu Zuomin, *Zongjinglide baogao, 1988* (President's report, 1988), cited in Lin Nan, "Local Market Socialism: Local Corporatism in Action in Rural China," *Theory and Society* 24 (1995): 315.

29. "Daqiu," Jinghai annals, 823.

30. Qiu Yongsheng, Xia Lin, and Du Jichang, "Daqiuzhuang xunli" (Daqiu-zhuang pilgrimage), *Guangming ribao* (Guangming daily), 10 June 1992.

31. Wu Wei and Wang Ke, "Daqiuzhuang de laoshao," 48.

32. Zhang Yuankui and Xu Youmei, "Dui 'Nonggongshang yitihua' de zhiyi" (Some doubts about the merger of agriculture, industry, and commerce), *Jianghan luntan* (Jiang Han forum), no. 2 (1981): 23–27.

33. "15 Questions," pt. 1.

34. Ma Licheng and Ling Zhijun, *Jiaofeng: Dangdai Zhongguo sanci sixiang jiefang shilu* (Crossed swords: Contemporary China's three thought liberations) (Beijing: Jinri Zhongguo chubanshe [Today's China Publishing], 1998), 144.

35. *TKP* series, pt. 5.

36. Zhang Yanjun, "Chuangxin bi zai jianjie" (The pressure is on to start anew), *PD,* 4 Aug. 1997, 2.

37. In Chinese, "Ren pa chu ming, zhu pa zhuang."

38. "Yanzhao Elegy," 42.

39. Daniel Kelliher, *Peasant Power in China: The Era of Rural Reform, 1979–1989* (New Haven: Yale University Press, 1992), 203.

40. "Yanzhao Elegy," 39.

41. On the incentives dispute, see "15 Questions," pt. 1; Yu Hongfeng, *Huihuangzhongde yinying,* 197; and "Yanzhao Elegy," 51.

42. "15 Questions," pt. 1; Yu Hongfeng, *Huihuangzhongde yinying,* 197.

43. On Li Bingkai, see *Jingji wanbao* (Economic evening news, Nanchang), 9 May 1993, *xingqi wenhui* (weekly journal), 1.

44. "Yanzhao Elegy," 22.

45. Ibid., 46, 49.

46. Ibid., 47.

47. Described in "15 Questions," pt. 1; *TKP* series, pt. 7; "Yanzhao Elegy," 47ff.

48. "Yanzhao Elegy," 46.

49. "15 Questions," pt. 1.

50. *Jingji wanbao*, 9 May 1993, *xingqi wenhui* (weekly journal), 1.

51. "Yanzhao Elegy," 52.

52. Ibid, 51.

53. "15 Questions," pt. 1.

54. Liu Linshan and Gao Xiufeng, "Shoushenzhongde Yu Zuomin" (Yu Zuomin under arrest), *Fazhi yu xinwen* (Law and news), 15 Nov. 1993, 11.

55. *TKP* series, pt. 7.

56. Ibid., pt. 5.

57. Interview with author by telephone from Tianjin, 14 Apr. 1998.

58. "Yanzhao Elegy," 32.

59. Tianjin shi difangzhi bianxiu weiyuanhui (Tianjin local annals editorial committee), "Daqiuzhuang," in *Chengxiang jianshe zhi* (City and town development) (Tianjin: Tianjin shehui kexueyuan chubanshe [Tianjin Academy of Social Sciences Press], 1996), 1277. Oi (*State and Peasant,* 218) describes a "relatively rich village" in northeastern Liaoning province where average income was Rmb 1,200 in 1985. My guess is that many villages were quietly prospering in the early 1980s, but they kept their success a secret given the memories of persecution of perceived capitalists in the country's recent past.

60. "Yanzhao Elegy," 31.

61. Ibid., 47.

62. Interview with author by telephone from Tianjin, 14 Apr. 1998.

63. "Yanzhao Elegy," 5.

64. Yu Hongfeng, *Huihuangzhongde yinying,* 168.

65. Associated Press, 23 Feb. 1985.

TWO. FOUR HENS AND A SLOGAN

1. Cited in Kate Xiao Zhou, *How the Farmers Changed China: Power of the People* (Boulder, Colo.: Westview Press, 1996), 106.

2. On this issue see Jean Oi, *Rural China Takes Off: The Institutional Foundations of Economic Reform* (Berkeley: University of California Press, 1999), 18–27.

3. See ibid., 27–47.

4. See Zhou, *How the Farmers Changed China,* 118.

5. On the symbiotic relationship between rural and state firms, see Pei Xiaolin, "Rural Industry: Institutional Aspects of China's Economic Transformation," in *Village Inc.: Chinese Rural Society in the 1990s,* ed. Flemming

Christiansen and Zhang Junzuo (Honolulu: University of Hawaii Press, 1998), 83–102.

6. Kelliher, *Peasant Power in China,* 212.

7. Cited in Zhou, *How the Farmers Changed China,* 106.

8. *PD,* 13 Jan. 1986, 5.

9. In Chinese, Daqiu Nonggongshang Lianhe Gongsi.

10. See Oi, *Rural China Takes Off,* chap. 4.

11. See the example of Fengjia village, Shandong province, described by Thomas Gold in "Still on the Collective Road: Limited Reform in a North China Village," in *Chinese Economic Policy,* ed. Bruce Reynolds (New York, Paragon House, 1988), chap. 2, 41–65.

12. Lin Nan, "Local Market Socialism," 327.

13. Cited ibid., 323.

14. Ibid., 317–18.

15. Details of the four companies are from "Daqiu," Jinghai annals, 823–31; and from company brochures distributed at a Daqiu press conference in Hong Kong in 1995.

16. *TKP* series, pt. 5.

17. Oi, *Rural China Takes Off,* fig. 6, 64.

18. Company figures from "Daqiu," Jinghai annals, 823–31; total figure from Yu Hongfeng, *Huihuangzhongde yinying,* 117.

19. *TVE News,* 16 Oct. 1987, 4.

20. Lin Nan, "Local Market Socialism," 320.

21. In Chinese: *Meiyou bu zheng zhi feng, jiu meiyou xiangzhen qiye.* Reported to this author by a Shandong province rural cadre, 1992.

22. "Yu Zuomin an xuanpan zhi hou" (After the verdict in the Yu Zuomin case), *Zhongguo nongmin* (China Peasant), Oct.–Nov. 1993, 6–9.

23. Liu Yuren, "Xian lijie zhengcede renmen: Yu Zuomin" (Those who understand the policies first: Yu Zuomin), in *Zhongguo xiangzhen qiye chenggong zhi lu* (The successful road of China's township enterprises) (Beijing: Zhongguo jianshe chubanshe [Construction Press], 1988), 41.

24. Interview in Daqiu, June 1992.

25. Cited in Zhou, *How the Farmers Changed China,* table 5.1, 112.

26. Yu Zuomin, "Shi nian gaige, shi nian ju bian" (Ten years of reform, ten years of great changes), *PD,* 13 Jan. 1989, 5.

27. Zhang Jianwei, "Zhongguo diyi cun jiemi" (Revealing the secrets of China's richest village) (7-part series), *Zhongguo qingnian bao* (China youth daily), 15–22 Jan. 1993, pt. 7 [hereafter cited as *CYD* series].

28. Liu Caiwen, "Daqiuzhuang yu Xiaoqiuzhuang" (Daqiuzhuang and Xiaoqiuzhuang), *Zhongguo huashang bao* (China business times), 5 July 1995, 2.

29. Yu Zuomin, "Wo kandaode riben" (The Japan I saw), *Xin guancha* (New observer) 10 (25 May 1985): 10.

30. Ibid.

31. These improvements excluded the growing numbers of migrant workers, who soon outnumbered the locals by four to one and manned the factories and fields. They lived in cramped bunkhouses and paid to see doctors. Yu claimed they were treated the same as locals in *TKP* series, pt. 3.

32. "Yanzhao Elegy," 34.

33. *CYD* series, pt. 6.

34. Quoted in both "Yanzhao Elegy," 41, and *TKP* series, pt. 7.

35. Yu Hongfeng, *Huihuangzhongde yinying*, 124.

36. "Yanzhao Elegy," 34.

37. *CYD* series, pt. 6.

38. In Chinese: "Tai tou xiang qian [future] kan. Di tou xiang qian [money] kan. Zhi you xiang qian [money] kan, cai neng xiang qian [future] kan."

39. *CYD* series, pt. 3.

40. "Yanzhao Elegy," 55. Yu's "money slogan" probably originated from one of his bitter exchanges with a cadre from Jinghai county in the early 1980s. The cadre had lectured Yu that his village should "concentrate on the future, not just on money." Yu had riposted with the slogan, and writer Jiang Zilong made sure to include it in "Yanzhao Elegy."

41. Details and quotations on the money slogan incident from: "15 Questions," pt. 1; *CYD* series, pt. 3; *TKP* series, pt. 5.

42. "15 Questions," pt. 1.

43. *Xueshu jiaoliu* (Academic Exchange), no. 2 (1987): 12–15.

44. Yu Hongfeng, *Huihuangzhongde yinying*, 171.

45. *TKP* series, pt. 5.

46. Details from the exchange with Bo Yibo in *TKP* series, pt. 5; *CYD* series, pt. 3; "15 Questions," pt. 1.

47. Yu Hongfeng, *Huihuangzhongde yinying*, 185.

48. *China Daily*, 14 Sept. 1987, 4.

49. *TVE News*, 14 Sept. 1987, 1; Xinhua (New China News Agency), 6 Sept. 1987.

50. *TVE News*, 23 Sept. 1987, 3.

51. *TVE News*, 11 Sept. 1987, 1.

52. Xinhua, 4 Apr. 1988.

53. *Tianjin ribao* (Tianjin daily), 22 May 1988, 1.

54. Tianjin shi difangzhi bianxiu weiyuanhui, "Daqiuzhuang," 1278.

55. Visitors included politburo member Hu Qiaomu, who led a hundred-person delegation to the village in June 1988; the minister of construction, Lin Hanxiong; and the minister of the State Science and Technology Commission, Song Jian; see Jinghai annals.

56. Ma and Ling, *Jiaofeng*, 261.

57. Yu Hongfeng, *Huihuangzhongde yinying*, 173.

58. *Christian Science Monitor*, 4 Nov. 1988, p. 18.

59. *CYD* series, pt. 3.

60. Yu Zuomin, "Shi nian gaige, shi nian ju bian," 5.

61. *CYD* series, pt. 2.

62. Li Yaowu and Liu Changhe, *A Glimpse of China's Rural Reform* (Beijing: Foreign Languages Press, 1989), 37–38.

63. Lin Nan, "Local Market Socialism," 329.

64. *Xiangzhen qiye nianjian* (TVE yearbook), 1990, 19.

65. Ma and Ling, *Jiaofeng*, 160.

66. *Xiangzhen qiye nianjian* (TVE yearbook), 1990, 20

67. *South China Morning Post*, 30 Aug. 1992, S3 [hereafter cited as *SCMP*].

68. "15 Questions," pt. 1.

69. *PD*, 13 Feb. 1990, 2.

THREE. LONG LIVE UNDERSTANDING!

1. Details of this incident can be found in Yu Hongfeng, *Huihuangzhongde yinying*, 37–43; Xu Rujin and Zhang Sutang, "Guofa bu rong"; Liu Linshan and Gao Xiufeng, "Shoushenzhongde Yu Zuomin," 10–13; Gao Xiufeng and Liu Linshan, "Fengkuang 'zhuangzhu': Yu Zuomin zuixing lu" (Crazy "village boss": Yu Zuomin's crimes), *Fazhi ribao* (Legal daily), 28 Aug. 1993, 2–4;

Huang Li and Wang Lin, "Daqiuzhuang shijiande qianqian houhou" (The whole story of the Daqiuzhuang incident), *Beijing qingnian bao* (Beijing youth daily), 20 Apr. 1993, *xinwen zhoumou* (news weekend), 1; Li Yanchun, "Yi ge lushide ban an shouji" (Case notes of a lawyer), *Yangcheng wanbao* (Yangcheng evening news), 9 Dec. 1995, 10; "Daqiu mingan zhongde Yu Zuomin" (Yu Zuomin amid the Daqiu murder case), *Jingji wanbao* (Economic evening news, Nanchang), 9 May 1993, *xingqi wenhui* (weekly journal), 1; "Daqiu tiemu shi ruhe qiaokaide" (How the iron curtain of Daqiu was pried open), *Qingnian bao* (Youth daily), 22 Aug. 1995, 7; "Qiaokai Daqiu 'tu quanzi'" (Knocking open the local circle of Daqiu), *Beijing qingnian bao* (Beijing youth daily), 18 Jan. 1994, 5; *CYD* series.

2. Lin Nan, "Local Market Socialism," 351n.90.

3. "15 Questions," 16 Oct. 1992 (pt. 3).

4. In Guangdong province, for example, only one-third of the thousand-odd rural cadres charged with crimes between 1995 and 1997 were prosecuted, according to the Xinhua news agency journal *Banyue tan* (Semimonthly talks), no. 7 (1998): 36–67. Very few of these cases were dropped for a lack of evidence, however; instead, politics intervened to spare the accused. "Higher-level authorities place too much emphasis on the 'talent' of local cadres and not enough on their 'morals,'" the journal reported.

5. Li Yanchun, "Yi ge lushide ban an shouji."

6. Ibid.

7. Liu Linshan and Gao Xiufeng, "Shoushenzhongde Yu Zuomin," *Qingnian bao* (Youth daily), 22 Aug. 1995, 7.

8. Yu Hongfeng, *Huihuangzhongde yinying,* 43.

9. "Qiaokai Daqiuzhuang 'tu quanzi.'"

10. Li Yanchun, "Yi ge lushide ban an shouji."

11. *New York Times,* 30 Mar. 1993.

12. Xinhua, 17 July 1992.

13. *TKP* series, pt. 7.

14. Xinhua, 21 Sept. 1992.

15. *Nanfang zhoumou* (Southern weekend), 5 Nov. 1999, 8.

16. *CYD* series, pt. 3.

17. Lin Nan and Ye Xiaolan, "Chinese Rural Enterprises in Transformation: The End of the Beginning," *Issues and Studies,* no. 34 (Nov./Dec. 1998): 17–18.

18. Qiu, Xia, and Du, "Daqiuzhuang xunli," 12 June 1992.

19. Indeed, on at least one occasion, Beijing's involvement was a disaster. At the urging of the Ministry of Agriculture, Daqiu contracted to farm a 47,000-hectare parcel of land in the newly independent Ukraine republic in mid-1992. Beijing was keen to see such deals as part of efforts to build ties with the countries of the former Soviet Union. But little Daqiu was hardly in a position to farm the Ukraine. Five village delegations were sent to survey the land before the whole deal finally collapsed in late 1992.

20. Interview with the author in Hong Kong, November 1992. See also Bruce Gilley, "The Richest Little Village in China," *Asia Inc.,* Jan. 1993, 56–63.

21. Interview in Hong Kong, November 1992.

22. *TKP* series, pt. 1; *Zhengming* (Cheng Ming weekly, Hong Kong), Dec. 1992, 58.

23. *Zhongguo renwu nianjian* (China personalities yearbook) (Beijing: Huayi chubanshe [Huayi Publishing], 1992), 334–35.

24. *SCMP*, 23 Nov. 1992.

25. Graham Hutchings, "Inside China: Some Become Less Equal Than Others," *Daily Telegraph,* 29 Dec. 1992, 12.

26. Sheryl WuDunn, "Daqiuzhuang Journal: A Chinese Village Discovers the Road to Riches," *New York Times,* 10 Jan. 1992.

27. Xinhua, 30 Sept. 1992.

28. Quoted in *China Daily,* 12 Dec. 1992, 4.

29. *TKP* series, pt. 4

30. On this incident, see Xu Rujin and Zhang Sutang, "Guofa bu rong"; Gao and Liu, "Fengkuang 'zhuangzhu.'"

31. *TKP* series, pt. 7.

32. Ibid.

33. In Chinese, "zheng guang, zheng qi"; ibid.

34. "15 Questions," pt. 2.

35. *TKP* series, pt. 7.

36. *CYD* series, pt. 4.

37. Yu Hongfeng, *Huihuangzhongde yinying,* 171.

38. Deng Xiaoping, *Selected Works,* vol. 1: *1938–65* (Beijing: Foreign Languages Press, 1992), 293. The yellow cats became white cats when the slogan became better known.

39. "15 Questions," pt. 1.

40. *TKP* series, pt. 7.

41. See Ma and Ling, *Jiaofeng*, 162–236; Gilley, *Tiger on the Brink*, 183–87.

42. *TKP* series, pt. 7.

43. "Yu Zuomin yong ren zhi dao" (Yu Zuomin's employment doctrine), in *Xiangzhen qiye shiyong daquan* (Big handbook of township and village enterprises), ed. Chen Yaobang (Beijing: Kexue chubanshe [Science Press], 1988), 596–97.

44. *TVE News*, 9 Sept. 1987, 1.

45. *CYD* series, pt. 5; emphasis added.

46. *TVE News*, 9 Sept. 1987, 1.

47. "15 Questions," pt. 2.

48. Lin Nan, "Local Market Socialism," 333.

49. *CYD* series, pt. 3.

50. Liu Linshan and Gao Xiufeng, "Shoushenzhongde Yu Zuomin," 10.

51. *CYD* series, pt. 5.

52. *SCMP*, 23 Nov. 1992, 2.

53. "15 Questions," pt. 3.

54. Wu and Wang, "Daqiuzhuang de laoshao 'zhuangzhu,'" 50.

55. *TKP* series, pt. 4.

56. WuDunn, "Daqiuzhuang Journal."

57. Lin Nan, "Local Market Socialism."

58. See, for example, Han, "Fengjian sixiang yingxiang."

59. *CYD* series, pt. 1.

60. Yu Hongfeng, *Huihuangzhongde yinying*, 190; *TKP* series, pt. 5.

61. "15 Questions," pt. 1.

62. *TKP* series, pt. 5.

63. Yu Hongfeng, *Huihuangzhongde yinying*, 173.

64. *CYD* series, pt. 1.

65. Ibid. In Chinese: "Ni shi daizhe qiong ren dadaole furen. Wo shi daizhe qiong ren bianchengle furen!"

66. Ibid.

67. See Lin Nan, "Local Market Socialism," 326–27.

68. *CYD* series, pt. 7.

69. *Zhenlide zhuiqiu*, 1991, 10, quoted in Ma and Ling, *Jiaofeng*, 178.

70. *TKP* series, pt. 1.

71. "15 Questions," pt. 1.

72. *TKP* series, pt. 7.

73. The Chinese idiom is "Ye gong hao long"; ibid.

74. Ibid., pt. 4.

75. Ibid., pt. 5.

76. "15 Questions," pt. 1.

77. *TKP* series, pt. 7.

78. Hutchings, "Inside China," 12.

79. *TKP* series, pt. 5.

80. On the spirtual culture campaign, see Gilley, *Tiger on the Brink,* 269–74.

81. "15 Questions," pt. 3.

82. On the Xiaojin incident, see Wang Yansheng, Zhang Ping, and Qiao Zhonglin, "Weiraozhe Xiaojinzhuang he Daqiuzhuang fashengde yi jian 'zuo' de gushi" (A story of "leftism" that happened in Xiaojinzhuang and Daqiuzhuang), *TVE News,* 13 July 1992, 1; Yi Bing, "Cong Baodi xianwei de 'pa' tanqi" (On the Baodi party committee's "fears"), *Jingbao* (Mirror magazine), Oct. 1996, 47–49; *TKP* series, pt. 6.

83. *TKP* series, pt. 7.

84. Wang, Zhang, and Qiao, "Weiraozhe Xiaojinzhuang."

85. Yi, "Cong Baodi."

86. *TKP* series, pt. 6.

87. Wang, Zhang, and Qiao, "Weiraozhe Xiaojinzhuang."

88. Yi, "Cong Baodi."

89. Wang, Zhang, and Qiao, "Weiraozhe Xiaojinzhuang."

90. On the Guo visit, see Zhang Ping, "Guo Fenglian laidao Daqiuzhuang" (Guo Fenglian comes to Daqiu Village), *TVE News,* 6 Nov. 1992, 1; *TKP* series, pt. 6; Xinhua, 25 Oct. 1992; *Window Magazine* (Hong Kong), 11 Dec. 1992.

91. Zhang Ping, "Guo Fenglian."

92. "92/10/23: Yu Zuomin he Guo Fenglian" (92/10/23: Yu Zuomin and Guo Fenglian), *Zhongguo nongmin* (China peasant), 1 (Nov. 1992): middle spread (n.p.).

93. Zhang Ping, "Guo Fenglian"; "92/10/23."

94. "Yu Zuomin an xuanpan zhi hou" (After the verdict in the Yu Zuomin case), *Zhongguo nongmin* (China peasant), Oct.–Nov. 1993, 6–9.

95. Yi, "Cong Baodi," 48.

96. Liu Linshan and Gao Xiufeng, "Shoushenzhongde Yu Zuomin."
97. "15 Questions," pt. 2.
98. Interview with former SERC official, Jan. 2000.
99. *Jingbao* (Mirror magazine), May 1994, 60.
100. "15 Questions," pt. 1.
101. "Qiaokai Daqiuzhuang 'tu quanzi.'"
102. Yi, "Cong Baodi," 48.
103. *CYD* series, pt. 7.
104. See Kelliher, *Peasant Power in China*, 247.
105. *CYD* series, pt. 1.
106. *TKP* series, pt. 7.

FOUR. OUTLAWS OF THE MARSH

1. This project was the brainchild of the village's chief agricultural adviser, the famous rocket scientist and CPPCC vice chairman Qian Xuesen. In early 1992 he asked Vice Premier Tian Jiyun to make the village a top-level experimental zone for animal husbandry. Tian, heeding the elder's advice, approved the suggestion within days and dispatched state councillor Chen Junsheng to the village to implement the plan. *CYD* series, pt. 2.
2. One factory manager from the Wanquan Group later told a Hong Kong newspaper that in forcing Wei to "speak out clearly" about the "unclear accounts," the questioners "might have been comparatively rude in their attitudes" and "beat him." Nothing illegal had taken place, the manager insisted, but "in the end he died." *Ming bao* (Ming Pao daily news, Hong Kong), 5 Mar. 1993.
3. Gao and Liu, "Fengkuang 'zhuangzhu.'"
4. Ibid.
5. Shi Naian and Luo Guanzhong, *Outlaws of the Marsh*, trans. Sidney Shapiro (Beijing: Foreign Languages Press, 1980), 55–56.
6. "Daqiuzhuang tiemu shi ruhe qiaokaide" (How the iron curtain of Daqiuzhuang was pried open), *Qingnian bao* (Youth daily), 22 Aug. 1995, 7.
7. Xinhua, 4, 12 Feb. 1993.
8. An Xian, "Daqiuzhuang mingan fasheng zhihou" (After the murder in Daqiuzhuang), *Nanfang zhoumo* (Southern weekend), 30 Apr. 1993, 1.
9. Gao and Liu, "Fengkuang 'zhuangzhu.'"

10. Ibid.; Xu Hui and Zhang Zhongxian, "Jinkan Daqiuzhuang" (A recent look at Daqiu Village), *Zhongguo jingji shibao* (China economic times), 30 Nov. 1998.

11. Huang Heng, "Daqiuzhuang shijian shimo" (The whole story of the Daqiuzhuang incident), *Xiaofei shibao* (Consumer times), 1 May 1993, *zhoumou ban* (weekend section), 1.

12. Gao and Liu, "Fengkuang 'zhuangzhu.'"

13. Ibid.

14. Xu Rujin and Zhang Sutang, "Guofa bu rong."

15. Gao and Liu, "Fengkuang 'zhuangzhu'"; Xu Hui and Zhang Zhongxian, "Jinkan Daqiuzhuang."

16. Huang Heng, "Daqiuzhuang shijian shimo"; Huang Li and Wang Lin, "Daqiuzhuang shijiande qianqian houhou."

17. Huang Heng, "Daqiuzhuang shijian shimo."

18. Ibid.

19. An, "Daqiuzhuang mingan fasheng zhihou."

20. Ibid.

21. *New York Times*, 30 Mar. 1993.

22. An, "Daqiuzhuang mingan fasheng zhihou."

23. Xinhua, 23 Dec. 1994; Gao and Liu, "Fengkuang 'zhuangzhu.'"

24. Gao and Liu, "Fengkuang 'zhuangzhu'"; Xu Hui and Zhang Zhongxian, "Jinkan Daqiuzhuang."

25. Lincoln Kaye, "Ugly Face of Reforms," *Far Eastern Economic Review*, 22 Apr. 1993, 19.

26. *Ming bao* (Ming Pao daily news, Hong Kong), 19 Mar. 1993.

27. *Beijing qingnian bao* (Beijing youth daily), 20 Apr. 1993.

28. An, "Daqiuzhuang mingan fasheng zhihou."

29. Huang Li and Wang Lin, "Daqiuzhuang shijiande qianqian houhou."

30. An, "Daqiuzhuang mingan fasheng zhihou."

31. "Daqiuzhuang mingan zhongde Yu Zuomin" (Yu Zuomin amid the Daqiuzhuang murder case), *Jingji wanbao* (Economic evening news, Nanchang), 9 May 1993, *xingqi wenhui* (weekly journal), 1.

32. Huang Heng, "Daqiuzhuang shijian shimo."

33. Moqi Feng, "Yu Zuomin bei ju hou de xinwen zhuizong" (News coverage since the arrest of Yu Zuomin), *Xiaofei shibao* (Consumer times), 1 May 1993, *zhoumou ban* (weekend section), 1.

34. Gao and Liu, "Fengkuang 'zhuangzhu.'"

35. Ibid.

36. Reuters, 8 Apr. 1993.

37. Gilley, *Tiger on the Brink,* 205–8.

38. *Huashang bao* (Chinese business times), 6 July 1993.

39. Wang Weigang, "Yu Zuomin zai jieshou shenxunde rizili" (Yu Zuomin's days of being interrogated), *Dubao cankao* (Newspaper reading reference), no. 158 (Feb. 1998): 1.

40. Gao and Liu, "Fengkuang 'zhuangzhu.'"

41. Xinhua, 16 Apr. 1993; *PD,* 17 Apr. 1993, 4.

42. *Beijing qingnian bao* (Beijing youth daily), 20 Apr. 1993.

43. Moqi, "Yu Zuomin bei ju hou."

44. *SCMP,* 26 Apr. 1993; UPI, 30 July 1993.

45. Xinhua, 31 July 1993.

46. An, "Daqiuzhuang mingan fasheng zhihou."

47. Gao and Liu, "Fengkuang 'zhuangzhu.'"

48. Liu Linshan and Gao Xiufeng, "Shoushenzhongde Yu Zuomin."

49. Li Yanchun, "Yi ge lushide ban an shouji." Tian Wenchang went on to found a successful law practice in Beijing, where his Web site listed "the successful prosecution of Yu Zuomin on behalf of the people of Daqiu Village" as among his greatest achievements. Wang Yaoting went on to act as the defense lawyer of several other enemies of the state, including the former party secretary of Beijing, Chen Xitong. See *Nanfang ribao* (Southern daily), 23 Sept. 1998, 4.

50. An, "Daqiuzhuang mingan fasheng zhihou"; emphasis added.

51. Gao and Liu, "Fengkuang 'zhuangzhu.'"

52. Xu Hui and Zhang Zhongxian, "Jinkan Daqiuzhuang."

53. Moqi, "Yu Zuomin bei ju hou."

54. Xu Hui and Zhang Zhongxian, "Jinkan Daqiuzhuang."

55. Gao and Liu, "Fengkuang 'zhuangzhu.'"

56. Ibid.

57. Ibid. See also the extended version of the report, Gao Xiufeng and Liu Linshan, "Fengkuang zhuangzhu" (Crazy village boss), in *Zhongnanhai sandai lingdao jiti yu gongheguo zhengfa shilu* (The third-generation collective leadership of Zhongnanhai and China's politics and law), ed. Yan Shuhan (Beijing: Zhongguo jingji chubanshe [China Economics Publishing], 1998), 2:236–65.

58. Fan Chunming, "Yu Zuomin deng wocang, fangai gongwu, xinghui, feifa jujin, feifa guanzhi an" (The case of unlawful detention, unlawful arrest, bribery, obstruction of justice, and harboring of criminals involving Yu Zuomin and others), in *Zhongguo shenpan anlie yaolan: 1994 nian zonghe ben* (China trial cases compendium: 1994 general edition) (Beijing: Zhongguo renmin gongan daxue chuban she [China People's Public Security University Press], 1995), 378–88.

59. Xu Hui and Zhang Zhongxian, "Jinkan Daqiuzhuang."

60. Associated Press, 27 Aug. 1993.

61. Xinhua, 27 Aug. 1993; *PD*, 28 Aug. 1993.

62. *Fazhi ribao* (Legal daily), 28 Aug. 1993.

63. Xinhua, 9 Oct. 1993.

64. Xinhua, 7 Apr. 1994.

65. Xinhua, 23 Dec. 1994.

FIVE. CONCLUSIONS

1. Jiang Zilong, "Nongmin diguo" (Peasant empire), *Nanfang zhoumou* (Southern weekend), 30 Apr. 1993, 1.

2. See Jean Oi, "The Role of the Local State in China's Transitional Economy," *China Quarterly,* no. 144 (Dec. 1995): 1132–49.

3. Bruce Gilley, "Pinstriped Farmers Rule in Beijiao," *Eastern Express* (Hong Kong), 4 Mar. 1995, 9.

4. Reuters, 6 Sept. 1999; Agence-France Press, 25 Oct. 1999; *Toronto Star,* 30 Sept. 1999, 1.

5. Chen Weixing, "Politics and Paths of Rural Development in China: The Village Conglomerate in Shandong Province," *Pacific Affairs,* Apr. 1998, 25–40; idem, "The Political Economy of Rural Industrialization in China: Village Conglomerates in Shandong Province," *Modern China,* Jan. 1998, 73–96.

6. I borrow liberally here from Donatella Della Porta and Mario Diani, *Social Movements: An Introduction* (Oxford: Basil Blackwell, 1999), chap. 1; and Louis Maheu, ed., *Social Movements and Social Classes* (London: Sage Publications, 1995), 1–17. However, the four-part classification is my own.

7. Even today, most media reports on collective action in rural China, and many scholarly articles, tend to focus almost exclusively on these two fac-

tors. For a study of a rural county where "perceived social injustice and unrest fuels political participation," see M. Kent Jennings, "Political Participation in the Chinese Countryside," *American Political Science Review,* June 1997, 361–85; also see Li Lianjiang and Kevin J. O'Brien, "Villagers and Popular Resistance in Contemporary China," *Modern China,* Jan. 1996, 28–61.

8. Della Porta and Diani, *Social Movements,* 8.

9. The so-called resource mobilization theory is most closely associated with Mayer Zald; see Zald and John D. McCarthy, eds., *Social Movements in an Organizational Society: Selected Essays* (New Brunswick, N.J.: Transaction Books, 1987).

10. See Della Porta and Diani, *Social Movements,* chap. 8, 193–225.

11. Kevin J. O'Brien, "Rightful Resistance," *World Politics* 49, no. 1 (1996): 31–55.

12. Della Porta and Diani, *Social Movements,* 16. Collective actions by a single village, even if sustained, cannot be called a social movement, since a village is a formal organization, not an informal network.

13. CASS Rural Development Institute office head Zhang Xiaoshan, quoted in "Yu Zuomin an xuanpan zhi hou" (After the verdict in the Yu Zuomin case), *Zhongguo nongmin* (China peasant), Oct.–Nov. 1993, 6–9.

14. Han Yi, "Fengjian sixiang yingxiang."

15. "Qian che zhi jian" (The warning up ahead), *PD,* 28 Aug. 1993.

16. Gilley, *Tiger on the Brink,* 272–73.

17. See David Zweig, "The 'Externalities of Development': Can New Political Institutions Manage Rural Conflict?" *Hong Kong University of Science and Technology, Working Papers in the Social Sciences,* no. 45, 1999.

18. See, for example, the cases of Minjiang in Gansu province, which defied repeated attempts by authorities to crack down on the village's logging operations throughout 1998 (*Zhongguo qingnian bao* [China youth daily], 29 Jan. 1999), and of Dadun village in Guangdong, which resisted repeated attempts by authorities to shut down its factories making counterfeit jeans under a Hong Kong label in the mid-1990s (Zhongguo zhongyang dianshi tai [Chinese central TV], 9 Nov. 1996), reported in British Broadcasting Corporation, *Summary of World Broadcasts, Far East,* 13 Nov. 1996), G55; and Zhongguo baoxian bao (China insurance news), reported in *SCMP,* 26 Nov. 1996.

19. *PD,* 11 Apr. 1997, 11.

20. *PD,* 20 June 1994, 5.

21. "Yu Zuomin an xuanpan zhi hou" (After the verdict in the Yu Zuomin case), *Zhongguo nongmin* (China peasant), Oct.–Nov. 1993, 6–9.

22. Lin Ping, "Nongcun chuxianle yi ge quanshi jieceng" (A power class has appeared in the countryside), *Guangjiaojing yuekan* (Wide angle monthly), Jan. 1999, 23–25.

23. *Nanfang nongcun bao* (Southern rural daily), 27 Jan. 1998, 2.

24. *Shanxi ribao* (Shanxi daily), 13 June 1996, 1, 3.

25. See the lengthy article in *Shenyang ribao wanbao zhoumouban* (Shenyang daily evening paper, weekend section), 20 Mar. 1999, 5.

26. Chen Weixing, "Politics and Paths," 34.

27. Several scholarly studies have noted the role of villager committees in providing the means for collective action. See Kevin J. O'Brien, "Implementing Political Reform in China's Villages," *Australian Journal of Chinese Affairs*, July 1994, 33–59; also Zweig, "'Externalities of Development.'"

28. *Dagong bao* (*Ta kung pao*), 18 Jan. 1999, A4.

29. Kevin J. O'Brien and Li Lianjiang, "The Politics of Lodging Complaints in Rural China," *China Quarterly*, no. 143 (Sept. 1995): 756–83.

30. *Yangcheng wanbao* (Yangcheng evening news), 25 Aug. 1999; Associated Press, 26 Aug. 1999.

31. See Herbert Yee and Wang Jinhong, "Grassroots Political Participation in Rural China," in *China in Transition: Issues and Policies,* ed. David Teather and Herbert Yee (London: Macmillan Press, 1999), 25–46; Zweig, "'Externalities of Development.'"

32. *New York Times*, 1 Feb. 1999, 1, 12.

33. *Renmin gongan bao* (People's public security news), 12 Aug. 1997, 3.

34. See Lucian Pye, "Chinese Democracy and Constitutional Development," in *China in the Twenty-First Century: Politics, Economy, and Society,* ed. Fumio Itoh (Tokyo: United Nations University Press, 1997), 205–18.

35. Xinhua, 11 Feb. 1999.

AFTERWORD

1. Xinhua, Photograph Series Number 0532, 17 Dec. 1998, General Introduction.

2. Ou Baoju became village head and Wei Zongjing was village party secretary.

3. In Chinese, *Daqiuzhuang cun* (Daqiu Village village) became *Daqiuzhuang zhen* (Daqiu Village town). The new designation was subsequently upgraded further to that of a "subcounty level" (*fu xian ji*) town. See Xu Hui and Zhang Zhongxian, "Jinkan Daqiuzhuang."

4. The five local members were all from the last village committee under Yu Zuomin, including his brother, Yu Zuoyao, who had dissented at a critical time during the standoff.

5. Lin Nan and Chen Chih-Jou, "Local Elites as Officials and Owners: Shareholding and Property Rights in Daqiuzhuang Industry," paper presented at conference on property rights in China, Hong Kong University of Science and Technology, 12–15 June 1996, 20.

6. Xu Hui and Zhang Zhongxian, "Jinkan Daqiuzhuang."

7. *Jinwan bao* (Evening news, Tianjin), 20 Jan. 1996.

8. *PD*, 15 July 1997.

9. *Jingji ribao* (Economic daily), 23 Oct. 1995.

10. *PD*, 27 Nov. 1995.

11. Ibid., 22 Feb. 1994.

12. Wang Xuexiao, "Jinri Daqiuzhuang (Today's Daqiuzhuang), *Renmin ribao haiwai ban* (People's Daily overseas edition), 3 Nov. 1995, 2. A separate report the following year put the figure at Rmb 5,600, or "twice the national rural average"; *Jinwan bao* (Evening news, Tianjin), 20 Jan. 1996.

13. The title went to Huaxi village in Jiangsu province.

14. Lin and Chen, "Local Elites as Officials and Owners," 16.

15. I have been able to identify the following post-1993 appointments from these three families: (1) Yu Zuozhang (cousin of Yu Zuomin), Yaoshun Group president; (2) Zhang Yuyin (cousin of patriarch Zhang Yupu), Wanquan Group president; (3) Liu Yongsheng (son of Liu Wanquan), Wanquan Group hotels and discos subsidiary Wanquan General Service Center president; (4) Yu Shaotong (son of Yu Zuozhang), Wanquan Group metals subsidiary Jiayuan Enterprise Company president; and (5) Zhang Yanlian (son of patriarch Zhang Yupu), Jinhai Group vice chairman.

16. Xu Hui and Zhang Zhongxian, "Jinkan Daqiuzhuang."

17. Lin and Chen, "Local Elites as Officials and Owners," 18.

18. Under an arrangement reached in 1995, the Four Hens paid a tax of 0.30 percent of net profits to the town and county governments (split one-third and two-thirds) in return for their limited services. The Four Hens in turn

levied taxes within their own groups and street districts to pay for education and welfare. See Lin and Chen, "Local Elites as Officials and Owners," 20.

19. A photo was featured on an official Tianjin government website in 1999.

20. Xinhua, 27 Aug. 1993.

21. *Xinwen zhanxian* (News frontline), 1 Feb. 1999, 2.

22. *Nanfang dushi bao* (Southern city news), 9 Jan. 1998, 22.

23. *Tianjin ribao* (Tianjin daily), 6 Feb. 1999, 1.

24. *Guangming ribao* (Guangming daily), 29 March 2000.

25. *PD,* 3 Nov. 1995.

26. In 1994, according to *Tianjin ribao* (Tinajin daily), 17 Dec. 1994, the Tianjin government included Daqiu among a dozen model "small towns" that would benefit from new infrastructure spending on things like paved roads, additional telephone lines, and social welfare facilities. In early 1995 Daqiu was included among fifty "industrial town demonstration zones" designated by the national Ministry of Agriculture "to guide the country's town and township enterprises toward concentrated and integrated development"; *PD,* 16 Feb. 1995; see also *Tianjin ribao,* 14 Mar. 1999, 1. Then in 1998, the Tianjin Fengli Elevator Guide Rail Company was included in the central government's National Torchlight Plan, a policy of government-supported high-technology development, according to a company advertisement seen in January 1999 on the Web site of the Tianjin marketing company Tianjin Yimo Arts and Communications Company: www.yimo.com.

27. Andrew Higgins, "'Corrupt Village Regains Its Glory," *Guardian,* 24 Nov. 1995.

28. These included a Rmb 20 million investment by Jinmei Group in a resort and industrial complex in the nearby coastal city of Nandaihe and a Rmb 65 million pressed steel tubes joint venture between Jinhai Group and a partner from Shandong province.

29. *Jingji ribao* (Economic daily), 23 Oct. 1995.

30. For the first time, the central government grouped TVEs with state-owned (*guoyou*) enterprises as well as the state's ownership stakes in private firms and foreign joint ventures under a new statistical and administrative category called the "publicly owned" (*gongyou*) sector. See *China Quarterly (Quarterly Chronicle and Documentation),* no. 152 (Dec. 1997): 909.

31. Xinhua, Photograph Series Number 0532, 17 Dec. 1998, General Introduction.

32. See Oi, *Rural China Takes Off,* 80–93; also Russell Smyth, "Recent Developments in Rural Enterprise Reform in China: Achievements, Problems, and Prospects," *Asian Survey,* Aug. 1998, 1–14.

33. These included Yaoshun Steel Pipes Enterprise Group, Yaoshun Non-Ferrous Metals Enterprise Group, and Jinmei Steel Industry Company.

34. The new company was named Tianjin Fengli Elevator Guide Rail Company after its main product.

35. Lin and Chen, "Local Elites as Officials and Owners," 16.

36. Ibid., 25–30; Lin and Ye, "Chinese Rural Enterprises in Transformation," 20–24.

37. Lin and Chen, "Local Elites as Officials and Owners," 3.

38. Ibid., 30.

39. *Nanfang ribao* (Southern daily), 23 Sept. 1998, 4.

40. On Yu's death, see *Wenhui bao* (*Wen wei po,* Hong Kong), 19 Oct. 1999, 4; *Wenhui bao* (Shanghai), 29 Oct. 1999, 11; *Dagong bao* (*Ta kung pao*), 1 Nov. 1999, 4; *Nanjing fuwu daobao* (Nanjing service reporter), 5 Nov. 1999; *Nanfang zhoumou* (Southern weekend), 5 Nov. 1999, 8.

41. Telephone interview with Wang Yaling, assistant to the president, Jinmei Group, 6 Nov. 1999.

REFERENCES

An Xian. "Daqiuzhuang mingan fasheng zhihou" (After the murder in Daqiu-zhuang). *Nanfang zhoumo* (Southern weekend), 30 Apr. 1993, 1.

Chen Weixing. "Politics and Paths of Rural Development in China: The Village Conglomerate in Shandong Province." *Pacific Affairs,* Apr. 1998, 25–40.

Christiansen, Flemming, and Zhang Junzuo, eds. *Village Inc.: Chinese Rural Society in the 1990s.* Honolulu: University of Hawaii Press, 1998.

Della Porta, Donatella, and Mario Diani. *Social Movements: An Introduction.* Oxford: Basil Blackwell, 1999.

Fang Ling. "'Zhongguo diyi cun' Daqiuzhuang jianwen" (Sights and sounds of "China's richest village," Daqiuzhuang) (7-part series). *Dagong bao (Ta kung pao)*, 11–17 Nov. 1992. [Cited as *TKP* series.]

Gao Xiufeng and Liu Linshan. "Fengkuang 'zhuangzhu': Yu Zuomin zuixing lu" (Crazy "village boss": Yu Zuomin's crimes). *Fazhi ribao* (Legal daily), 28 Aug. 1993, 2–4.

Gilley, Bruce. "The Richest Little Village in China." *Asia Inc.,* Jan. 1993, 56–63.

———. *Tiger on the Brink: Jiang Zemin and China's New Elite.* Berkeley: University of California Press, 1998.

Han Yi. "Fengjian sixiang yingxiang shi xiangzhen qiye fazhande jiban" (The effects of feudal thinking are a yoke on the development of township and village enterprises). *Dongfang luntan* (Eastern forum) (Qingdao shiwei [Qingdao party committee]), no. 3 (1993): 56–58.

Hinton, William. *Shenfan: The Continuing Revolution in a Chinese Village.* New York: Vintage Books, 1984.

Huang Heng. "Daqiuzhuang shijian shimo" (The whole story of the Daqiuzhuang incident). *Xiaofei shibao* (Consumer times), 1 May 1993, *zhoumou ban* (weekend section), 1.

Huang Li and Wang Lin. "Daqiuzhuang shijiande qianqian houhou" (The whole story of the Daqiuzhuang incident). *Beijing qingnian bao* (Beijing youth daily), 20 Apr. 1993, *xinwen zhoumou* (news weekend), 1.

Hutchings, Graham. "Inside China: Some Become Less Equal Than Others." *Daily Telegraph,* 29 Dec. 1992.

Jiang Zilong. "Yanzhao beige" (Yanzhao elegy). *Renmin wenxue* (People's literature) 7, no. 298 (1984): 5–55. [Cited as "Yanzhao Elegy."]

Jinghai xianzhi bianxiu weiyuanhui (Jinghai county annals editorial committee). *Jinghai xian zhi* (Jinghai county annals). Tianjin: Tianjin shehui kexue yuan (Tianjian Academy of Social Sciences), 1995. [Cited as Jinghai annals.]

Kelliher, Daniel. *Peasant Power in China: The Era of Rural Reform, 1979–1989.* New Haven: Yale University Press, 1992.

Li Yanchun. "Yi ge lushide ban an shouji" (Case notes of a lawyer). *Yangcheng wanbao* (Yangcheng evening news), 9 Dec. 1995, 10.

Lin Nan. "Local Market Socialism: Local Corporatism in Action in Rural China." *Theory and Society* 24 (1995): 301–54.

Lin Nan and Chen Chih-Jou. "Local Elites as Officials and Owners: Shareholding and Property Rights in Daqiuzhuang Industry." Paper presented at conference on property rights in China, Hong Kong University of Science and Technology, 12–15 June 1996.

Lin Nan and Ye Xiaolan. "Chinese Rural Enterprises in Transformation: The End of the Beginning." *Issues and Studies,* no. 34 (Nov./Dec. 1998): 1–28.

Liu Linshan and Gao Xiufeng. "Shoushenzhongde Yu Zuomin" (Yu Zuomin under arrest). *Fazhi yu xinwen* (Law and news), 15 Nov. 1993, 10–13.

Liu Yuren. "Xian lijie zhengcede renmen: Yu Zuomin" (Those who understand the policies first: Yu Zuomin). In *Zhongguo xiangzhen qiye chenggong zhi lu* (The successful road of China's township enterprises), 38–46. Beijing: Zhongguo jianshe chubanshe (Construction Press), 1988.

Ma Licheng and Ling Zhijun. *Jiaofeng: Dangdai Zhongguo sanci sixiang jiefang shilu* (Crossed swords: Contemporary China's three thought liberations). Beijing: Jinri Zhongguo chubanshe (Today's China Publishing), 1998.

Moqi Feng. "Yu Zuomin bei ju hou de xinwen zhuizong" (News coverage since the arrest of Yu Zuomin). *Xiaofei shibao* (Consumer times), 1 May 1993, *zhoumou ban* (weekend section), 1.

Oi, Jean C. *Rural China Takes Off: The Institutional Foundations of Economic Reform.* Berkeley: University of California Press, 1999.

―――. *State and Peasant in Contemporary China: The Political Economy of Village Government.* Berkeley: University of California Press, 1989.

"Qiaokai Daqiuzhuang 'tu quanzi'" (Knocking open the local circle of Daqiuzhuang). *Beijing qingnian bao* (Beijing youth daily), 18 Jan. 1994, 5.

Qiu Yongsheng, Xia Lin, and Du Jichang. "Daqiuzhuang xunli" (Daqiuzhuang pilgrimage). *Guangming ribao* (Guangming daily), 9–12 June 1992.

Sun Qitai and Xiong Zhiyong. *Dazhai hongqide shengqi yu zhuiluo* (The rise and fall of the red flag of Dazhai). Zhengzhou: Henan renmin chubanshe (Henan People's Publishing House), 1994.

Thaxton, Ralph A. *Salt of the Earth: The Political Origins of Peasant Protest and Communist Revolution in China.* Berkeley: University of California Press, 1997.

Tianjin shi difangzhi bianxiu weiyuanhui (Tianjin local annals editorial committee). "Daqiuzhuang." In *Chengxiang jianshe zhi* (City and township development annals), 1277–79. Tianjin:Tianjin shehui kexue yuan (Tianjian Academy of Social Sciences), 1996.

Wang Yansheng, Zhang Ping, and Qiao Zhonglin. "Weiraozhe Xiaojinzhuang he Daqiuzhuang fashengde yi jian 'zuo' de gushi" (A story of "leftism" that happened in Xiaojinzhuang and Daqiuzhuang). *Zhongguo xiangzhen qiye bao* (China township and village enterprise news), 13 July 1992, 1.

Wu Wei and Wang Ke. "Daqiuzhuang de laoshao 'zhuangzhu'" (The old and young leaders of Daqiuzhuang). *Zhonghua ernu* (Sons and daughters of China) 1 (1993): 44–52.

WuDunn, Sheryl. "Daqiuzhuang Journal: A Chinese Village Discovers the Road to Riches." *New York Times,* 10 Jan. 1992.

Xu Hui and Zhang Zhongxian. "Jinkan Daqiuzhuang" (A recent look at Daqiu Village). *Zhongguo jingji shibao* (China economic times), 30 Nov. 1998.

Xu Rujin and Zhang Sutang. "Guofa bu rong: Yu Zuomin fanzui jishi" (A case that the national law will not tolerate: An account of the crimes of Yu Zuomin). *Renmin ribao haiwai ban* (People's Daily overseas edition), 28 Aug. 1993.

Yang, Dali L. *Calamity and Reform in China: State, Rural Society, and Institutional Change since the Great Leap Famine.* Stanford: Stanford University Press, 1996.

Yi Bing. "Cong Baodi xianwei de 'pa' tanqi" (On the Baodi party committee's "fears"). *Jingbao* (Mirror), Oct. 1996, 47–49.

Yu Hongfeng. *Huihuangzhongde yinying: Zhongguo "shou fu cun" Daqiuzhuang jiemi* (The shadow amid splendor: Revealing the secret of China's "first rich village," Daqiuzhuang). Beijing: Jingguan jiaoyu chubanshe (Police Officer Education Press), 1993.

Yu Zuomin. "Shi nian gaige, shi nian ju bian" (Ten years of reforms, ten years of great changes). *People's Daily,* 13 Jan. 1989, 5.

———. "Wo kandaode riben" (The Japan I saw). *Xin guancha* (New observer) 10 (25 May 1985): 10.

"Yu Zuomin xiao da 15 wen" (Yu Zuomin happily answers 15 questions) (3-part series). *Zhongguo xiangzhen qiye bao* (China township and village enterprise news), 12, 14, 16 Oct. 1992. [Cited as "15 Questions."]

Zhang Jianwei. "Zhongguo diyi cun jiemi" (Revealing the secrets of China's richest village) (7-part series). *Zhongguo qingnian bao* (China youth daily), 15–22 Jan. 1993. [Cited as *CYD* series.]

Zhang Ping. "Guo Fenglian laidao Daqiuzhuang" (Guo Fenglian comes to Daqiu Village). *Zhongguo xiangzhen qiye bao* (China township and village enterprise news), 6 Nov. 1992, 1.

Zhou, Kate Xiao. *How the Farmers Changed China: Power of the People.* Boulder, Colo.: Westview Press, 1996.

Zweig, David. "The 'Externalities of Development': Can New Political Institutions Manage Rural Conflict?" *Hong Kong University of Science and Technology, Working Papers in the Social Sciences,* no. 45, 1999.

———. *Freeing China's Farmers: Rural Restructuring in the Reform Era.* Armonk, N.Y.: M.E. Sharpe, 1997.

INDEX

put of, 61–62; 1998 statistics on, 149; privatization of, 174–76; "publicly owned" status of, 173, 204n30; rectification campaign against, 69–71; share of labor force in, 15, 37; staffing levels of, 46; TVE term for, 40. *See also* Daqiu rural enterprises
Russia, 82, 83

Salaries. *See* Incentives
San jiudi (three locals) policy, 14
Schools, 23, 53
Search for Truth (magazine), 103
Shandong province, 2, 150
Shareholding system *(gufen zhidu)*, 83, 133, 174–76, 205n33
Shedui qiye (brigade enterprises), 15, 40. *See also* Rural enterprises
Shengchan dadui (production brigades), 5
Shengchan dui (production teams), 5
Shi Jiaming (Mistress Shi), 9, 17, 118, 137; nepotism of, 97; on PAP's mobilization, 126; post-purge status of, 178; public relations role of, 88, 106–7; trial of, 140, 143; and Yu, 74
Shui hu zhuan (Outlaws of the marsh), 122–23
Sichuan province, 14
Socialist economy: Deng's theory of, 91, 92–93, 103; Yu on, 62, 92, 103–4, 156, 157
Song Jian, 192n55
South China Morning Post, 85, 96, 138
Southern Weekend, 138, 141
Southwestern Yangtze Column of the Anti-Corruption Army of the People's Workers and Peasants, 162–63
Starvation, 5–7
State Economic Reform Commission, 113
State firms: bribing of, 48–49; inefficiencies of, 38, 39; in "publicly owned" sector, 173, 204n30; rural firms versus, 23–24, 61–62
State Science and Technology Commission, 68

Steel pipes factory (Daqiu Industrial Company), 22, 43–44, 47, 184 table. *See also* Yaoshun Group
Steel strip factory (Wanquan Industrial Company), 19–20, 21, 43, 44, 47, 174, 184 table. *See also* Wanquan Group
Su Nan (southern Jiangsu), 15
Sun Yat-sen, 52
Supply-push factors of collective action, 152, 154–55, 200n7

Taiwan, 82
Ta Kung Pao (newspaper), 85, 87–88, 89, 90
Tan Shaowen, 76, 124
Tao Siju, 135
Taxes: of Daqiu village, 1978-1997, 182 table; of Four Hens, 45 table, 203–4n18
Three locals *(san jiudi)* policy, 14
Tiananmen Square demonstrations (1989), 69, 94, 146–47; and rectification campaign, 70–71
Tianjin, 4, 84, 113; Daqiu trial in, 139–44; inspection teams from, 29–31, 134–35, 154, 168; model town program of, 172, 204n26; 1963 flooding in, 8. *See also* Tianjin police
Tianjin Cold-Rolled Steel Strip Mill, 19, 20, 21
Tianjin Color Television Factory, 53
Tianjin Paper Mill, 8
Tianjin police: Liu Linshan's interview with, 123; and Wei Fuhe's murder, 121–23, 124–25, 129; Yu's detention by, 136–37, 138–39
Tianjin Tobacco Company, 172
Tianjin Trust and Investment, 83, 133
Tian Jiyun, 60, 197n1
Tian Wenchang, 76–80, 141, 199n49
Tong Zemin, 29–31, 35
Township and village enterprises (TVEs). *See* Rural enterprises
Townships *(xiang),* 5, 38
Trial of Daqiu, 139–44

Text:	11/15 Granjon
Display:	Granjon
Composition:	Impressions Book and Journal Services, Inc.
Printing and binding:	Edwards Brothers, Inc.
Index:	Patricia Deminna